PHILOSOPHER KINGS?

PHILOSOPHER KINGS?

THE ADJUDICATION OF CONFLICTING HUMAN RIGHTS AND SOCIAL VALUES

GEORGE C. CHRISTIE

UNIVERSITY PRESS

Oxford University Press, Inc., publishes works that further Oxford University's objective of excellence in research, scholarship, and education.

Oxford   New York
Auckland   Cape Town   Dar es Salaam   Hong Kong   Karachi   Kuala Lumpur   Madrid   Melbourne
Mexico City   Nairobi   New Delhi   Shanghai   Taipei   Toronto

With offices in
Argentina   Austria   Brazil   Chile   Czech Republic   France   Greece   Guatemala   Hungary   Italy
Japan   Poland   Portugal   Singapore   South Korea   Switzerland   Thailand   Turkey   Ukraine
Vietnam

Copyright © 2011 by Oxford University Press, Inc.

Published by Oxford University Press, Inc.
198 Madison Avenue, New York, New York 10016

Oxford is a registered trademark of Oxford University Press
Oxford University Press is a registered trademark of Oxford University Press, Inc.

All rights reserved. No part of this publication may be reproduced, stored in a retrieval system, or transmitted, in any form or by any means, electronic, mechanical, photocopying, recording, or otherwise, without the prior permission of Oxford University Press, Inc.

_____

Library of Congress Cataloging-in-Publication Data

Christie, George C.
 Philosopher kings ? : the adjudication of conflicting human rights and social values / George C. Christie.
  p. cm.
 Includes bibliographical references and index.
 ISBN 978-0-19-534115-7 (hardback : alk. paper)
 1. Human rights—Cases. I. Title.
 K3240.C4748 2011
 341.4'8—dc22   2010039887

_____

1 2 3 4 5 6 7 8 9

Printed in the United States of America on acid-free paper

Note to Readers
This publication is designed to provide accurate and authoritative information in regard to the subject matter covered. It is based upon sources believed to be accurate and reliable and is intended to be current as of the time it was written. It is sold with the understanding that the publisher is not engaged in rendering legal, accounting, or other professional services. If legal advice or other expert assistance is required, the services of a competent professional person should be sought. Also, to confirm that the information has not been affected or changed by recent developments, traditional legal research techniques should be used, including checking primary sources where appropriate.

(Based on the Declaration of Principles jointly adopted by a Committee of the American Bar Association and a Committee of Publishers and Associations.)

You may order this or any other Oxford University Press publication by
visiting the Oxford University Press website at www.oup.com

To Serge, Rebecca, and Nick

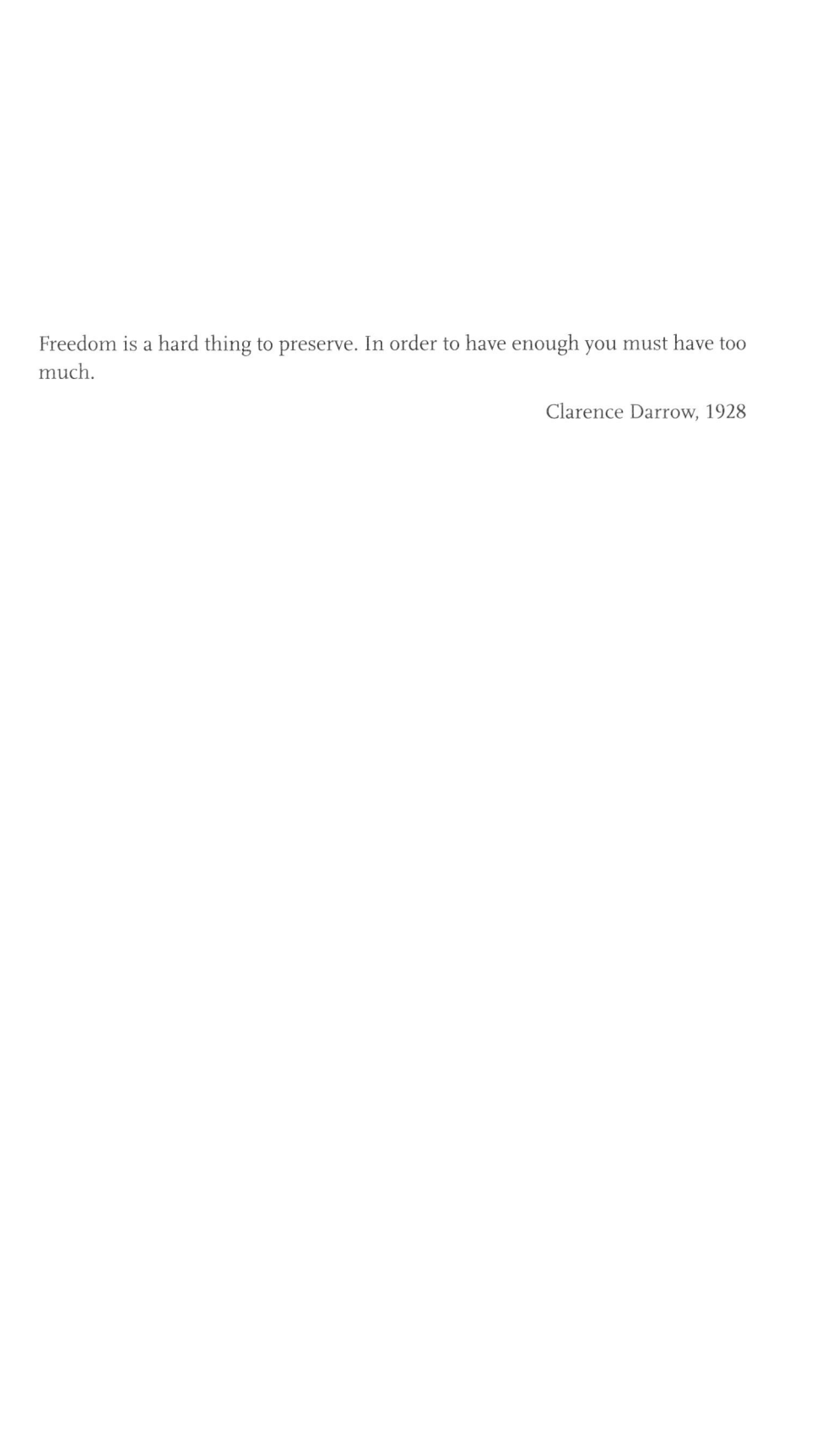

Freedom is a hard thing to preserve. In order to have enough you must have too much.

Clarence Darrow, 1928

CONTENTS

Acknowledgments   xi
Preface   xiii

PART I. PROLEGOMENA   1

Chapter 1. Introduction   3
Chapter 2. "Rights" Discourse   13
Chapter 3. Structural Impediments to Consistent Application
    of "Universal" Human Rights   21

PART II. THE DIFFICULT ISSUES   35

Chapter 4. The Enlarged View of Rights in Contemporary Constitutions
    and Human Rights Conventions—The Notion of Defeasible Rights   37
Chapter 5. Litigation Involving a Conflict of Rights, Each
    of Equal Value   51

PART III. THE LIMITED HELP FROM PHILOSOPHY
AND THE SOCIAL SCIENCES   75

Chapter 6. The Epistemology of Judicial Decision Making   77
Chapter 7. The Unsuccessful Attempt to Find a Philosophical
    "North Star" to Aid in Judicial Decision Making   89
Chapter 8. The Use of Balancing Tests and Factor Analysis—The Inevitable
    Tendency to Resort to Bright-Line Tests   105

PART IV. CASE-BY-CASE ADJUDICATION   117

Chapter 9. An Overview of Case-by-Case Adjudication, Its Possible Goals,
    and the Influence of Legal Traditions   119
Chapter 10. The Optimal Conditions for Case-by-Case Adjudication
    and Its Limits   129
Chapter 11. Case-by-Case Adjudication of Contentious Human Rights
    Controversies   147

PART V. CONCLUSION   165

Chapter 12. What If We Must Choose?   167

Bibliography 177
Table of Cases   183
Index   189

ACKNOWLEDGMENTS

Many people have assisted me in the preparation of this book. A number of them were students at the Duke Law School. My principal student research assistants on this book have been Maciej Borowicz and Tom Watterson, and I also received valuable assistance from others, particularly Karen Beach and Greg McDonough. I owe a great debt to the reference librarians at the Duke Law Library, especially to Kristina Alayan, Jennifer Behrens, Molly Brownfield, and Katherine Topulos. Their prompt and efficient response to my inquiries significantly eased my burdens. Very special thanks must go to the friends who read this book in draft form: Peter Glazebrook, who also helped me on matters of British law, Michael Mirande, a former student of mine, and H. Jefferson Powell, who had the patience to read two plus drafts of this book. Without the moral support of Jeff Powell and of my wife, Deborah, who also very painstakingly went over the draft manuscript, I have some doubts whether I could have persevered in what I have come to appreciate in retrospect was a very ambitious project. I would be remiss if I did not also acknowledge the help on French law provided by John Bell, or if I did not express my gratitude to the judges and staff of the European Court of Human Rights who were kind enough to welcome me on a visit to observe the Court in June 2007. Of the many people who worked on the manuscript, Dana Norvell and Balfour Smith, both of whom read and helped edit the entire manuscript, are particularly deserving of mention. I must also thank Pat Roz, who was always ready to pitch in whenever needed. Finally, I should like to express my appreciation of the support provided by the Eugene T. Bost, Jr. Research Professorship of the Charles A. Cannon Charitable Trust No. 3, which enabled me to take a research leave for the spring 2007 semester and of the Duke Law School for providing me with a sabbatical leave during the fall semester of 2009.

PREFACE

The ambitious goal of this book, as suggested by its alternate title, is to examine how, if at all, courts can deal with cases involving the intersection and even outright conflict between freedom of expression and the growing number of other individual and social rights and values that developed societies have accepted as worth protecting through the judicial process. As someone whose academic concerns have always centered around the subject of legal reasoning, an interest in what has become the subject of this book was initially piqued when, as I describe in Chapter 3, I saw that significant differences existed between common law and civil law methods of legal argumentation and that, as a result, the same legal text might be applied differently in a common law system than it would be in a civil law system. I soon realized that not only were there different approaches to legal problems entrenched in those legal cultures, but also, and more importantly, that these differences were the result of different views of the nature and function of the state. These views of the nature and function of the state have become particularly visible as nations on the international as well as the national level choose to delegate to courts the difficult job of providing context to a wide range of so-called human rights that are vaguely worded, explicitly declared to be defeasible, and that, in some cases, are expressly declared to be of equal value to other similarly defined rights with which they might inevitably come in conflict. Given the increasing recognition of the existence of what might be called universal human rights, it is a subject that can only adequately be approached from a comparative perspective. I have focused much of my attention on decisions in the United States and on decisions in Europe rendered by courts in the United Kingdom and by the European Court of Human Rights.

The need to consider at the international level the decisions of the European Court of Human Rights is obvious. As of 2006, the number of judgments issued by the European Court of Human Rights had exceeded by a factor of at least twenty the number of judgments issued by the Inter-American Court of Human Rights. The third and only other international court of human rights, the African Court on Human and Peoples' Rights, issued its first judgment in December 2009. The European Court of Justice also deals with what might be called human rights. This is a natural consequence of the fact that the Treaty of Rome does contain a "Social Chapter" and that Article 6 of the Lisbon Treaty expressly adopts the European Charter of Fundamental Rights of 2000, as "adapted at Strasbourg on December 12, 2007," and directs the European Union to accede to the European Convention for the Protection of Human Rights and Fundamental Freedoms. Not surprisingly, the European Court of Justice has accepted the decisions of the European Court of Human Rights as part of its jurisprudence although there is no formal requirement for it to have done so. In doing so, it declared that "respect for fundamental rights forms an integral part of the general principles of law protected by the Court of Justice. The protection of such rights, whilst inspired by the constitutional traditions common to the Member states, must be ensured within the framework of the structure and objectives of the Community."[1] Thus far many of the European Court of Justice's decisions in this area have focused on discrimination in the workplace.[2] This is understandable because the treaties that originally established the jurisdiction of the organs of the European Union did not explicitly refer to individual rights and particularly not the individual rights on which we shall largely be focusing as the discussion proceeds.[3]

The reason for including many references to United States law is that the American decisions often conflict with those of European courts and this conflict provides a valuable platform for a comparative study. Finally, the decisions of the courts of the United Kingdom are also an obvious choice for major consideration not only because of their own intrinsic interest but also because they represent a major and good-faith effort to accommodate values long given primacy in the common law to the more complex and diffuse system of values enshrined in the European Convention.

The point of this book is to examine how the courts can deal with a world in which many values increasingly compete with freedom of expression, including freedom of religious expression, without the courts themselves taking on the role of moral arbiter. I will discuss ways in which this might be successfully done in contexts in which rights of privacy or important state interests are in potential conflict with freedom of expression, but I also will be obliged to acknowledge the possibility that we may in the end not be able to come up with a completely satisfactory method. In that case, we may be forced either to abandon our commitment to a regime of multiple basic rights some of which are of equal value, or accept that, despite our protestations to the contrary, we are in practice implicitly favoring one right or social value over another.

---

1. Case 11/70, Internationale Handelsgesellschaft v. Einfuhr und Vorratsselle für Getreide und Futtermitel, [1970] ECR 1125, 1133.

2. *See*, e.g,. Case C-50/96, Deutsche Telekom v. Schröder, [2000] ECR I-743.

3. For a good summary of all but the most recent of these developments, see Elizabeth F. Defeis, *Human Rights and the European Court of Justice: An Appraisal*, 31 FORDHAM INT'L L.J. 1104 (2008). *See also* Suzanne Burri, *The Position of the European Court of Justice with Respect to the Enforcement of Human Rights, in* CHANGING PERCEPTIONS OF SOVEREIGNTY AND HUMAN RIGHTS: ESSAYS IN HONOUR OF CEES FLINTERMAN 311–27 (Ineke Boerefijn and Jenny E. Goldschmidt eds., 2008); Andrew Williams, *Respecting Fundamental Rights in the New Union: A Review, in* THE FUNDAMENTALS OF EU LAW REVISITED (Catherine Barnard ed., 2007).

PART I

PROLEGOMENA

1. INTRODUCTION

One of the most important characteristics of the contemporary world is the growing acceptance of the idea that there are truly universal human rights, and that courts—whether on the international or the national level—are the appropriate bodies to adjudicate disputes as to the content of those rights and their application to concrete situations. This is a book about how courts might perform that task. It begins with a description of how courts have thus far tried to perform that task, then examines the problems that are encountered as they try to perform that task, and finally explores the several ways that have been suggested as to how they might more satisfactorily perform that task in dealing with the ever-expanding volume of litigation, particularly in Europe, on the content and scope of any such rights.

Because, as explained in the preface, the most developed jurisprudence on the content, scope, and application of human rights law is in Europe and the United States, this book will focus primarily, but not exclusively, on decisions from the United States and from European courts such as the House of Lords[1] and particularly the European Court of Human Rights, which has handled more human rights disputes than all other international courts combined over the entire course of human history.[2] The book focuses in large part, but not exclusively, on disputes involving the right to freedom of expression, the right to religious practice and expression, and the right of privacy, not only because these rights are involved in many contemporary disputes, but also because there is much disagreement as to the reach of these rights, since the exercise of any one of these three categories of rights often comes in conflict with the exercise of another of those rights or with certain important state interests. The problem faced by the courts here is one of interpretation and the resolution of conflicts between important human interests. These sorts of conflicts are generally not involved in cases involving the enforcement of what most people would accept as incontrovertible human entitlements such as not to be enslaved nor to be the victims of genocide or of torture—matters where, as a practical matter, the only real issue is normally the enforcement of these broadly accepted universal legal prohibitions by political means, including sometimes the application of force.

---

1. The appellate jurisdiction of the House of Lords ceased to exist as of July 30, 2009. Its successor, the Supreme Court of the United Kingdom, became operational on October 1, 2009. There are no substantive changes in jurisdiction or in the mode of hearing appeals. *See* note 15, *infra*.

2. *See* Karen J. Alter, *Delegating to International Courts: Self-Binding vs. Other-Binding Delegation*, 71 LAW & CONTEMP. PROBS. 37, 57–60 (2008).

The notion of human rights, and even of universal human rights, has a long history. We shall have occasion to refer to some of the historical development of the notion of human rights in the next chapter. What we might remark on here is the breathtaking expansion of the range of asserted universal human rights and the use of courts to protect those rights, a phenomenon that took wing in the last quarter of the twentieth century.[3] Undoubtedly the increasing globalization of the world economy has made it easier to envision a body of enforceable human rights law that, like trade law, transcends national boundaries. So has our rapidly changing vision of the role of the state and its growing responsibility for not only the economic but also the emotional welfare of its citizens, as well as, perhaps inevitably, the increasing dependence on courts to facilitate the smooth functioning of all these changes on both a national and an international level. This accelerating reliance on courts is a particularly prominent feature of the burgeoning field of human rights. On the national level, entrusting courts to resolve contentious and often extremely complex issues reflects a growing social demand for state recognition and protection of what are coming to be considered basic human rights. At the same time, this trend also reflects a mistrust of the ability of the legislative and executive arms of government to recognize and protect those rights adequately. On the international level, it also reflects the view that there are issues which transcend the authority of individual nation-states and which therefore can only be governed by a universal law that, though influenced by the actions of nation-states, must ultimately be discovered and declared by courts whose members are in some way independent of the political control of any individual nation-state. Since, however, there is no truly functioning world government, this in practice means courts that are subject to no effective legally sanctioned political control.

This resort to courts rather than political action to define and resolve the fundamental issues underlying the expansion of human rights law that is the focus of this book reminds one, in a way, of medieval natural-law theories in which there was no necessary connection between politics and law. There is, however, a major difference. In a dynamic world such as the one in which we live, it is the courts as expositors of an evolving law that are at the apex of the system, rather than a relatively static natural law which is not dependent on any human institutions for its authority. What is shared by these two situations is the belief that there are universally known or, at least, universally knowable norms of universal application.

Considering human beings in their capacity as discrete individuals, it is hard to deny that we each believe in some sort of universal values. As Chaïm Perelman noted, this appeal to universal values is implicit in our references to beauty,

---

3. *See* SAMUEL MOYN, THE LAST UTOPIA (2010).

justice, or even truth.[4] This human characteristic of appealing to universal values is what he tried to capture in what he called discourse directed to the "universal audience,"[5] a feature of human communication and argumentation that was also captured by George Herbert Mead's notion of "universal discourse."[6] As the discussion proceeds, we shall have several occasions to discuss this feature of human belief and practice at greater length.[7] What is even more crucial to the inquiry of this book, however, is the additional assumption—repeatedly made by many people and again reminiscent of natural law theory—that there is actual agreement on the content of many of our basic social values, and especially those that underlie the modern notion of universal human rights.

That many human beings have long believed in the potential knowability of universal and concretely applicable moral truths is undeniable. We may, for example, recall Cicero's response to the contention that there cannot truly be a universal natural law because there is no universal agreement as to the nature of its divine source. To this objection, Cicero replied that the fact that all people believe in some kind of divinity—even if they are mistaken about what kind of divinity it is—indicates that there is such a divine source for the moral excellence that resides in God and in man, and for the knowledge of which, despite inconsistencies and errors in their thinking, intelligent people turn to philosophy and reason in order to gain knowledge of the truth.[8] This is an argument picked up in the mid-seventeenth century by John Locke in his Essays on the Law of Nature;[9] and it was followed up by Locke's further assertion that the content of the law of nature is to be determined through the process of rational discourse taking as its starting point our sense experiences.[10] The point was further refined

---

4. CH. PERELMAN AND L. OLBRECHTS-TYTECA, THE NEW RHETORIC: A TREATISE ON ARGUMENTATION § 7 (J. Wilkinson & P. Weaver trans., 1969) [hereafter THE NEW RHETORIC]. This work was originally published in French in 1958 as TRAITÉ DE L'ARGUMENTATION, now in its 6th edition (2008). It is commonly referred to as Perelman's work. Olbrechts-Tyteca was Perelman's research assistant whose invaluable contribution included assembling many of the massive number of rhetorical examples contained in the work.

5. See ibid, and passim.

6. GEORGE HERBERT MEAD, MIND, SELF, AND SOCIETY 195 (1934).

7. See Chapter VI, infra.

8. MARCUS TULLIUS CICERO, LAWS, Bk. I, §§ 24–35, 47–63, Oxford World's Classics edition, THE REPUBLIC AND THE LAWS (N. Rudd trans., 1998).

9. JOHN LOCKE, ESSAYS ON THE LAW OF NATURE 115 (Essay I) (trans. from the Latin by W. von Leyden, 1954). Dr. von Leyden dates the ESSAYS to the period 1663–64 and states that they were probably delivered in Latin as lectures at Oxford at the end of 1664. Id. at 12–13.

10. Id. at 147–59 (Essay IV).

in Pufendorf's assertion that natural law consists of propositions propounded by the learned which the unlearned are unable to refute.[11]

In less obviously elitist terms, the belief in the hypothetically knowable content of a concrete normative order is captured in Adam Smith's notion of "an impartial spectator"[12] and in the nineteenth century legal philosopher John Austin's assertion that the convergence theory of truth applied not only to scientific inquiry but to deontological inquiry as well.[13] Finally, in our contemporary world, those who are not complete relativists but, like Jürgen Habermas, are nevertheless unwilling to impose their own view of moral truth on others can, by referring to an "ideal speech situation," hold out the promise that in such a situation, with unlimited time for discussion, universal agreement as to what is the appropriate resolution to social disagreement will eventually emerge.[14] Indeed, the belief that there is a core of knowable universal human rights may be proceeding on the assumption that such an ideal speech situation capable of dealing with a multitude of often competing ethical values actually can be created in the here and now simply by referring to the judiciary the difficult questions presented when important human interests and values come in conflict. The validity of any such assumption will be among the issues that will be discussed in this book.

The modern movement of enunciating certain general rights of all persons, in what might be called "constitutional" or "basic" or "fundamental" documents, and then actually resorting to courts to enforce these rights clearly raises important questions. This increasing reliance on courts, on the international as well as the national level, to meet the rising expectations of people around the world highlights the need to determine the proper social role of courts. If the judicial forum is to serve as the institutional setting in which disputes about contentious and often complex social issues are to be settled, we must face up to the question of how courts might be able to fill that role. This means that we must first

---

11. SAMUEL VON PUFENDORF, DE JURE NATURAE ET GENTIUM, Bk. II, Ch. I, 513, first published in 1672. Hugo Grotius also relied on the agreement of "advanced" civilizations as the means for discovering the content of natural law in his great treatise on international law, DE JURE BELLI AC PACIS, Bk. I, Ch. I, xii, first published in 1625.

12. ADAM SMITH, THE THEORY OF MORAL SENTIMENTS 118, 131, 134, 137 and *passim* (1759) (Liberty Fund facsimile edition, 1982). Smith sometimes refers to this imagined observer as the "indifferent spectator," as for example in *id.* at 85.

13. JOHN AUSTIN, I LECTURES ON JURISPRUDENCE, LECTURE III at 122–40 (Fifth rev. ed. by R. Campbell, 1885). The first six of Austin's lectures, which of course includes this one, have been reprinted a number of times under the title, THE PROVINCE OF JURISPRUDENCE DETERMINED.

14. *See* JÜRGEN HABERMAS, BETWEEN FACTS AND NORMS 185–86 (W. Rehg trans., 1996). A good discussion of what in English is called Habermas' notion of the ideal speech situation is contained in RAYMOND GUESS, THE IDEA OF A CRITICAL THEORY: HABERMAS AND THE FRANKFURT SCHOOL 64–70 (1981).

determine, in as concrete a way as possible, what are the questions society wants the courts to decide. We must then explore how courts might try to go about deciding those contentious questions. Finally, we must confront the difficult issue of whether courts can decide those questions in a way that satisfies the expectations of the public at large and the judges themselves as to the appropriate social role of judges.

It is axiomatic that, in any decisional context in which only a yes or no answer is required, any decisional body with an odd number of members will come up with a decision. If one is not troubled by a process in which, for example, five-to-four decisions of the United States Supreme Court or three-to-two decisions of panels of the House of Lords, or its successor, the Supreme Court of the United Kingdom,[15] are no longer an unusual outcome in controversial cases, there is no problem. One merely has to accept that social issues, no matter how contentious, must nevertheless be decided. The fact that one group of nine or five judges might very likely decide the issue differently than would another group of nine or five judges is either not a matter of consequence or something that cannot be avoided. After all, no one questions that judges are given authority by society to make such decisions, and every society needs a mechanism for deciding even controversial issues.

Recent declarations by judges sitting on the United States Supreme Court and in the House of Lords have indeed explicitly acknowledged that the particular composition of those final appellate courts in these highly contentious and emotionally charged cases will often lead to a decision different from that which would be reached by a tribunal composed of different judges. One might say that this is merely to recognize the inevitable. For example, in *Parents Involved in Community Schools v. Seattle School District No. 1*, a five-to-four decision of the United States Supreme Court involving race-based criteria in the assignment of students to public primary and secondary schools, Justice Stevens declared in his dissent that "[i]t is my firm conviction that no Member of the Court that I joined in 1973 would have agreed with today's decision."[16] In a similar but less emotionally charged vein, in an English case pitting the plaintiff's right of privacy

---

15. *See* Sir Richard Buxton, *Sitting en Banc in the New Supreme Court*, 125 L.Q. Rev. 288 (2009). The title is ironic because, as the writer, a retired Court of Appeal Judge notes, the new court, like its predecessor, will never sit en banc. Although composed of twelve judges, it appears that it will normally continue to sit in panels of five, although occasionally perhaps in larger panels as the House of Lords did in *Regina v. Bow Street Metropolitan Stipendiary Magistrate, ex parte Pinochet Ugarte (No. 3)*, [2000] A.C. 147 (1999) (panel of seven) and in *Secretary of State v. AF (No. 3)* [2009] 3 All E.R. 643 (H.L.) (panel of nine). Sir Anthony Mason, *Envoi to the House of Lords—A View From Afar*, 125 L.Q. Rev. 584, 595–96 (2009), believes "that there is certainly a case for sitting no less than seven judges in any case and nine, or even eleven, in controversial cases or cases of exceptional importance."

16. Parents Involved in Community Schools v. Seattle School District No. 1, 551 U.S. 701, 803 (2007).

against the defendant-newspaper's right to freedom of expression, Lord Carswell conceded that "[w]eighing and balancing these factors is a process which may well lead different people to different conclusions, as one may readily see from consideration of the judgments of the courts below and by several members of the Appellate Committee of your Lordships' House."[17] That case, *Campbell v. MGN Ltd*, was a three-to-two decision in which the majority, of whom Lord Carswell was one, ruled in favor of the privacy claim. We shall have occasion to consider the *Campbell* case at greater length at several places later in this book. For present purposes, it is enough to note that the *Campbell* case was heard by nine judges as it wound its way through several layers of courts. Five of the judges—all three judges in the Court of Appeal and the two dissenters in the House of Lords—ruled in favor of the freedom of expression claim. Four judges—the trial judge and the three-judge majority in the House of Lords—ruled in favor of the privacy claim which was the claim that eventually prevailed.

As the House of Lords was increasingly required to decide cases involving serious basic issues of social policy, not all of them what we would call "human rights" issues, it is not surprising that it should have produced an increasing number of three-to-two decisions on at least some issues.[18] Nor should it be surprising that the conflicts between the rights of privacy and of freedom of expression should be among these closely divided decisions. If, however, one expects something more from those who perform judicial functions than simply deciding difficult and emotionally charged controversies, there are serious issues to be resolved and serious difficulties to overcome. Many of the most important questions that will be discussed concern disputes involving hotly contested issues concerning what are considered basic human rights. These developments force us to consider whether means exist by which courts might decide those issues such that the judges would, in the end, not so frequently be forced to admit that different and equally diligent judges might in good conscience reach the opposite conclusion.

---

17. Campbell v. MGN Ltd, [2004] A.C. 457 at ¶ 168. On the continued use of panels by the Supreme Court of the United Kingdom, *see* note 15, *supra*.

18. Research done by my research assistant, Greg McDonough, reveals that there were 25 three-to-two decisions in the House of Lords in the ten-year period 1950–59, and 32 in the ten-year period 1990–99. But in the nine-year period 2000–08, if one includes three cases decided by the Privy Council, all of which included human rights issues and in two of these three the Privy Council split five-to-four, there were 51 cases in which there were such sharp divisions on at least some of the key issues. A significant number of all the sharply divided cases decided in the more recent period involved human rights issues. As is well known, the Judicial Committee of the Privy Council was largely and often exclusively composed of judges who sit in the House of Lords, and this practice of having judges of the highest appellate court sit in the Judicial Committee has not changed with the establishment of the Supreme Court of the United Kingdom.

In order to approach those ultimate questions, we shall have to consider first, in the context of legal discourse, what we mean by the term "right." More specifically, what do we mean by the term "human rights"? Are there any philosophical principles that might help us provide reasonably concrete and objective answers to all these questions? The study of all these questions is not made any easier by the fact that they also bring into play questions concerning the relationship of the state to its citizens and the role of the courts in the evolution of that relationship. If the state is not only required to refrain from certain sorts of interference in the lives of its citizens and to protect those citizens from third parties who might physically injure their persons and property, but is also required to provide them with certain judicially determined levels of economic and social welfare as well as emotional tranquility, the range of questions that might require judicial resolution expands greatly. Such a requirement obliges us to consider whether we might be approaching, at least in the so-called developed nations, a world in which, because of the enormous reach of the state's power to act, anything which the state allows anyone to do that affects others is traceable back to the state. This was Bentham's view of the logical nature of law at a time when the actual power of the state to intervene in the lives of its citizens was much less than it is today.[19] It is one of the issues underlying what, in the United States, is called the state-action problem,[20] a subject at one time much mooted but now relatively quiescent, perhaps because, being largely thought difficult if not impossible to answer, it was best ignored on the ground that "sleeping dogs are best left quiet."

If almost nothing that anyone can do that affects other people, and even to a large extent himself, can be done without the help of either resources or facilities provided by the state, almost everything is, in a practical sense as well as in the logical sense espoused by Bentham, quite plausibly either state action or, to adopt an alternate paradigm, potentially subject to state regulation. That, in turn, at the very least has the awkward consequence of making the individual in his actions the agent of the state and subject to all the duties and restraints imposed on public officials. By thus opening up an ever-broadening range of activities of private actors to state regulation, the number of instances in which courts will be asked to decide contentious social issues will only increase. This is a vast subject. A thorough treatment of it, were it even possible, would require a very extended discussion that is obviously beyond the scope of this work. Nonetheless, some of the conclusions reached in this book may be relevant to that inquiry and thus

---

19. JEREMY BENTHAM, OF LAWS IN GENERAL, Ch. II, § 6 (H.L.A. Hart ed., 1970).

20. One of the few recent discussions of the issues raised by the state-action problem provides a very good summary of the issues it raises and the problems it encounters. *See* Stephen Gardbaum, *The "Horizontal Effect" of Constitutional Rights,* 102 MICH. L. REV. 387, 411–34 and *passim* (2003).

justify the brief further discussion of this broader social issue in later portions of this book.[21]

It is no use denying or even decrying the fact that, in an increasingly urbanized society, the state is constantly expanding its role in the economic and social lives of its inhabitants. This development only accentuates the importance of perennial questions such as what are the differences not only in the roles of courts and legislatures but also in the decision-making processes of courts and legislatures. Certainly, the increased use of courts operating at the international level, even further removed from any meaningful political control than are national judicial tribunals, only heightens the urgency of dealing with these issues. Furthermore, with the increased involvement of courts in the details of governmental operations, are courts becoming just another part of an enormous, growing, and nominally democratically established administrative apparatus; or is judicial decision making something different in kind from that of an administrative organ of the state, however honest, efficient, and competent that administrative organ might be? Indeed, at the international level, where, outside of the area of world trade, there is very little of an efficient and effective administrative apparatus, are the courts, by default, in fact being asked to serve as essentially unreviewable, and therefore unaccountable, organs of administration as much as they are judicial bodies in the traditional sense?

These, of course, are all issues that transcend human rights adjudication and relate to all types of litigation, whether on a national or international level, but the issues involved in discussions about the proper role of courts are currently more prominently raised in contemporary human rights adjudication. In some of the most controversial cases, courts have had to deal with questions such as whether religious believers can wear head scarves or other indicia of religious belief in public buildings or whether it can be made a crime to deny that the events described by the term Holocaust ever took place.[22] Given the emotive reactions that these types of cases generate, it is no wonder that human rights litigation attracts the attention of the general public because non-lawyers not only have strong feelings on these sorts of issues but can even envision how the outcome of that type of litigation might affect them in both positive and negative ways.

We must finally not forget that, to be useful, our study must not only eventually bring the discussion to bear on some relatively concrete contexts, but must, if possible, also try to suggest concrete ways in which the methods of adjudicating actual clashes between competing human rights can be either improved or changed to address the current difficulties presented by that type of adjudication. In particular, we shall explore the repeated suggestion in the cases that we shall

---

21. *See*, in particular, the closing portions of Chapter 10, *infra*.
22. These are matters that we shall discuss in Chapter 4, *infra*.

be discussing that a process of case-by-case adjudication can serve as the means for arriving at a satisfactory solution to these difficult matters. All this we shall do by examining problems and issues that have already surfaced in human rights litigation. We must begin, however, at a more basic level in order to understand better the complexity of the problems before us. In the next two chapters, we shall start the discussion by examining first what we mean when we label something a right, particularly a human right, and then explore whether the existence of different legal traditions facilitates or inhibits the development of a truly universal human rights law. We shall then proceed to a detailed discussion of contested and controversial human rights cases, starting with cases involving the interaction between freedom of speech, including religious expression, and other important social interests and then moving on to an examination of cases involving a conflict between rights of privacy and freedom of expression. In the course of that discussion, we shall see that it has come to be generally accepted that these disputes will have to be resolved by some sort of balancing process in a continuing course of case-by-case adjudication.

We shall then turn to the task of describing a process of case-by-case adjudication that might be adequate to the task entrusted to it and what if any assistance can be provided by contemporary legal philosophy. The project is not an easy one, and it is quite possible that we shall not be able to come up with a process of case-by-case adjudication that completely meets our expectations. We shall finally consider what other options might be open to us if we wish to construct a more intellectually satisfying procedure for resolving disputes involving conflicting human rights and social objectives.

2. "RIGHTS" DISCOURSE

Although there is much talk of rights in all kinds of discourse, it is not at all clear that people are consistent in what they mean to say when they speak of rights. And, of course, if any given individual is not always consistent in his own usage of the language of rights, it would be chimerical to expect that, when people are arguing among themselves about the existence and ambit of some asserted right, they are necessarily engaging in a discussion in which all the participants have the same conception of what a right is. The concept of "rights" in legal discourse has at least two important functions. The first is the substantive function of describing what the right-holder is entitled to and, to be truly helpful, of also identifying the person or persons who are required to respect that entitlement. Entitlement, however, is a word that can have both a legal as well as a moral connotation. In the human rights litigation that forms the principal focus of our discussion, the concept of entitlement that underlies the notion of "a right" clearly carries both connotations. If anything, the moral connotation is the dominant one even in legal discourse.[1] The second function of the concept of "rights," particularly in human rights litigation, is to suggest that, in applying or even recognizing a right, the courts are not exercising the authority granted to them in order to impose their own views on the members of the society which they serve but are, instead, merely recognizing and applying some generally accepted entitlement. We should begin then by getting some idea of what we are referring to when, as we so often do, we start speaking in terms of human rights.

In legal analysis, it has been customary to use Wesley Newcomb Hohfeld's schema when analyzing what it means to have a right.[2] For Hohfeld, any talk about a right necessarily implied a corresponding duty. That is, a Hohfeldian right is always a right by one person, X, that another person, Y, should do something or refrain from doing something. Hohfeldian rights are often called "claim rights." In the Hohfeldian framework conventionally followed in legal reasoning, there are no rights "to" anything or even simply "to do" something. A right to social welfare is simply a right that the state must do something, which, in the analysis generally followed in scholarly discussions, must be translated into a right of the claimant, X, that some official of the state, Y, should pay him some

---

1. This overlap between the moral and legal meaning of right in human rights discourse is, as we shall note several times as this book progresses, a source of confusion and difficulty in any attempt to construct an appropriate model for the judicial resolution of hotly contested human rights issues.
2. WESLEY N. HOHFELD, FUNDAMENTAL LEGAL CONCEPTIONS (1919) (hereafter HOHFELD).

money, a situation that can be described as one in which the official, Y, is under a duty to pay X some money.[3] In the law, a right to have something, say ownership of a physical object, is treated as a right *in rem*, that is the set of rights that some individual or some collective with legal status has against an indefinite number of other discrete individuals that they not, for example, interfere with the right-holder's possession.

By contrast, in the Hohfeldian scheme, what are commonly called rights *to do* something are not really rights at all but rather what he calls "privileges." To say that someone has a right, i.e., a privilege, such as for example to speak, is to say that he is under no duty not to speak. Hohfeld was insistent that to know what the practical implications of a privilege are one must know what rights, if any, that person has that others should not interfere with the exercise of his privilege. For example, if one simply has a privilege to speak, it does not imply that anyone is under a duty to listen to him or even to stop making so much noise that no one can make out what the speaker is saying. Likewise, a person's "right" to marry does not imply that anyone is under a duty to marry him or even necessarily to facilitate his getting married. It only means that other people cannot interfere with his making use of the existing institutional mechanisms to get married. Whether he has a right that someone should ultimately make it possible for him to actually utilize those mechanisms to get married is still another, and separate, question.

This lack of substance in what Hohfeld called privilege cannot be avoided by simply asserting that what Hohfeld would have called a privilege to speak is really a right to "freedom of speech" or "freedom of expression." This would be an attempt to retain the apparent analytical rigor of Hohfeld's analysis of what rights are while at the same time ignoring the essential implications of his intellectual endeavor. Hohfeld's purpose in constructing his analytical framework was to avoid confusion, and, in particular, the confusion between rights and privileges. It is certainly evident that one of the reasons there is so much talk of rights in legal philosophy and legal argument is precisely to attach the emotive features of the term "right" to legal relations that are quite amorphous and, in Hohfeld's view, were quite lacking in content. Thus, for Hohfeld, standing by itself, the most that a *constitutional* right to freedom of speech or expression can possibly connote, if it is to be more than the mere absence of a duty not to speak, is a right that persons exercising the power and authority of the state may not punish him for speaking or expressing himself. That, in the abstract, without the enunciation of some detailed additional rights, is the extent of the duty that is the

---

3. That this was a necessary implication of Hohfeld's work was pointed out from the beginning. *See* Arthur Corbin, *Legal Analysis and Terminology*, 29 YALE L.J. 163 (1919). It is also, of course, the way Kelsen deals with the problem of the rights and duties of juristic persons. *See*, e.g., HANS KELSEN, GENERAL THEORY OF LAW AND STATE 95, 93–109, 182–201 (A. Wedberg trans., 1949) (1945).

corollary of a so-called constitutional right of freedom of speech or expression. Likewise, a right to one's bodily integrity, either against the state or against private persons, is only a right that neither state officials nor private persons may invade one's bodily integrity; and, if they do, that the law will give one a remedy against them. To sum up, as Hohfeld correctly pointed out in a criticism he made of some of the work of John Chipman Gray, abstract rights to have something or to do something, if they are to have anything more than a rhetorical function, are really nothing more than privileges to do something or to have and enjoy something.[4] As a logical matter, references to these sorts of abstract rights do not tell us very much.

The law does of course provide individuals with rights in the Hohfeldian sense against the actions of state officials that interfere with their person, property, or some of their activities, as it does against the actions of private individuals interfering with those interests and activities, by providing the accompanying state-provided remedies for their violation. Furthermore, as a historical matter, where the existence of some such remedies was the *only* basis for asserting the existence of such a legal right, it was generally accepted that the state was not under any legal obligation to provide any such remedies. There were thus situations in which the integrity of a person's body or property or other interests could be threatened with injury and even actually damaged in which no legal remedy was available at all; and to some extent there still are. Moreover, with the rise of legal positivism and the decline of natural law theories and the consequent sharp separation of law from morality, it also generally came to be accepted by many lawyers and philosophers that the state itself was the creator of all so-called legal rights, from which it followed that only constitutional texts, or statutes, or legal decisions could be the sources of legally recognizable rights. Over time, an increasing number of such rights, with the attendant remedies for their violations, came to be established but, until the moment of such recognition, no legal right and therefore no corresponding legal duty existed at all.

Thomas Hobbes was one of the first thinkers to present this position in such a stark form,[5] which still expressly figures in some discussions of tax and other economic policies. If, for example, one accepts that property rights are basically the creations of the state, then, if the implications of this proposition are carried to their logical conclusion, one is forced to conclude that what the state gives, it can take away. Proponents of what others might conceive of as confiscatory taxation have based much of their argument on such a view.[6] If the bundle of rights we call property is simply a matter of state creation, one whose property is taken

---

4. HOHFELD, *supra*, note 2, at 40–42.
5. *See,* e.g., THOMAS HOBBES, LEVIATHAN Ch.13, at 66 (Everyman's Library 1914) (1651).
6. *See,* e.g., LIAM MURPHY & THOMAS NAGEL, THE MYTH OF OWNERSHIP 8 and *passim* (2002).

from him for the sake of funding some social initiatives has no complaints, even on moral grounds, if the benefits from those social initiatives far outweigh the injury suffered by the person whose property is taken. That is not to say that, in deciding to abrogate an existing property right, it would be inappropriate to consider the expectations of people who have organized their affairs on the basis of the existence of that right; but, in the last analysis, the abrogation of legal rights, as well as their creation, depends on the pragmatic, prudential decisions of those exercising political power.

Someone for whom the implications of the position that all rights are the creation of the state are difficult to accept, might wish to take a less stark view of the origins of legal rights. Such a person might contend that legal rights are not the mere products of the exercise of political power, but rather have their origin in social practice. Under this view, all that is asked of the courts or other organs of the state is that they should recognize and enforce rights that have been validated by an established general social practice. Rights of property and of official recognition of marriage between heterosexuals would fall into this category. Rights of homosexuals to take advantage of state-provided mechanisms in order to marry—whatever the justice of recognizing those rights—have not yet received such wide approbation although they may perhaps now be on the road to receiving such recognition. For the moment, if they are to have any basis as existing universal human rights, it must be on the ground that such rights are not mere creations of the state but are instead, to use Joachim Hruschka's words, "an a priori extension of practical reason."[7] What are the rights that the state is obliged to introduce and protect is an enormous question and is not one that I propose to examine in depth in this work even if I had the competence to attempt to do so. For present purposes, the point is that, if one is going to try to make sense of the notion of rights as used in contemporary litigation, one must at some point be prepared to accept that rights are either purely the product of political decisions by those in control of the organs of the state, or that they are those aspects of general social practice adopted and enforced by the state, or that they reflect universal moral imperatives that the state is morally obliged to recognize and enforce.

With this general background in mind, we can now return to our principal concern, namely how the concept of "rights" figures in contemporary legal theory and how that concept might figure in human rights litigation. Traditionally, as we have noted, the basic paradigm of a legal dispute has involved a claim by one person that another has wronged him by invading some established and socially accepted interest that the legal system of society has undertaken to protect against interference by others. For example, someone has hit the claimant or taken or

---

7. Joachim Hruschka, *The Permissive Law of Practical Reason in Kant's Metaphysics of Morals*, 23 LAW & PHILOSOPHY 45, 71 (2004).

damaged his property. It is taken for granted that, except in exceptional circumstances, such as where defense of one's own person or that of another is involved, no one has any legal right to hit another or to take or damage his property. It is also taken for granted that people should honor their commitments, at least when the legal procedures governing the making of contracts have been followed. There may be a dispute as to who actually owns some real or personal property or whether the legal requirements governing the making of contracts have been followed, but once these issues are resolved, the claimant is normally considered to be entitled to a legal remedy. He is the person who has the right and the defendant has the duty not to violate that right. The claimant has a legal right to receive compensation because it is his rights that have been infringed by the defendant's failure to fulfill his duty to refrain from the offending conduct.

The current enthusiasm for focusing on the notion of rights in an attempt to explain why judges are not trespassing on the domain of legislators when they decide difficult and emotionally laden questions is not, however, primarily concerned with these traditional sorts of legal disputes. This is nowhere more apparent than in the contemporary interest in protecting a broad range of what are now considered to be "basic human rights." The tradition of seeking recognition for basic rights of citizens against often politically motivated state interference has a long history in Western civilization that, in the English-speaking world, can be traced back to the Magna Carta issued in 1215, the English Bill of Rights of 1689, and, of course, the American Bill of Rights of 1791 that consists of the first ten amendments to the United States' Constitution. Most of these rights were narrowly focused and for the most part concerned procedural protections for persons involved not only in criminal prosecutions but also in civil litigation.

The global recognition of what are now called human rights, a much broader category, can certainly be traced back to that most famous of all such documents, the Declaration of the Rights of Man approved by the French National Assembly in August of 1789, whose assertion of the existence of universal human rights was repeated in December 1948, in the promulgation of the Universal Declaration of Human Rights by the General Assembly of the United Nations. But, although global in reach, both the Declaration of the Rights of Man and the Universal Declaration of Human Rights, unlike the American Bill of Rights, were merely hortatory with no immediate legal effect in any nation state. This largely hortatory or aspirational character of most enunciations of universal human rights gradually changed as more nations in the post-World War II era inserted express protections for the rights of individuals into their national constitutions. And now, finally, the European Convention for the Protection of Human Rights and Fundamental Freedoms, with its enunciations of specific legally protected "rights," covers the 47 countries that have thus far ratified it. What has not changed over time, however, is the general belief among the drafters of all these documents that the rights they set forth are not the creations of the state but are rather features and requirements of civilized society to which the state is merely being asked to give legal recognition. This certainly is the universal understanding of the purpose of the European Convention. Furthermore, many people believe that not only are these rights not simply the creations of an all-powerful state but also that the decisions of courts in interpreting and applying these rights are not the last word as to what might be the content and scope of these rights. The huge uproar in the United States when the Supreme Court, in *Kelo v. City of New London*,[8] claiming with some justification to be applying settled law, held that a sufficient public purpose can justify a government's using its power of eminent domain to acquire property to be turned over to a private developer as part of a plan to facilitate the renaissance of a moribund urban area, is proof enough of that. Many American states reacted by expressly forbidding any such use of the eminent domain power, and the United States House of Representatives adopted a resolution prohibiting any funds provided by the fiscal 2006 Appropriations Act for the Department of Housing and Urban Development to be used for the enforcement of the Court's judgment in *Kelo*.[9]

For the moment, we can describe the tasks now facing the courts in dealing with human rights litigation as follows: First, there are the traditional sorts of situations in which a person seeks relief against other individuals or even the state for injuries to his person or property as well as relief for the violation of other long-recognized legal rights entitled to legal protection. Violations of rights to bodily integrity and denial of the right to legal counsel in a criminal prosecution clearly fall into this category and of course continue to be involved in a significant though less controversial subset of human rights litigation. The history of academic writing about the law has until recently largely been concerned with this category of rights which also most clearly fits within the Hohfeldian model. It is obvious that this book will only be concerned with these traditional sorts of rights in an ancillary way.

The book instead focuses on two other broad categories of rights. One of these other categories of rights is concerned with "rights to something." As was pointed out earlier in this chapter, assertions of the existence of any such right would not be considered a true right under a Hohfeldian analysis unless it were accompanied by a description of exactly what it is that the claimant is entitled to and who is required to provide that something to the claimant. As to who is required to provide the claimant with his entitlement, it would normally be some agent of the state. To that extent, the claimant's action would resemble an action by one individual against another for breach of contract or possibly for the

---

8. 545 U.S. 469 (2005).

9. This largely symbolic gesture was H. Amdt. 427 to H.R. 3058, adopted on June 30, 2005. For a contemporary comment on this and the state reactions to *Kelo, see* Bernard W. Bell, *Legislatively Revising* Kelo v. City of New London: *Eminent Domain, Federalism, and Congressional Powers, available at* http://ssrn.com/abstract=800174.

tortious deprivation of a property right. The difference between a private breach of contract action and an action for the failure of the state to honor a person's abstract right to decent housing or affordable healthcare, or some other general welfare right, is that there is nothing resembling a contract or a statutorily prescribed formula to enable a court to determine exactly what the claimant is entitled to. Ideally, one would expect that questions of what and how much would have been settled by legislation, such as by a statutory minimum wage, or by administrative regulation, such as a scale for reimbursement of medical expenses. There is no question that a court could decide such questions but would it then still be acting as a court rather than as an organ of administration. Moreover, in a country, like the United States, that gives the power to tax exclusively to the legislature and forbids spending of public monies that have not been authorized and appropriated for the purpose in question, serious separation of powers issues would arise. As the discussion proceeds, something more will be said on this subject.

The second of these other broad categories of human rights litigation concerns rights which, though recognized, are treated as defeasible for important public purposes or rights whose exercise is likely to come in conflict with the exercise of other recognized human rights. Such defeasible rights do not seem to fit very easily into the sharply defined Hohfeldian concept of the logical structures of legal rights. As is the case under the European Convention on Human Rights[10] and other similar multinational treaties[11] and many post-World War II national constitutions,[12] the recognition of these types of defeasible rights forces courts to consider a wide range of state interests and to navigate a path through the overlapping and often conflicting rights of privacy, freedom of religious expression and practice, and freedom of expression in general. What makes these types of cases unusually difficult is that the courts are, in a sense, again being asked to perform a traditional legislative or administrative function. Simply put, in balancing individual rights against state interests or in resolving a conflict between the competing human rights of different individuals, the courts are required to engage in an exercise of practical wisdom to a particularly heightened extent that seems at odds with traditional notions of the judicial role. This category of situations will be the

---

10. European Convention for the Protection of Human Rights and Fundamental Freedoms, §§ 8, 9, and 10 (hereafter European Convention or European Convention on Human Rights).

11. *See*, e.g., International Covenant on Civil and Political Rights (1966), Articles 18 and 19; American Convention on Human Rights (1969), Articles 11, 12, 13, 27, and 29. Some of these rights (and duties) are covered in Articles 8 to 11 and 27 to 29 of the African Charter on Human and People's Rights (1981).

12. *See*, e.g., Canadian Charter of Rights and Freedoms (Part I of the Constitution Act, [U.K.] 1980), § 1; New Zealand Bill of Rights Act, 1990, § 5; Constitution of South Africa (1996), as amended to 2007, §§ 36, 39.

major focus of this book. That discussion will examine not only how well the courts might decide what we might wish to characterize as the "merits" of a dispute, but also how in doing so they might nevertheless claim to be applying something like the traditional Hohfeldian-based notion of what legal rights are to this new field of legal controversy. That is to say, that they are not taking upon themselves the role of philosopher kings prescribing what is good for society but rather trying to conform to what has been traditionally accepted as the function of the judiciary.

With the adoption of human rights conventions and the establishment of international courts not subject to any meaningful effective political control, one might plausibly argue that modern democracies may have reached a world characterized by the joint sovereignty of legislatures and courts.[13] I proceed on the contrary assumption, however, namely that, in a modern democracy, sovereignty resides in the people and that whatever primacy is accorded to the legislature rests on the fact that its members are chosen by the people and that the ability of the legislature in a modern democratic society to exercise its authority to act on behalf of the people who have elected it rests on the continued acquiescence of the people in its actions. That said, I in no way mean to deny that courts have always made law in the process of deciding concrete cases and will inevitably always continue to do so. What I am saying is that how they do something is as important as what they do. This is the price courts must pay to justify their comparative insulation from politics. This is particularly true in the emotionally charged areas of the law that we shall be discussing.

With this background in mind, we shall review the recent expansion of the universe of human rights. As we embark on that task, it is important to understand that how courts try to perform the tasks entrusted to them will be influenced not only by abstract notions of justice or notions about the nature of the judicial role or even by the felt importance of the values underlying various accepted human rights, but also by the traditions, often of very long standing, of the legal culture from which these courts arise and by the different styles of adjudication followed in different legal traditions. How these factors will materially influence human rights litigation will therefore be the subject of the next and final chapter of the introductory portion of this book. Once we have done that, we shall then be in a position to enter into the heart of what is certainly a complex and emotionally charged subject.

---

13. *See* C. J. S. Knight, *Bi-Polar Sovereignty Restated*, 68 CAMBRIDGE L.J. 361 (2009), for a discussion of how this vision might capture the current situation in the United Kingdom. One might say that acceptance of such a vision captures some aspects of the Austinian view that if there is no "legal" limitation of the exercise of power by an entity, be it a person or a collective body, that entity is a "sovereign." But Austin required such an entity to be able actually to enforce its mandates. Sovereignty for Austin was not solely a logical conception.

3. STRUCTURAL IMPEDIMENTS TO CONSISTENT APPLICATION OF "UNIVERSAL" HUMAN RIGHTS

The effect of the increasing globalization of the world's economic and political structure on the development of law and legal institutions is nowhere more publicly visible than in the burgeoning field of human rights. Whatever might be the downside of globalization, it is a development that raises in the minds and aspirations of many the prospect that, not only will the issues surrounding the proper role of the courts in an increasingly globalized world be resolvable, but that, in the process, we shall also develop a truly universal law of human rights. The purpose of this chapter is to remind us that, even if that ambitious goal of developing a truly universal law of human rights were realizable—as will be explored in the succeeding chapters, there are reasons to believe that such an achievement is unlikely in the foreseeable future—there are still serious structural reasons why it might never result in the consistent application of any such universal law across national boundaries. However much we might desire to attain the goal of consistent application, even among nation states that share the same basic values there are historical and cultural factors that will materially affect our ability to achieve a true congruence in the application of a transnational human rights law. These historical and cultural factors include not only notions about the proper role of government in a modern democratic society, but also notions about more mundane but practically more important matters such as how the legal process should be organized. As long as the procedural traditions that reflect these historical and cultural factors continue to maintain their current importance in national legal systems, even if the more substantive problems to be discussed in the later chapters of this book are satisfactorily dealt with and we have achieved a world in which there is universal agreement on the actual linguistic expression of a universal human rights law, we shall still not necessarily succeed in establishing either a universal understanding as to what those rights actually entail or uniformity in the application of such rights.

One of the most striking structural differences between the common law countries of the English-speaking world and the continental European countries that follow the civil law tradition is the deference given by appellate courts to the factual determinations of trial courts. Scholars such as Mirjan Damaška consider this as just one aspect of the fact that historically the governmental structures in common law countries have, on the whole, been less hierarchically organized than those in civil law countries.[1] Whatever its historical roots, this tolerance of

---

1. Mirjan Damaška, The Faces of Justice and State Authority 16–65 (1986).

looser control over subordinate decision-makers certainly continues to be a feature of judicial organization in the common law world when it is a question of the weight to be accorded to the findings of fact made by trial courts, although it is also evident in other areas of the law. For example, in a case involving a ruling by school authorities that a Muslim girl must wear at least a modified version of the school dress uniform rather than what she claimed was traditional clothing prescribed by her religion, Lord Hoffmann declared that, under English law,[2] the exercise of judicial review by the courts of such decisions by entities such as school boards would normally focus on "whether the decision-maker reached his decision in the right way rather than whether he got what the court might think to be the right answer," whereas under the European Convention for the Protection of Human Rights and Fundamental Freedoms, which the House of Lords was obliged to apply in the case before it, the focus of the reviewing court was on whether the "result" was right, not the particular way that result was reached.[3]

Historically, some of the deference to the decisions of trial courts, particularly on factual matters, is undoubtedly owing to the use of juries in civil cases. Although, in England and in most common law countries, the use of juries in civil cases has, with few exceptions, been abolished—the most notable exception being defamation where in England, for example, juries are still required except in narrowly defined circumstances[4]—some of the traditional deference to factual determinations made by a jury has, as we shall soon note in greater detail, been carried over to civil cases tried by a judge alone.[5] Furthermore, while trial by jury is still quite common in the United States, trial by a judge alone is also frequent, not only in equity and admiralty cases that were supposedly tried under what purportedly were civil law methods of trial, but also in common law cases. Over the years, however, rather than common law cases tried in federal courts without a jury being handled according to equity and federal admiralty procedure, with few exceptions the opposite took place.[6] Under the Federal Rules of Civil

---

2. In the United Kingdom, traditionally, if an administrative body is acting within its legal authority and has not committed any procedural improprieties and if its decision can be said to be reasonable in the sense of not irrational or unreasonable its decisions will be upheld. *See* HILAIRE BARNETT, CONSTITUTIONAL & ADMINISTRATIVE LAW Ch. 25 (2009).

3. R (Shabina Begum) v. Denbigh High School, [2007] A.C. 100 (2006) at ¶ 68. *See also* In Re G, [2009] 1 AC 173 (2008) at ¶ 119 (per Lady Hale).

4. *See* Supreme Court Act 1981, c. 54, § 69, which provides that actions for defamation, fraud, malicious prosecution, and false imprisonment "shall be tried with a jury, unless the court is of the opinion that the trial requires any prolonged examination of documents or accounts or any scientific or local investigation which cannot conveniently be made with a jury."

5. *See* text at notes 9–11, *infra*.

6. This American as well as the English history is discussed at greater length in George C. Christie, *Judicial Review of Findings of Fact*, 87 Nw. U. L. REV. 14 (1992). In England,

Procedure that now apply to *all* civil litigation in United States federal courts, and are the predominant model followed by the states, a trial judge's findings of fact must be accepted by appellate courts unless the findings are "clearly erroneous."[7] The only major apparent exceptions are certain findings of fact that determine whether someone may suffer civil or criminal punishment for speech acts. Thus, someone who has been found by a jury to have defamed another by publishing false facts about him can ask the trial court and later an appellate court to review the record in the case and make an independent judgment on whether the alleged defamatory statement was in fact false.[8] If the jury finds the statement true, however, the disappointed litigant can only succeed if he can convince the trial judge or the appellate court that no reasonable jury could have reached that conclusion. The plaintiff cannot ask the judge to substitute his view of the matter for that of the jury. The undoubted explanation for what has become a pro-defendant bias is that, because freedom of expression is a constitutionally preferred value, the key factual issue that the statements in question are false must be proved by "clear and convincing" evidence.[9]

There are no such severe limitations on the authority of civil law appellate courts, at least at levels below that of a *cour de cassation*, where review is limited to questions of law. This is not to deny that the extent to which intermediate appellate courts in civil law countries can in theory or in actual practice hear new evidence and make new findings of fact can vary from country to country.[10] With the abandonment of juries in most civil cases, one might have supposed that this aspect of civil law procedure that permits appellate courts to substitute their own findings of fact would also have prevailed in England, particularly since, under the Judicature Act of 1873, and unlike in the United States, appeals from the

---

when cross-examination of witnesses was deemed essential, juries were sometimes utilized in equity cases but only in an advisory capacity. The Chancellor was under no obligation to accept the jury's findings of fact. In the United States, a few states have used and even still use juries in equitable proceedings. *See* HENRY L. MCCLINTOCK, EQUITY 29–30 (2d ed. 1948). Admiralty proceedings are within the exclusive purview of the federal courts and have never involved the use of juries.

7. FED. RULES CIV. P. § 52 (a).

8. The principal cases are *New York Times v. Sullivan*, 376 U.S. 254 (1964) and *Bose Corp. v. Consumers Union of the United States, Inc.*, 466 U.S. 485 (1984).

9. This is how the Supreme Court's declaration in *New York Times v. Sullivan, supra* note 8, that the issue of knowledge of falsity or reckless indifference to truth or falsity must be proved by "convincing clarity," was interpreted by the lower courts and eventually by the Court itself in the *Bose* case, *supra* note 8.

10. For current German law, *see* ZPO §§ 529, 531, and 540. As will be seen in the discussion that follows, what is important for present purposes is the difference between how common law courts and civil law courts treat evaluative judgments such as the defendant's "negligence" or his "intention" to injure the plaintiff that are also typically treated as questions of fact and, as such, given a degree of deference that is largely not present in civil law countries.

decisions of trial judges in England are now supposed to be "rehearings" in which an appellate court, such as the Court of Appeal, can even hear new evidence.[11] The complete adoption of the civil law attitude to trial court findings of fact has not, however, been the case. The House of Lords has expressly held that not all findings of fact made by trial judges are subject to such reexamination in appellate courts.[12] Their lordships distinguished primary facts—what Lord Simonds called "the finding of a specific fact"—from inferences based on those facts where appellate courts might have more leeway. Even then, when considering factual findings on the reliability of witnesses—and here one should note the common law's preference for live testimony rather than testimony in the form of depositions and affidavits—their lordships agreed that an appellate court should substitute its conclusions for those of the trial court only in cases of "clear error."[13] Undoubtedly, the common law preference for an adversarial form of trial process largely controlled by counsel, rather than a process largely controlled and dictated by the judge, also greatly contributes to this continued deference to trial courts on factual issues.

The question therefore naturally arises as to what would happen if a decision turning largely on factual determinations made in a jurisdiction in which considerable deference is given to the determinations of a trial court, as in the United Kingdom, is eventually appealed to an international tribunal staffed largely by judges trained in the civil law tradition and which basically follows a civil law procedure, such as the European Court of Human Rights. In *McLeod v. The United Kingdom*,[14] following a divorce, there was a highly bitter confrontation that arose over the distribution, pursuant to a judicial order, of the personal property in the matrimonial home which, under the terms of the divorce, was to be transferred to the ex-wife upon her paying the ex-husband the value of his interest in their home. The applicant, the ex-wife failed to deliver to her ex-husband the property mentioned in the court's order. The ex-wife also failed to deliver the property to the ex-husband's solicitor within the allotted time. A new order to deliver the property was entered by the court, this time under threat of penal sanction. She again failed to comply. An order committing her to prison was issued, but she was first given an extra week to voluntarily comply with the court's order. At the conclusion of that hearing, the ex-husband suggested to his ex-wife that he would come by three days before the expiration of that time limit to collect the property assigned to him. She in turn said that she would have to consult with her solicitor before agreeing because she wanted her solicitor to be present at that time.

---

11. *See* Arthur L. Goodhart, *Appeals of Questions of Fact*, 71 L. Q. Rev. 402, 407 (1955).
12. Benmax v. Austin Motor Co., [1955] A.C. 370.
13. *Id.* at 373.
14. Application No. 24755/94, decided Sept. 23, 1998, 27 Eur. H.R. Rep. 493 (1999).

Believing that the ex-wife had agreed to his proposal, the ex-husband arrived at the premises on the day he had suggested, with a representative of his solicitors and two police constables whom his solicitors had asked to be present in case there was any trouble. At the time, the ex-wife was not present but her elderly, infirm mother was. Upon being informed by the constables of the court order, she stepped aside and the ex-husband, assisted by his two siblings, started removing the property assigned to him while one of the constables checked to make sure that only property mentioned in a list supplied by the ex-husband's solicitors was taken. As the ex-husband and his helpers were about to drive away with the second and last load of personal property, the ex-wife returned home and demanded that the property which had been removed be returned to the house. One of the constables intervened and insisted that she permit the property to be removed. He let her inspect the contents of the van. The ex-wife subsequently instituted criminal proceedings against her ex-husband and his brother and sister. These were dismissed. She then brought civil actions for damages against her ex-husband and his brother and sister, against the ex-husband's solicitors, and against the London Metropolitan Police. The first two actions were tried in the county court and resulted in judgments in favor of the ex-wife for trespass to her land and property. The judge found that there had been no agreement that the ex-husband could take the property on a date certain.

The third action—the one against the police that reached the European Court of Human Rights—was tried in the High Court and ultimately turned on the question of whether the police, in entering the premises of the ex-wife, now the applicant, did so in the exercise of the common law privilege of the police to enter private property over the objection of the owner to prevent a breach of the peace. The trial judge found that the police constables had reasonable grounds for believing that a breach of the peace might take place and that therefore their entry was privileged. Accordingly, he dismissed the case. An appeal was taken to the Court of Appeal. As we have already noted, since the Judicature Acts of the latter part of the nineteenth century, even though appeals from the decisions of trial judges sitting without a jury are considered rehearings, considerable deference is nevertheless accorded to the factual findings and conclusions of the trial judges. In the Court of Appeal, Lord Justice Neill set out the trial judge's findings of fact and reasoning in a judgment with which the two other judges concurred. Lord Justice Neill concluded, "I, for my part, can see no basis for upsetting his decision on these facts."[15] The Court of Appeal refused permission to appeal to the House of Lords. When the applicant sought leave from the appeals committee of the House of Lords, that body also refused her request for leave to appeal.[16]

---

15. [1994] McLeod v. Comm'r of Police of the Metropolis, 4 All E.R. 553, 560 (C.A.).
16. *Id.* at 561.

Finding herself foreclosed from further relief in Great Britain, the ex-wife, now the applicant, sought relief from the now defunct European Commission of Human Rights on the grounds that, *inter alia*, the actions of the police constables were in violation of Article 8 of the European Convention. Article 8 provides, in relevant part, that

> [e]veryone has the right to respect for his private ... life [and] his home. There shall be no interference by a public authority with the exercise of this right except such as is in accordance with the law and is necessary in a democratic society in the interests of national security, public safety or the economic well-being of the country, [or] for the prevention of disorder or crime.

By a vote of fourteen to two, the European Commission declared its opinion that there had been no violation of the applicant's rights under Article 8 of the European Convention.[17] The case was then referred by the Commission to the European Court of Human Rights. That court, in a seven-to-two decision, noted the findings of the European Commission and the British courts and then made its own finding that, although British law could provide for entry into someone's property against that person's objections to prevent a breach of the peace, under the circumstances presented, the entry by the constables was not necessary. The applicant's rights under Article 8 were therefore violated.

The English judge on the European Court, Sir John Freeland, joined by one of his colleagues, dissented in an opinion which gave much greater emphasis to the findings and conclusions of the British trial judge. The dissent chided the majority for giving "insufficient weight" to certain findings of the trial judge, such as the finding that, although the applicant had not been present when the initial entry was made to remove the property, the constables could not know whether she might return while the property was being removed and therefore could conclude that they should remain in the driveway until the removal of the property had been completed.[18] The majority had concluded, in contrast, that upon being informed that the applicant was not at home, the constables should not have entered the home because there was "little or no risk of disorder." According to the majority, the fact than an altercation occurred upon her return home was "immaterial in ascertaining whether the police officers were justified in entering the property initially."[19]

I am not concerned with the question of whether the constables were or were not justified in what they did. My point is a different one. In a common law jurisdiction such as the United States, a finding by the trial judge on a matter, such as the existence of a reasonable belief in the possibility of a breach of the peace,

---

17. The proceedings before the European Commission are reported in *McLeod v. United Kingdom*, *supra* note 15, ¶¶ 30–31.
18. 27 Eur. H.R. Rep. at 519 (¶ 5 of the dissent).
19. *Id.* at ¶ 57.

would be considered primarily a finding of fact. It is hard to conceive how an ultimate appellate court, particularly if it were applying a clearly erroneous standard, could possibly overturn such a finding by the trial court. It is even more unthinkable that an ultimate appellate court in such a legal tradition could possibly make its own contrary determination regarding a finding that had been made by a trial judge, affirmed unanimously by a three-judge intermediate appellate court, deemed unworthy of review by the three-judge appeals committee of the House of Lords, and accepted fourteen to two by the European Commission of Human Rights, a body like the European Court of Human Rights, entitled to make its own findings of fact. I use the *McLeod* case also to illustrate my point that common law appellate judges even when, as in England, they do have the power to substitute their findings of fact and conclusions for those of the trial court, might be much more reluctant to do so than civil law judges. That is, they are more prepared to tolerate the sort of variability of result which was inevitable when trial by jury was the norm in civil cases (as it largely still is in the United States) than are judges trained in the civil law tradition. Indeed, in the United States, examples may be found in which not only have different juries reached different decisions on cases arising out of the same factual circumstances but cases arising out of the same accident, and tried without a jury before different judges, have also been decided differently.[20]

On a more theoretical level, the *McLeod* case would seem to be an excellent example of what George Fletcher, a prominent contemporary student of comparative law, calls "a preference for pluralism in legal thought ... in the thinking of Anglo-American lawyers," a quality which he finds lacking in civil law adjudication.[21] Fletcher notes that the "prominence of reasonableness" as a crucial category of legal thought in common law adjudication illustrates that, unlike the civil law, "the common law does not insist upon the right answer at all times but only a reasonable or acceptable approach" to a problem, that is, an approach that accepts that "there are many reasonable answers to any problem." What Fletcher

---

20. *Compare* Socash v. Addison Crane Co., 346 F.2d 420 (D.C. Cir. 1965), affirming *per curiam* a judgment by the trial judge for the defendant on the ground that his findings were not clearly erroneous, *with* Dempsey v. Addison Crane Co., 247 F. Supp. 584 (D.D.C. 1965), in which the trial judge found for the plaintiff, but nevertheless agreed that the findings of the trial judge in the *Socash* case were not clearly erroneous. Both cases involved injury to workers when a piece of heavy machinery fell on both of them. In the first case the worker was killed; in the second the worker was severely injured. The trial judge in the second case noted that "just as two juries may reach different conclusions on the same facts, so may two judges." *Id.* at 589. In what seems like a sop to the losing party, he noted that the plaintiffs in his case were represented by different counsel who had claimed that some evidence introduced in his case had not been introduced in the prior case. He did not in any way describe what that evidence was.

21. George P. Fletcher, *Comparative Law as a Subversive Discipline*, 46 AM. J. COMP. L. 683, 699 (1998).

is driving at is that, when discretion is entrusted to judges or administrative officials, the common law is generally prepared to accept any reasonable solution provided that, in the decisional process, the appropriate proceedings were followed. This is the point underlying Lord Hoffmann's comments, noted earlier in this chapter, about the different roles English judges play depending on whether they are reviewing decisions of English administrative bodies governed solely by domestic law or are instead applying the European Convention. Now that in order to meet the proportionality requirement adopted by the European Court of Human Rights the British courts must apply a stricter standard of judicial review to the ultimate factual conclusions, and to the exercise of discretion by administrative bodies on the basis of those findings, the question has arisen whether this will lead to a stricter standard of judicial review in matters not covered by the European Convention.[22]

It is one thing for an appellate court to accept any reasonable or even any not clearly incorrect finding of fact by a trial court. That does not, however, mean that the same or even any deference at all should be accorded to a trial court's or an administrative body's ruling on a question of law and most especially when the issue is of constitutional dimensions. Because it is germane to any discussion of the basic value choices underlying the practices we have been discussing, we must also note an important related matter that will figure frequently in succeeding chapters. In its interpretation of the European Convention, the European Court has often held that a "margin of appreciation" should be allowed for policy decisions of individual states which can be made either by legislation, administrative regulation, or judicial decision. In so doing, as we shall see in succeeding chapters, the European Court is acknowledging that, when a state is permitted to

---

22. This question is discussed by Barnett, *supra* note 2 at 687–94, 723–27, in which he indicates that there seems to be a division of opinion with some strongly expressed views that, on matters not subject to potential review at the European level, the traditional more "objective" approach should continue to be applied on the ground that proportionality review would get the courts too involved in the administrative process and force them to become more embroiled in policy. *Id.* at 725–27. For a more recent discussion of some of these issues, *see* Merris Amos, *Problems with the Human Rights Act 1998 and How to Remedy Them: Is a Bill of Rights the Answer?*, 72 MOD. L. REV. 883, 901–02 (2009).

In the United States, the Administrative Procedure Act, 5 U.S.C. § 706 (2) (E), provides that findings of fact made in formal proceedings, whether judicial or rulemaking in nature, will be upheld if supported by "substantial evidence." In non-formal proceedings the more deferential "arbitrary or capricious" test is employed. *See* II RICHARD J. PIERCE, JR., ADMINISTRATIVE LAW TREATISE, § 11.2 (4th ed. 2002). When the issue is an agency's interpretation of its statutory mandate, following the doctrines set forth in *Chevron U.S.A., Inc. v. National Resources Defense Council, Inc.*, 467 U.S. 837 (1984), if the statute is silent or ambiguous with respect to the issue the agency's interpretation will be upheld if it is a "permissible" interpretation of the statute in question. *See* I RICHARD J. PIERCE, JR., *supra* at § 3.2.

rely on the margin of appreciation given to it under the Convention to derogate from many of the rights guaranteed by that document, it is, as Lady Hale expressed, because "[n]ational authorities are better able than Strasbourg to assess what restrictions are necessary in the democratic societies they serve."[23] The use of the Convention term "necessary" rather than the common law "reasonable" shows that it is not an abandonment of the view, exemplified in the Court's refusal to accept the factual findings of subordinate decision-makers in *McLeod*, that there is a correct answer to the question at issue or even an acknowledgement that there may be several right answers to that question.[24] It is in no way an acknowledgement that the Court is prepared to accept a not unreasonable conclusion of national authorities even if the Court itself would have reached a different conclusion. What is confusing about the concept of margin of appreciation, as we shall further explore as the book proceeds, is that, as Lord Hoffman and Lady Hale have said, it seems to look for correct decisions but at the same time to accept that the correct decision, even on questions of law, may differ from jurisdiction to jurisdiction so that what is protected as freedom of expression in one jurisdiction is not protected in another. That is one of the quandaries with which we shall have to wrestle. It seems to combine the worst elements of the common law and civil law traditions. One might even say that a multi-national legal regime based on a concept of defeasible rights and correct answers to legal questions which also accepts that each nation-state is often in the best position to decide what derogations from those rights is necessary in its particular society seems to be a somewhat modest achievement for a system of human rights law based on the notion of human rights that transcend national borders.

The clash of legal cultures can arise perhaps even more starkly when the common law decision whose validity is being challenged is the result of a jury's verdict in a criminal case. In this situation, it is more than the importance of respecting long entrenched methods of procedure, but also of how to reconcile some conflicting basic values. In *A v. The United Kingdom*,[25] for example, a nine-year-old boy had been "hit with a stick by his stepfather" on probably more than one occasion and hit sufficiently severely to leave a number of bruises on the boy's body. The stepfather was charged with assault occasioning actual bodily harm and tried in an English court before a judge and jury. The stepfather's defense was based on the admitted fact that the victim was a "difficult boy" and that the beating had been a necessary and reasonable exercise of parental

---

23. In re G, [2009] 1 A.C. 173 (2008) at ¶ 118. The standard jargon of course is that to get the benefit of the margin of appreciation the challenged measures must not be disproportionate as well as necessary in a democratic society.

24. As noted, *supra* note 21, this was one of Fletcher's contentions about the differences between common law and civil law adjudication.

25. A. v. United Kingdom, Application No. 25599/94, decided Sept. 23, 1998, 27 Eur. H.R. Rep. 611 (1999).

discipline. The trial judge instructed the jury that the burden was on the prosecution to prove, beyond a reasonable doubt, that the force used was unreasonable. The jury thereupon, by a majority verdict, voted to acquit the defendant stepfather. Subsequently, a proceeding on behalf of the boy against the United Kingdom was brought before the European Commission of Human Rights. The case was eventually referred to the European Court of Human Rights. In reliance on Article 3 of the European Convention, which declares that "[n]o one shall be subject to torture or to inhuman or degrading treatment or punishment," the European Court of Human Rights found that the stepfather's acquittal violated the European Convention because the boy had not been provided adequate protection against the "treatment or punishment" that he had received. It noted that children were "entitled to State protection, in the form of effective deterrence." In that regard, the Court specifically noted that "despite the fact that the applicant had been subjected to treatment of sufficient severity to fall within the scope of Article 3, the jury acquitted his step-father."[26] The boy sought and received compensation not only for the grave physical abuse he had suffered but also for the emotional distress of enduring the trauma of criminal proceedings which resulted in the acquittal of his stepfather. The court awarded the boy £10,000 as compensation for nonpecuniary damages and up to £20,000 in costs.[27]

Although this is not the place for an extended discussion of *A v. United Kingdom*, the Court's apparent recognition that being obliged to witness a criminal proceeding in which his stepfather was acquitted violated the boy's rights is perplexing. Undoubtedly, as in the *McLeod* case, it evidences a predilection to assert hierarchical control over subordinate decision-makers that is lacking in common law jurisdictions. Moreover, the situation is likely to reappear despite the fact that in the course of the proceedings the government of the United Kingdom advised the Court that it would amend its domestic law;[28] and in fact United Kingdom law was amended in 2004 to forbid any punishment of children if actual bodily harm is caused.[29] I am of course not in any way challenging the wisdom of protecting children from actual bodily harm. I am concerned rather with a broader procedural issue, namely, what happens if a jury perversely acquits despite overwhelming evidence of guilt. It seems extremely doubtful that the United States would ever enter into arrangements under which it could be brought before an international tribunal by its own citizens because a jury was unwilling to convict a person who, we will assume, clearly deserved to be convicted. The common law tolerance of jury nullification, however much it has

---

26. *Id.* at ¶ 23.
27. *Id.* at ¶¶ 32–37.
28. *Id.* at ¶ 33.
29. Children Act 2004, § 58.

been criticized, is too deeply entrenched in its law.[30] Indeed, now that a criminal defendant can, in almost all American jurisdictions, choose to be tried by a judge alone, the same conclusive effect is accorded to a judgment of acquittal by a trial court.

As is well known, civil law jurisdictions take a less absolute position. German law, for example, is not atypical in allowing retrial of a previously acquitted defendant after the prosecution has successfully appealed the trial court's decision.[31] German law also allows a subsequent prosecution in a new proceeding, despite a prior acquittal, in cases where false statements were made at the original trial, as well as after a subsequent admission of guilt by the acquitted person.[32] Indeed, Article 4 of Protocol No. 7 of the European Convention specifically allows for the reopening of the case of an acquitted person if "there is evidence of new or newly-discovered facts or if there has been a fundamental defect in the previous proceedings." In a departure from traditional practice in common law countries, Canada now also permits prosecutorial appeals and subsequent retrials of acquitted defendants when errors of law have been made at trial, including misdirection of the jury by the trial court.[33] In addition, as a result of recent legislation, enacted over bitter dissent, prosecutorial appeals and retrial of an acquitted defendant is possible in some limited circumstances in the United Kingdom as well.[34] It is of course possible that the European Court might some day decide that, under the European Convention, a blanket double-jeopardy provision with no exceptions is not acceptable; and, if the proposals that have been made for an international court of human rights ever come to fruition, however unlikely that may now seem, such a court might also decide likewise.[35]

---

30. What made this nullification possible as a practical matter was the decision in *Bushell's Case*, 6 State Trials 999, 124 Eng. Rep. 1006 (C.P. 1670), which held that a judge who believed the jury had rendered a perverse verdict contrary to the evidence or the law could not fine any of the jurors in question.

31. *See* German Code of Criminal Procedure, StPO § 296 [hereafter StPO].

32. *See* StPO § 362.

33. *See* R.S.C.C. C-46, § 676 (1985).

34. Criminal Justice Act 2003 permits the Court of Appeal, on application of the prosecution, to permit the retrial of an acquitted person for certain (serious) listed offenses if there is "new and compelling" evidence (§ 78) and "it is in the interests of justice" (§ 79). Part 7 of this act (§§ 43–50) also provides that the prosecution may apply for a trial without a jury in complex fraud cases and in cases where there is a danger of jury tampering.

35. One should note that, because the world is made up of multiple sovereignties, the possibility exists of a person acquitted in one jurisdiction being retried in another. This possibility is explicitly recognized in German law. *See* StPO § 153c (1)(3). Thus far, this has probably been a bigger issue in the United States which, unlike some other federal nation-states, such as Germany and Canada, has separate state and federal systems of criminal law, so as to make successive prosecutions possible, particularly with the continued extension of federal criminal law to cover matters that at one time were considered of concern only to the states. Congress, however, has made state judgments of conviction or

Some of the reasons for these present differences of approach to the sanctity of a trial court acquittal, are, of course, historical and cultural. The traditional common law prohibition against double jeopardy under any circumstances undoubtedly reflects a particularly heightened uneasiness about again subjecting to the rigors of criminal prosecution even someone who has admitted to having committed or has been indisputably shown to have committed a crime. In the seventeenth and eighteenth centuries, when the prohibition against the retrial of a person acquitted by a jury had become firmly entrenched in English and American law, the belief that the application of public force against an individual was itself an evil was certainly not unreasonable. Nor, as we shall suggest as the book unfolds, is it necessarily one that must be discarded now that people are prepared to take a more benign view of the state and to welcome its more active role in directing the behavior of its citizens.

At any rate, and more generally, these cases have been presented to remind us that, as the process of globalization brings more and more legal proceedings under the jurisdiction of international tribunals, the different methods of legal argumentation and judicial decision making followed in common law countries and civil law countries may prove to be as great a stumbling block to achieving uniformity of decisions as are substantive disagreements as to the content of the law. However much most people in the western world accept that there are fundamental human rights, and are generally in agreement on what many if not most of those rights are, and often even agree on how those rights apply in particular contexts, they are not in agreement on how disputes as to the violation of those rights should be tried. In the cases we have examined, they have disagreed as to how much deference is to be paid to the conclusions of the bodies that made the initial decisions in those disputes. Achieving agreement on these questions, so as to establish a uniform enforcement process that is truly universal, may prove much harder than many people think.[36] Matters such as the style of

---

acquittal on the merits conclusive with regard to a number of crimes. *See* UNITED STATES ATTORNEYS MANUAL § 9–2.031. As to all other crimes a successive federal prosecution must be based on a finding of a substantial federal interest which the state prosecution left unvindicated and on a belief that there is sufficient evidence to persuade an unbiased trier of fact to convict. Furthermore, any such successive prosecution must be approved by "the appropriate Assistant Attorney General." *Ibid.* State practice is sometimes more restrictive than federal law. In New York, "any prior prosecution in any jurisdiction of the United States" bars any subsequent prosecution in the New York state courts. N.Y. CRIM. PROC. L. § 40.30. With the greater integration of the economic and social structure of the member states of the European Union, the issue of multiple prosecutions in different jurisdictions may likewise achieve increased prominence. *See* SAMUEL MIETTINEN, CRIMINAL LAW AND POLICY IN THE EUROPEAN UNION (2010).

36. An Italian scholar has argued that, in the field of administrative law, failure to tolerate procedural diversity is at variance with the declaration in Article 22 of the Charter of Fundamental Freedoms of the European Union that the EU "respects" cultural diversity.

judicial reasoning, which may seem unimportant to those who think in terms of the big picture, can assume crucial importance in practical life. One ignores such factors at one's peril. If one has any doubts on that score, he need go no further than to examine the bitter controversy that has arisen, and continues to arise, in Great Britain when the Government has tried, and to some limited extent has succeeded, as we have just noted, in restricting jury trials in some criminal cases and in softening the common law regarding enforcement of the prohibition against double jeopardy.[37] To sum up: Traditional notions as to how the legal process should function can be part of a society's concept of what the notion of human rights encompasses. That is to say, procedural law can reflect some deep underlying substantive values.

Giacinto della Cananea, *Beyond the State: The Europeanization and Globalization of Procedural Administrative Law*, 9 EUR. PUB. LAW 563, 570–71 (2003).

37. In reporting on the conviction of the first person to have been prosecuted under the provisions of the Criminal Justice Act 2003, discussed *supra* note 34, *The Economist* noted that those provisions were "pushed through" by the government "[d]espite strong opposition from some civil liberties campaigners, lawyers and backbench MPs." THE ECONOMIST, Sept. 16, 2006, at 66.

PART II

THE DIFFICULT ISSUES

4. THE ENLARGED VIEW OF RIGHTS IN CONTEMPORARY CONSTITUTIONS AND HUMAN RIGHTS CONVENTIONS—THE NOTION OF DEFEASIBLE RIGHTS

As we have already noted,[1] one common characteristic of typical post-World War II constitutions and of the European Convention and other international conventions is that they not only set forth the rights of individuals but also expressly allow derogation from many of the rights specified in those documents when it is "necessary" to do so "in a democratic society" for a number of reasons, including what may be broadly characterized as national security and public safety, as well as the social, economic, or even moral welfare of the community. This is a considerable departure from the Hohfeldian notion of rights that is the basis of the idea of rights as "trumps."[2] Under the new regime of defeasible rights, many so-called rights are merely express statements of the interests of the individuals and social collectives that make up a political society. Calling some particular interests of individuals or social collectives "rights" is undoubtedly to assert that a political society accepts that these interests should play an important role in the construction and application of social policies. As such, however, these renamed rights are not trumps at all but, at most, merely considerations to which decision-makers, including courts, must give serious attention. This automatically entails that courts, asked in the name of justice to provide protection of an individual's rights under such documents, will often be put in the position of having to balance the interests of an individual against the competing interests of the

---

1. *See* Chapter 2, *supra*, at p. 19.

2. The frequent use of the expression "rights as trumps" owes much of its current popularity to Ronald Dworkin. *See*, e.g., Ronald Dworkin, *Rights as Trumps, in* THEORIES OF RIGHTS 153–68 (Jeremy Waldron ed., 1985). But as we develop more fully later in Chapter 7, *infra*, for Dworkin the fundamental right is that society should show equal concern for each of its members as human beings. It is comparable to the notion of the "inviolability of human dignity" (*Die Würde des Menschen ist unantastbar*) contained in Article 1.1 of the Basic Law of the Federal Republic of Germany. These concepts obviously involve an inquiry loaded with wide-ranging and controversial moral and philosophical issues. Hohfeld, in contrast, was concerned with concrete rights, such as the right that someone not enter his property where the applicability of the right depends on the largely factual findings of a jury or other trier of facts. *See* WESLEY NEWCOMB HOHFELD, FUNDAMENTAL LEGAL CONCEPTIONS 38–39 (1919).

community and against the competing interests of other individuals. That is a difficult enterprise in the best of circumstances.

One might perhaps say that this difficult task must inevitably be undertaken regardless of the language used in asserting the existence of a right. After all, no right is really absolute. But that contention, though in practice not without a substantial factual basis, is of course not always legally true. The prohibition against torture enshrined in an international treaty which has received close to universal adoption, and is also included in the European Convention, allows for no exceptions.[3] And indeed there are many provisions in the United States Constitution that are equally absolute, such as the parties' ability to insist on trial by jury in both criminal and civil cases and the prohibition against double jeopardy that we have just discussed.[4] It is striking that, in granting these particular absolute protections, neither the international treaty nor the European Convention nor the United States Constitution uses the language of rights at all. These documents merely declare what the state may not do and the procedures that the state must not, under any circumstances, decline to follow. Whatever legal rights an individual may have are derived from those prohibitions and procedural requirements. In Hohfeldian terms, it is the duty imposed on the state, and consequently on human beings acting in its name, that is primary, and it is from that duty whatever legal rights an individual has are derived.

Furthermore, although not similarly absolute in effect, the freedom of expression contained in the First Amendment of the United States Constitution, which also does not use the word "right" at all but merely provides that "Congress [and now, by extension, the several states] shall make no law . . . abridging the freedom of speech, or the press," is universally accepted as giving more protection to freedom of expression than is provided by Article 10 of the European Convention, which expressly recognizes the "right to freedom of expression." It will thus be helpful, as the discussion proceeds, to explore why this is the case. An examination of why the Convention, with its express references to "rights," gives less protection to freedom of expression than not only the First Amendment to the United States Constitution, but also traditional English common law, will highlight the crux of the problem confronting courts administering a rights-based jurisprudence that, to a considerable extent, is based on the notion of rights expressly declared to be defeasible for certain presumably laudable purposes. In making our comparison, we shall focus on the jurisprudence generated by the European Convention because its provisions are not only typical of post-World War II international and national declarations of human rights, but also because,

---

3. Convention Against Torture and Other Cruel, Inhuman or Degrading Treatment of Punishment, U.N. GAOR, 39th Sess., Supp. No. 51, art. 2(2), at 197, U.N. Doc. A/RES/39/46 (1984); European Convention on Human Rights, Art. 2.

4. *See* Chapter 3, *supra*, at pp. 29–32.

at the international level, that convention has generated the most comprehensive jurisprudence concerning the interpretation of such documents.[5]

The European Court of Human Rights has been forced to consider the protection given to freedom of expression in a variety of circumstances which can roughly be divided into two broad categories. The first concerns instances in which rights guaranteed by the Convention, including freedom of expression, have been regulated and even suppressed for certain important public purposes. These are the types of cases, which I have grouped together under the rubric "defeasibility of rights," that will be discussed in this chapter. The other category encompasses cases in which the Court has been called upon to restrict and even punish the attempt to exercise rights protected by the Convention, including, again, freedom of expression, in order to protect some other right guaranteed by the Convention. While the issues that will be discussed under these categories are certainly interrelated and, in some instances even the same, it will be useful, at least initially, to consider each category separately. We shall begin in this chapter with the "defeasibility of rights." The problems that arise in adjudication involving a conflict between or among competing rights will be reserved for the following chapter.

After enumerating a host of rights that are protected under its aegis, the European Convention for the Protection of Fundamental Rights and Freedoms proceeds, in Article 15, to permit a state to derogate in "time of war or other public emergency threatening the life of the nation" from the rights set forth in the Convention to the extent that such derogation is "strictly required by the exigencies of the situation," provided that such measures are "not inconsistent with its other obligations under international law." Furthermore, except "in respect of deaths resulting from lawful acts of war" there may be no derogation from Article 2's protection of the "right to life," nor does Article 15 permit derogation from Article 3's protection against torture or inhuman or degrading treatment or punishment, nor Article 4's prohibition of slavery, nor Article 7's prohibition of punishment without law—with law defined broadly to include "the general principles of law recognized by civilized nations." Freedom of expression is among the rights not excluded from the sweep of Article 15. When a state adopts measures under the authority of Article 15, it must also inform the Secretary General of the Council of Europe of those measures and the reasons for them as well as when those measures have ceased to operate.

In the *First Cyprus Case*[6] concerning measures taken in the 1950s that were alleged to include executive detentions, rough treatment of detainees, destruction

---

5. *See* Chapter 1, *supra*, note 2.
6. Greece v. United Kingdom, Application 175/56, Report of 26 September 1958. This case and the *Second Cyprus Case*, which is about to be mentioned in the text, are extensively discussed in A. W. BRIAN SIMPSON, HUMAN RIGHTS AND THE END OF EMPIRE: BRITAIN AND THE GENESIS OF THE EUROPEAN CONVENTION 924–1052 (2004). There is also

of property and even worse transgressions, the European Commission of Human Rights refused to accept a challenge by Greece to this exercise of Article 15 powers in Cyprus by the United Kingdom. In refusing to accept the application, the Commission expressed its reluctance to substitute its judgment for that of the British government as to whether there was a public danger that threatened the life of the nation. That question was said to be a question of appreciation and the Commission was not prepared to second-guess the conclusion of the British authorities who had a better grasp of the situation. A *Second Cyprus Case*[7] was brought by Greece before the Commission but was eventually mooted after Greece and the United Kingdom, in December 1958, reached a political settlement on the Cyprus issue, although not before some further applications—including one alleging that a detained doctor had been released from detention with broken ribs—had been declared inadmissible. Subsequent to these Cyprus cases, the European Court of Human Rights held that the Republic of Ireland had not violated the convention by detaining an IRA sympathizer without trial for six months.[8] In several other cases against the United Kingdom, the Court also refused relief to persons who had been detained after a declaration of an emergency in Northern Ireland, although relief was given to applicants who were able to show a violation of Article 3 through the use of interrogation techniques such as hooding, noise, sleep deprivation, and denial of food and drink.[9]

Subsequently, there were cases against Turkey arising out of its use of Article 15 to support measures taken to deal with Kurdish separatists.[10] As in the cases against the United Kingdom, the Court was prepared to accept the Turkish government's conclusion that there was a public emergency but less willing to accept at face value denials of the abuse of rights in implementing the measures taken to deal with the emergency. Since it is not a central purpose of this book to deal with Article 15, it is unnecessary to continue this discussion much further. Enough has been said to illustrate that, in deciding the Article 15 cases, when the issue is the existence of a "public emergency threatening the life of the nation" and, in deciding whether the measures taken to deal with any such emergency are "strictly required," the Court, through the use of "margin of appreciation," is,

---

a much shorter but also helpful discussion in MARIE BÉNÉDICTE DEMBOUR, WHO BELIEVES IN HUMAN RIGHTS? 41–45 (2006).

7. Greece v. United Kingdom, Application 299/57, Report of 8 July 1959.

8. Lawless v. Ireland, Judgment of 1 July 1961, Application No. 332/57, 1 Eur. H.R. Rep. 15 (1979–80). This case and *Ireland v. United Kingdom*, cited in the following note, are also discussed in SIMPSON, *supra* note 6, at 1081–85 and DEMBOUR, *supra* note 6, at 47–49.

9. Ireland v. United Kingdom, Series A, No. 25, Application No. 5310/71, Judgment of 28 January 1978, 2 Eur. H.R. Rep. 25 (1979–80).

10. *See*, e.g., Aksoy v. Turkey, Application No. 21987/73, Judgment of 18 December 1996, 23 Eur. H.R. Rep. 553 (1997). This case and the other similar Turkish cases are discussed in DEMBOUR, *supra* note 6, at 49–53.

at best, performing functions more akin to those performed by an *extremely* deferential super-administrative tribunal which does not have before it the detailed record normally available to a domestic court reviewing an administrative decision for abuse of discretion.[11] In this context, the doctrine of margin of appreciation accepts that national governments are normally in a better position to determine whether an emergency that threatens the life of the country actually exists as well as, perhaps more importantly, the appropriateness of the measures taken to deal with that emergency. Only when the issue is whether or not someone was mistreated or left without effective relief for such abuse at the national level does the Court become less deferential and start to assume again its customary role of trying to achieve, in a particular case, what it believes justice requires.

Cases involving the application of Article 15 have always been rare and, as one would expect and certainly hope, are likely to become even more so as the European Union becomes more prosperous, self-confident, and more firmly established. Of greater interest are the far larger number of cases dealing with Articles 8, 9, and 10 which concern, respectively, rights "to respect for private and family life," "to freedom of thought, conscience, and religion," and "to freedom of expression." As we shall soon see in greater detail, all three of those rights are expressly subject to defeasibility for important social reasons whose application to particular situations will be examined as the discussion proceeds. The European Court of Human Rights and national courts have, to cite a few instances, thus had to struggle with whether women may wear some form of Muslim attire in public institutions,[12] such as state-supported schools and universities and also government offices, and whether people may be punished for denying the existence of the Holocaust, even sometimes in a fairly private context.[13] One justification that has been used by the Court to justify its declaring

---

11. The amorphous nature of the notions of margin of appreciation and proportionality as evidenced in the Cyprus and Irish cases is noted in YUTAKA ARAI-TAKAHASHI, THE MARGIN OF APPRECIATION DOCTRINE AND THE PRINCIPLE OF PROPORTIONALITY IN THE JURISPRUDENCE OF THE ECHR 182–88 (2002).

12. We shall begin an extensive discussion of some of these cases shortly.

13. *See* Garaudy v. France, Application No. 65831/01, Judgment of 24 June 2003; Witzsch v. Germany, Application No. 41448/98, Judgment of 20 April 1999. Witzsch v. Germany, Application No. 7485/03, Judgment of 13 December 2005 [hereafter *Witzsch* (2005)]. What is particularly odd about the German cases is the limited nature of the publication of the proscribed statements. In the earlier case the statements denying the existence of the Holocaust were in an attachment to a letter Witzsch had written to politicians complaining about a proposed amendment to § 130 of the penal code, which proscribed incitement to hatred, that would add an additional clause proscribing the express denial of "national socialist mass killing." In the second *Witzsch* case the offending statements were contained in a letter he had written to a well-known historian who had authored a magazine article about Hitler's having wanted "the murder of the Jews." The recipient of

42 PHILOSOPHER KINGS?

inadmissible the applications of persons convicted of denying the Holocaust has been based on Article 17 of the Convention, which states that nothing in the "Convention may be interpreted as implying . . . any right to engage in any activity or perform any act aimed at the destruction of any of the rights and freedoms set forth herein or at their limitation to a greater extent than is provided for in the Convention."[14] Given the broad wording of the various articles of the Convention, could one perhaps possibly argue that what is "provided for in the Convention" is what the Court rules that the Convention prescribes? If so, as absurd as it seems, one could also, perhaps, plausibly argue that once the Court has given a ruling recognizing the existence of a particular right in a particular situation or a ruling resolving a conflict between two rights protected by the Convention, it would be wrong for anyone to agitate for such a ruling to be overturned in a factually indistinguishable case because, if it were overturned, a right protected by the Convention would be more limited in operation than the Court had previously held that it was. After all, it is not merely the Holocaust that cannot be denied. In 2006, the French National Assembly voted to make denial of the "Armenian Genocide" of 1915 a criminal offense.[15] It was not, however, passed by the French Senate. Indeed, a Swiss Court in fact convicted a Turkish politician under Swiss law[16] for denying the Armenian Genocide. It finally should be noted that a government-backed bill criminalizing the public incitement to extreme thinness passed the French National Assembly on April 15, 2008.[17] It does not appear that the French Senate has thus far acted on that bill.

One might of course correctly note that the European Court of Human Rights and the national courts of the countries that are parties to the Convention—many

---

the letter showed it to the police but he explicitly refused to lodge an application for Witzsch's prosecution. The police, however, showed the letter to a person whose grandparents had died in a concentration camp who then lodged an application for prosecution. We shall return to these cases again in later chapters when we try to outline what would be a more satisfactory decision-making process for these sorts of cases. For the moment it suffices to note the extremely limited public danger posed by Witzsch's letter.

14. *See*, e.g., *Witzsch* (2005) at ¶ 3.

15. The 2006 Bill was approved by the National Assembly on October 12, 2006. Assemblée Nationale (12ème legisl.): 3030 rectifié, 3074 et T.A. 610.

16. *See* Case X, Judgment (in French) 6B-398/2007/rod of the Tribunale federale, of 12 December 2007. An English language report of his conviction on March 9, 2007 in Lausanne is contained in a Reuters report, *Swiss convict Turk of denying Armenian genocide*, of March 9, 2009, www.reuters.com/article/latestCrisis/idUSL09197269.

17. *See* Angelique Chrisafis, *French MPs back law to bar media from promoting anorexia*, GUARDIAN, Apr. 16, 2008, *available at* www.guardian.co.uk/world/2008/apr/16/france. law (last visited Nov. 21, 2009). In a recent case, *Lautsi v. Italie*, Application No. 30814/06, Judgment of 3 November 2009, the European Court of Human Rights declared that the Italian custom of putting a crucifix on the walls of classrooms violated the rights of students who were of other religions or who professed no religion. Would agitation to overturn that ruling be proscribed?

of them not members of the European Union—are forced to struggle with these questions, whether they would like to or not, because they are required to do so by the express language of many provisions of the European Convention, including Article 10 which protects freedom of expression. Since Article 10 will be the provision of the European Convention that will figure most prominently in our discussion, it may be helpful to set forth the complete text of that article at the outset.

> 1. Everyone has the right to freedom of expression. This right shall include freedom to hold opinions and to receive and impart information and ideas without interference by public authority and regardless of frontiers. This article shall not prevent States from requiring the licensing of broadcasting, television or cinema enterprises.
>
> 2. The exercise of these freedoms, since it carries with it duties and responsibilities, may be subject to such formalities, conditions, restrictions or penalties as are prescribed by law and are necessary in a democratic society, in the interests of national security, territorial integrity or public safety, for the prevention of disorder or crime, for the protection of health or morals, for the protection of the reputation or rights of others, for preventing the disclosure of information received in confidence, or for maintaining the authority and impartiality of the judiciary.

As the discussion proceeds, it will also be helpful to keep in mind Article 8, which, as we have already noted, deals with the "right to respect for private and family life," and Article 9, which, as we have also noted, deals with "the right to freedom of thought, conscience and religion." Article 9 will be particularly important for our immediate discussion. Sometimes, in the form of freedom of religious expression, it supports the general freedom of expression protected by Article 10; at other times, it is used to justify the suppression of expression because that expression offends religious sensibilities. Like Article 10 and Article 8, which will be discussed in greater detail in the next chapter, Article 9 allows for derogation. With regard to Article 9, "[f]reedom to manifest one's religion or beliefs shall be subject only to such limitations as are prescribed by law and are necessary in a democratic society in the interests of public safety, for the protection of public order, health or morals, or for the protection of the rights and freedoms of others."

In 2005, the European Court of Human Rights was called upon to decide a case that arose in Turkey and involved a female medical student who insisted on covering her hair while attending a university in Istanbul. She had been doing so at her prior university in another part of Turkey and also, for a time, at her university in Istanbul until, as accepted by the Court as having been "prescribed by law," regulations were published by the university authorities forbidding her to attend classes and from performing the other duties of a medical student while so attired. After being unable to obtain relief in Turkey, she applied to the European Court of Human Rights. That court is currently comprised of 47 judges, one for each nation that is currently a party to the European Convention, and it normally sits in panels of seven. In the case in question, *Leyla Sahin v. Turkey*,[18] the Court sat as a "Grand Chamber," that is, currently and at the time of the *Sahin* case, as a panel of seventeen. In a sixteen-to-one judgment, the Court accepted the Turkish government's contention that the regulations and Sahin's exclusion in reliance on those regulations were necessary to uphold and preserve Turkey's commitment to secularism. Although Sahin had continued and successfully completed her studies in Austria, the European Court's decision apparently made it impossible for Sahin, under present Turkish law, to practice medicine in Turkey.

The one dissenting judge, Françoise Tulkens of Belgium, thought that the restrictions imposed on Sahin were not "necessary in a democratic society" under Article 9. She also noted[19] that a few years earlier the Court, in the *Gündüz* case,[20] had found an infringement of freedom of expression in a case in which a Muslim religious leader had been convicted for "violently criticizing the secular regime in Turkey, calling for the introduction of *sharia* and referring to the children born of marriages performed solely before secular authorities as 'bastards,'" a case which also demonstrates that the Court certainly does consider freedom of expression a very important value. Nevertheless, as we shall have occasion to discuss at greater length in subsequent chapters, the checkerboard pattern of upholding derogation from rights guaranteed in the Convention in some cases while striking them down in other not too dissimilar cases is troubling. For the moment, it suffices to note Judge Tulkens' suggestion in the *Sahin* case that, while there were important differences between that case and the *Gündüz* case, whether those differences were important enough to justify a different conclusion is another matter. Judge Tulkens' belief that Sahin had a stronger case for claiming a right to freedom of religious expression than did Gündüz is not easily dismissed. As Judge Tulkens noted, Article 9 of the Convention as applied to cases such as Sahin's is concerned not with the "freedom to have a religion (inner conviction), but to manifest one's religion (the expression of that conviction)," which for many people of almost all religions is an important aspect of their religious beliefs.[21]

Sahin contended that the Turkish regulations not only interfered with her right to manifest her religious beliefs as guaranteed by Article 9 but also with her general right to freedom of expression as guaranteed by Article 10, as well as her

---

18. Sahin v. Turkey, Application No. 44774/98, Judgment of 10 November 2005, 44 Eur. H.R. Rep. 5 (2007) [hereafter *Sahin*].
19. *Id.* at ¶ 9 of the dissent.
20. Gündüz v. Turkey, Application No. 35071/97, Judgment of 4 December 2003.
21. *Sahin* at ¶ 6 of the dissent.

"right to respect" for her "private life" as guaranteed by Article 8, and also her right to an education free of discrimination guaranteed under Article 14, and her right to an education as expressly guaranteed under Article 2 of Protocol No. 1 to the Convention. The Court, however, focused its attention on Article 9, and to a much lesser extent on Article 2 of Protocol No. 1. Neither the Court nor the dissent separately considered Sahin's arguments that the Turkish regulations interfered with her rights under Articles 8 and 10. The Court's stated reason for refusing to do so was that the arguments pro and con would merely duplicate those under Article 9. It is odd that the Court did not consider whether the fact that the Turkish regulations interfered with other rights protected by the Convention should increase Turkey's burden of justifying the restriction imposed on Sahin. Sahin's contention that her challenge to the measure in question is strengthened by the fact that it also infringed other rights protected by the Convention is not one that is easily dismissed. Leaving aside for the moment the interference with her general right to freedom of expression under Article 10, the Turkish measures, by not permitting her to cover her hair, surely interfered with her right to respect for her private life as guaranteed by Article 8. As to the claim under Article 14 that the measures in question discriminated against her on the basis of her religion, contrary to the guarantee of Article 14, the cursory assertion that the measures in question were not aimed at her religious affiliation but at "the legitimate aim of protecting order and the rights and freedoms of others and were manifestly intended to preserve the secular nature of educational institutions"[22] does seem rather curious. It is doubtful if Sahin thought it very persuasive.

The issue in the *Sahin* case boiled down to whether the interference with her rights under the Convention was necessary in a "democratic society." Even if one accepts that, under previous precedent, "secularism" is an overriding social and political goal in a democratic society,[23] to meet the Court's proportionality test it is not enough that the goal be legitimate. It is also required, under the doctrine of proportionality, that the means chosen to further that goal should not only be rationally connected to it but also no more than are necessary to achieve that goal. The latter is a particularly hard determination for any court to make under any circumstances but surely the fact that a rational justification could be given for a state's enacting measures that restrict a person's religious expression should not be enough. To permit a defeasible right to have the sort of bite that would

---

22. *Sahin* at ¶ 165. Judge Tulkens joined in this part of the judgment (¶ 14 of her dissent).

23. *See* Refah Partisi v. Turkey, Application No. 41340/98 et al., Judgment of 13 February 2003 (Grand Chamber), 37 Eur. H.R. Rep. 1 (2003). This was the case in which the Court upheld Turkey's banning of what in English was called the "Welfare Party" on the ground that it supported a religious agenda and was thus a threat to the principle of secularism enshrined in Turkey's constitution.

enable it to serve as something like a Hohfeldian right, a measure in derogation of that right should be the least restrictive alternative. It is no wonder that the European Court of Human Rights' reliance on both margin of appreciation and proportionality has been met with some sharp criticism.[24] In the *Sahin* case, the Court relied on assertions by politicians about the importance of secularism, the gravity of the threat it faces and the need to protect the rights of women, as well as the mention of certain historical events. These may well, for some, be sufficient political justifications. But, for a court purporting to reach the "right" decision in deciding whether restrictions on the rights expressed in the Convention were "proportionate," finding such broad generalizations to be sufficient certainly seems debatable.

Following the Court's decision in the *Sahin* case there have been several other cases involving Muslim dress for women. In two cases involving France,[25] the Court unanimously ruled that there had been no violation of the right to freedom of religious expression guaranteed by Article 9 of the Convention when two girls were expelled from school for refusing to remove their headscarves during "physical education and sport classes." The teacher who had requested them to remove their headscarves did so on the basis that wearing a headscarf was incompatible with physical education classes.[26] The expulsion was enforced even after the girls offered to wear hats rather than headscarves during such classes.

Leaving aside whether the assertion that wearing a headscarf (or a hat) was incompatible with the safe participation in physical education or sports classes or that allowing the girls this privilege would undermine school discipline, one must compare these French decisions with the more nuanced approach of the House of Lords in a similar case.[27] This British case involved a girl who attended a school which required students to wear a school uniform. The girl had already taken advantage of a uniform option that permitted her, in addition to wearing "a headscarf of a specified color and quality," to wear a shalwar kameeze. That was, as described in the judgment, "a combination of the kameeze, a sleeveless smock-like dress with a square neckline, revealing the wearer's collar and tie, with the shalwar, loose trousers tapering at the ankles," together with "a long-sleeved white

---

24. On Muslim dress, *see* Tom Lewis, *What Not to Wear: Religious Rights, the European Court, and the Margin of Appreciation*, 56 INT'L & COMP. L. Q. 395 (2007). For criticism on a more general level, *see* Gunnar Beck, *The Mythology of Human Rights*, 21 RATIO JURIS 312 (2008). For further critical comments with additional citations to critical literature, *see* GEORGE LEFTSAS, A THEORY OF INTERPRETATION OF THE EUROPEAN CONVENTION ON HUMAN RIGHTS 80–98 (2007).

25. Dogru v. France, Application No. 27058/05, Judgment of 4 December 2008 [hereafter *Dogru*]; Kervanci v. France, Application No. 31645/04, Judgment of 4 December 2008. Both judgments were rendered in French, but only the *Dogru* decision was issued in English as well.

26. *See Dogru* at ¶ 13.

27. R (Shabina Begum) v. Governors of Denbigh High School, [2007] A.C. 100 (2006).

shirt . . . worn beneath the kameeze and, save in hot weather, a uniform long-sleeved school jersey . . . worn on top."[28] After two years of wearing such attire she, and her older brother who was her guardian, insisted that she be permitted to wear "a long coat-like garment known as a jilbab" because it concealed the contours of the female body more than the shalwar kameeze.[29] Since the school refused to give her that permission, she no longer attended school. After exhausting administrative avenues of review, she and her guardian sought a judicial order requiring the school to allow her to attend school wearing the jilbab. This was refused by the trial court, whose decision was reversed by the Court of Appeal on the ground that it had not reached its decision through an appropriate process of reasoning. The House of Lords in turn reversed the Court of Appeal and reinstated the order of the trial court. Great stress was laid by the House of Lords on the fact that there were several schools which the girl could conveniently attend that would permit her to wear the jilbab. It was certainly a much more modest and fact-bound judgment. In a later English case, a girl wanted to continue attending her school wearing a "niqab," described as "a veil that covers her entire face save for her eyes."[30] That permission was refused. The authorities did find the girl a place in another selective entry school with similar academic standards about 25 minutes away, to which the authorities would provide transportation. She refused the offer and her subsequent resort to the courts to compel her re-admission to her original school was denied.

If, as the European Court suggested in the *Sahin* case, the effect of permitting women to cover their hair in a public institution would increase the moral compulsion on other Muslim women to wear a headscarf, is it completely far-fetched to suggest that perhaps the public observance of religiously required dietary restrictions in public institutions could be outlawed because of the moral suasion it might exert on co-religionists? The importance of the matter requires serious empirical support before accepting both the truth and the practical importance of such alleged threats to social order. At the very least, one would want to see more than anecdotal evidence as support if one were prepared to accept it as a plausible argument. It should be noted that Sahin did not challenge the legitimacy of establishing secularism as an important policy. What was at stake was the application of those regulations and the public policy underlying them to the facts of her case. One can accept that there are very few, if any, rights that are absolute under any and all possible factual conditions, but if the right of freedom to manifest one's religious beliefs, and the more general right to freedom of expression—even if sometimes defeasible—are in any meaningful way to serve as true Hohfeldian rights rather than as merely the recognition of

---

28. *Id.* at ¶ 6 (statement of agreed facts in speech of Lord Bingham).
29. *Id.* at ¶ 9.
30. R (on the application of X) v. Head Teacher and Governors of Y School, [2008] 1 All E.R. 249 ¶ 1A (Q. B. 2007).

generally accepted important social values, they must surely have a more robust application.

The factual dependence of so many of the hotly contested human rights cases is a matter whose implications will be further explored as the discussion proceeds throughout the remainder of this chapter as well as in subsequent chapters. The problems created by that dependence arise not merely when the question is whether a specific right is subject to defeasance for reasons of public policy in some particular case but also in the cases, to which we shall shortly turn in the next chapter, that involve private parties and deal with a conflict between two generally recognized human rights. Before leaving the present discussion concerning the defeasibility of rights for reasons of public policy, however, it may also be helpful to consider *Müller v. Switzerland*,[31] decided by the European Court of Human Rights in 1988, a case which suggests that not only are many of the rights guaranteed by the Convention not very robust, they are also possibly very ephemeral in the sense of easily being affected by changing public sentiment.

Müller was one of a group of artists invited, in 1981, to make art on the spot between early August and mid-October 1981 as part of the celebration of the 500th anniversary of the Canton of Fribourg's entry into the Swiss Confederation. Müller produced three large paintings. On the day of the public opening, the principal prosecutor for the Canton initiated proceedings under Article 204 of the Swiss Criminal Code which prohibited obscene publications and also required that they be destroyed. The authorities had been prompted to act by a man whose daughter had "reacted violently" to the paintings.[32] Müller was the named (or lead) applicant but nine other artists were also involved in the proceedings. According to the Swiss trial court, the paintings produced by Müller, while not sexually arousing, were "undoubtedly repugnant to say the least."[33] The Swiss courts found all ten artists guilty under Article 204 and fined them each 300 Swiss Francs. The Swiss courts did not, however, order Müller's paintings destroyed, but instead allowed them to be placed in the custody of a museum whose curator was required not to put them on public display and to permit them to be seen only by "a few serious specialists capable of taking an exclusively artistic or cultural interest in them as opposed to a prurient interest."[34] The Swiss courts relied on testimony of art critics that Müller was a "serious" artist and on the fact that similar paintings of his had been exhibited in Basel with no public outcry or prosecution.

---

31. Müller v. Switzerland, Application No. 10737/84, Judgment of 24 May 1988, 13 Eur. H.R. Rep. 212 (1991).
32. *Id.* at ¶ 2.
33. *Id.* at ¶ 14.
34. *Ibid.*

Five years after Müller had failed in his appeals to the Fribourg Cantonal Court and then to the Criminal Cassation Division of the Federal Court, a Swiss district court, in January 1988, ordered Müller's paintings returned to him. In that interim, Müller and his co-applicants in 1984 had applied for relief to the now defunct European Commission of Human Rights on the ground that both their convictions and the confiscation of their paintings were violations of Article 10 of the Convention. The Commission found that the confiscation of the paintings was a violation but that the convictions were not. The European Court of Human Rights, however, disagreed with the Commission and held that the convictions of the artists as well as the confiscation of Müller's paintings, which by this time had been returned to him, were not violations of Article 10. The Court did so even while recognizing that before and after the Fribourg exhibition, paintings by Müller had been exhibited in various places in Switzerland and abroad and that in 1980 a Swiss court, in returning the pictures of others that had been confiscated in 1960, had recognized that "the public's ideas" had become "more liberal in recent times." Indeed, as already indicated, while the *Müller* case was pending before the European Court, Müller had already obtained a judicial order from a Swiss court for the return of his paintings in January 1988.[35] For the European Court, the fact that in 1988, when it issued its judgment, the convictions and confiscation of the paintings might be considered by some Swiss courts to violate Article 10, even in Fribourg, did not mean that the Fribourg prosecution and confiscation in 1981 were in violation of Article 10. The Court recognized that although it was empowered to give the final ruling[36] "the requirements of morals vary from time to time and from place to place, especially in our era," and declared that it was not for international judges to give opinions on the content of those requirements.[37] The paintings, "with their emphasis on sexuality in some of its crudest forms were liable grossly to offend the sense of sexual propriety of persons of ordinary sensibility."[38] Not only were the convictions not a violation but "having regard to their margin of appreciation, the Swiss courts were entitled to hold that confiscation of the paintings in issue was 'necessary' for the protection of morals."[39]

The only conclusion one can draw from the *Müller* case, and cases like the *Otto-Preminger-Institut*[40] case upholding Austria's banning the showing of a movie on the ground that it was blasphemous, is that, where there is no clear European consensus, any good reason for restricting freedom of expression

---

35. *Id.* at ¶ 19.
36. *Id.* at ¶ 32.
37. *Id.* at ¶ 35.
38. *Id.* at ¶ 36.
39. *Ibid.*
40. Otto-Preminger-Institut v. Austria, Application No. 13470/87, judgment of 20 September 1994, 19 Eur. H.R. Rep. 34 (1995).

under one of the enumerated criteria permitting defeasibility, even if such justifying reason is subject to major change over a relatively short period of time, has a good chance of satisfying the margin of appreciation given to national courts and legislatures in deciding that these restrictions are necessary in a democratic society.[41] That again is not a very robust view of the purportedly universal "basic rights" protected by the European Convention.

To say that the problems that have been highlighted will be somehow resolved through the process of "case-by-case" adjudication, such as that which operates in common law jurisdictions, does not get one very far unless one explains in some detail what one means by case-by-case adjudication and how it will meet the challenges we have identified. This will be among the subjects that will be discussed in increasing detail as this book proceeds as we confront the question of how, if at all, a process of case-by-case adjudication might be designed that would enable a legal regime of defeasible rights to produce a scheme of rights with true bite. In the next chapter we shall discuss situations where resorting to case-by-case adjudication is likely to arise considerably more frequently, namely in disputes between private parties involving a conflict of rights protected by the Convention.

---

41. A key case in this evolution is *Handyside v. United Kingdom*, Application No. 5493/72, Judgment of 7 December 1976, 1 Eur. H.R. Rep. 737 (1979–80). In that case, which had been brought in England, a reference book for teenagers on sex had been found to be obscene and was confiscated. A similar case in Scotland had failed and no proceeding had been brought in Northern Ireland, the Isle of Man, or the Channel Islands, nor in Denmark or in other European countries where translations of the book had been circulated. *Id.* at ¶¶ 19, 57. The Court nevertheless held that, given that the situation in each jurisdiction on these matters was different, the proceedings in London were within the margin of appreciation allowed to local authorities.

5. LITIGATION INVOLVING A CONFLICT OF RIGHTS, EACH OF EQUAL VALUE

Looking only at the text of the European Convention, one could easily conclude that the rights to privacy, freedom of religion, and freedom of expression protected, respectively, by Article 8, 9, and 10 of the Convention, are only directed at state interference with the rights recognized and protected by those provisions. Thus, given that each of these rights is defeasible for important public purposes, the only balancing that courts applying those provisions would be required to do to reach the just solution in a particular case would be between the interests of the person with whose rights the state is interfering and the interests of the state, as representative of the social collective, which are claimed to justify that interference. The issues then before the courts would have the same logical structure as those considered in the *Sahin* and *Müller* cases discussed in the preceding chapter. There would be one right or a set of rights, all possessed by the defendant, and the issue before a court would be whether that right or set of rights was subject to defeasance by the state for some important public purpose. As a matter of logic, it would certainly not have been a necessary implication of the language of the provisions which we have been discussing that the courts would also have to resolve disputes between private parties in which the claimant asserts that the exercise by another of rights protected by the Convention interferes with a different right of the claimant that is also protected under the Convention. As is very well known, however, the decisions of the European Court have clearly established that the states that are parties to the Convention also have a legally enforceable general duty to secure the individual rights protected by the European Convention from interference by other private persons. It is this additional responsibility of the state to secure the rights enumerated in the Convention against persons who are not considered state actors that exacerbates the tensions which the courts must address and resolve in deciding such cases. Because the United States Constitution imposes no such broad responsibility on the United States government or on state governments, the task of the United States Supreme Court is much easier than that faced by the European Court of Human Rights, and the courts of the states that are parties to the Convention.

We have already seen an example of the more difficult task faced by European courts during our discussion in Chapter 3 of *A v. United Kingdom*,[1] which is one of the early cases that established this extended doctrine of state responsibility.

---

1. A. v. United Kingdom, Original Application No. 2599/94, judgment of Sept. 23, 1998, 27 Eur. H.R. Rep. 611 (1999).

In that case, the European Court of Human Rights suggested that a state might be held responsible for not providing a person adequate protection from "inhuman treatment or punishment," contrary to Article 3 of the Convention, when it did not provide an adequate deterrent to parental abuse of disciplinary authority; and then did not provide a remedy for the anguish of a child in witnessing the jury's verdict acquitting the step-parent accused of using excessive force in disciplining his stepchild, the applicant in that case.[2] As we noted earlier, under the common law and as is still the law without exception in the United States, the only right involved in a case like this was the right of the defendant not to be tried twice for the same offense. No one else, not the victim or the state, had any applicable rights. Now, however, under the jurisprudence generated by the European Convention, what was once the enforcement of a single right guaranteed by the Convention becomes a case ultimately involving the resolution of conflicting rights. In that case it was the conflict between the right of the acquitted stepfather not to be tried twice for the same offense and the right of the child subjected to inhuman or degrading treatment to secure compensation for the state's failure to give him redress for such treatment by providing some appellate or other procedure to remedy a perverse jury acquittal of the person who had inflicted the degrading treatment. It is hard to maintain, either on principle or by resort to the notion of rights, that it is easy to resolve the conflict between the right of the injured boy not to be subjected to inhuman treatment, including the witnessing of a perverse acquittal, and the right of the defendant in the criminal proceedings against him to be judged solely by a jury of his peers. Moreover, as we have already noted, while one may grant that a jury, although composed of private citizens, is participating in a public proceeding, many people might still be puzzled as to why the state should be held responsible for the actions of private citizens, whose exercise of discretion is beyond control or correction, because of something like a double jeopardy provision whose purpose, as noted previously in Chapter 3, is to protect individuals from the overwhelming power of the state which has the means to continue to retry someone until his financial and emotional resources are completely exhausted.

The question of state responsibility for the actions of private persons has been presented more starkly and much more frequently, however, in litigation between private parties and particularly in cases in which one person is claiming that his right to protection of his private life under Article 8 of the Convention requires the state to give him a remedy against the publication by another person of statements or photographs concerning what the claimant asserts is his private life. The opposing party in any such dispute will of course argue that the remedy sought by the plaintiff would violate his right to freedom of expression under Article 10 of the Convention. Each of the parties has a plausible claim that justice

---

2. *Id.* at ¶ 22.

is on its side. Resolving this dispute is made even more difficult and complex by the declaration of the European Parliamentary Assembly[3] and the decisions of the European Court of Human Rights that the rights granted by the Convention under Articles 8 and 10 of the Convention are of equal value.[4] This is in contrast with what had been the traditional primacy given to freedom of expression in all common law countries, even in those without written constitutions. Moreover, there is a certain asymmetry at play here. All the cases thus far have involved a claimant asking the state to punish someone for exercising his freedom of expression in order to protect the claimant's right to respect for his private life. None have involved a situation in which the state itself was asked to punish a person for trying to maintain his privacy in order to protect the freedom of expression of another person.

An examination of the tension between the right of privacy and the right of freedom of expression is thus as timely and appropriate a choice as one could find in a study that seeks to understand whether the modern, enlarged concept of human rights can facilitate the judicial resolution of important and emotionally charged social conflicts in a way that produces results that both satisfy our sense of social justice and are compatible with the traditional view of the role of courts, namely that they are neither super-legislators nor administrative agencies. In discussing conflicts between the rights protected under Article 8 and the rights guaranteed under Article 10 of the European Convention in disputes between private parties, one must begin by recognizing that all legal systems enforce some legal protection of what might be called privacy interests. The issue which is now being litigated in Europe is whether, in the name of justice or some other moral imperative captured by the notion of "a right," a person can be restrained or even punished for publishing information that is not false and that has not been obtained unlawfully or under any actual or implied promise of confidentiality. To assist the discussion, it will be helpful to start by first considering two judicial decisions, one by the European Court of Human Rights, the other by the House of Lords, both of which were rendered in 2004. These have become leading cases in this area of the law and, as such, will accordingly continue to figure in our discussion throughout the remainder of this book.

The earlier of these two cases is *Campbell v. MGN Ltd*,[5] decided by the House of Lords in May 2004. The plaintiff in that case was a famous fashion model who had previously publicly disparaged the apparently not uncommon practice among elite fashion models of using drugs as a means of coping with the pressures of the fast-paced life that they were obliged to lead. In making her

---

3. Resolution 1165, ¶ 11 (1998) of the Parliamentary Assembly of the Council of Europe.

4. *See*, e.g., von Hannover v. Germany, Application No. 59320/00, Judgment of June 24, 2004, 40 Eur. H.R. Rep. 1 (2005), at ¶ 42.

5. Campbell v. MGN Ltd, [2004] 2 A.C. 457 (hereafter *Campbell*).

comments, the plaintiff had emphasized that she herself did not use drugs. In point of fact, that assertion was false. A British tabloid, the *Daily Mirror*, learned not only that the plaintiff was attending Narcotics Anonymous meetings but also the exact location at which the meetings were held. In the first of three articles, the *Daily Mirror* took a somewhat disingenuously sympathetic tack in reporting that the plaintiff was seeking treatment for her condition and, to accompany the article, published a photograph of Campbell taken as she emerged from the building in which the meetings were held. The plaintiff immediately commenced legal proceedings against the *Daily Mirror*. In response, the paper published two further articles, the first of which was accompanied by another photograph taken in the street outside the Narcotics Anonymous meeting place. Both of these articles were critical of the plaintiff. They accused her of hypocrisy in criticizing others for doing what she herself was doing. The case was brought under the Data Protection Act of 1968 and also under the common law for breach of confidence. Campbell recovered some not very substantial damages in the trial court. A unanimous Court of Appeal reversed but it, in turn, was reversed by a divided House of Lords.

In the House of Lords, the case was characterized as one in which the plaintiff was seeking damages for breach of confidence and, in so doing, their lordships treated the case as one in which it had to resolve a conflict between the plaintiff's right to protection of her private life under Article 8 of the European Convention and the right of the defendant to freedom of expression under Article 10 of that Convention. Their lordships accordingly accepted that they were being called upon to weigh the conflicting rights of the parties and took it as a given that, under the European Convention, the rights involved, namely the right to respect for one's private life and the right to freedom of expression, were of equal value. In short, the case involved an instance of what in the United States is called "ad hoc balancing." Each of the five law lords who comprised the panel accordingly struggled to find the right balance, with the ultimate result being a three-to-two decision that the plaintiff's Article 8 rights prevailed over the defendant's Article 10 rights. The publication of the photographs, which it was conceded were not illegally obtained, was considered particularly blameworthy by those in the majority. As in the decisions of the European Court of Human Rights that we have already discussed and shall discuss further as this book proceeds, it was recognized by their lordships that, more than is the case in most judicial decision making, ad hoc balancing is extremely fact dependent. It is, therefore, important to examine closely how the individual law lords looked at the factual situation out of which the case arose to see what they thought were the decisive elements.

There was no express identification of how the *Daily Mirror* learned the details of Campbell's seeking assistance from Narcotics Anonymous. It was, however, accepted by their lordships, to use Lord Nicholls' words, that the "source of the newspaper's information was either an associate of Miss Campbell or a fellow addict attending meetings of Narcotics Anonymous."[6] Since British law did not recognize any general right of privacy as it was assumed existed in the United States,[7] their lordships focused on the developing law of breach of confidence and held, in reliance on previous late twentieth-century cases, that the "cause of action [for breach of confidence] has now firmly shaken off the limiting constraint of "[t]he need for an initial confidential relationship," and that "[n]ow the law imposes a 'duty of confidence' wherever a person receives information he knows or ought to know is fairly and reasonably to be regarded as confidential."[8] At the same time, as Lord Nicholls conceded, "the use of the phrase 'duty of confidence' and the description of information as 'confidential' is not altogether comfortable." Recognizing that information about a person's private life "would not, in ordinary usage be called 'confidential'," he thought "the 'more natural description' was that such information is 'private' and that the tort is better

---

6. *Id.* at ¶ 6.

7. *Id.* at ¶¶ 11, 22. This assumption was based upon the belief that *Restatement (Second) of Torts* § 652D accurately represented the law of the United States. As will be seen as the discussion proceeds, this assumption is clearly erroneous. Several of their lordships discussed the possibility of defining the tort as did § 652D as covering the disclosure of private facts that "would be highly offensive to a reasonable person," but the general consensus was the one to be described shortly in the text which, as we shall see, is certainly more in line with the position taken by the European Court of Human Rights and, in my opinion, is also more faithful to the facts of the *Campbell* case.

8. *Campbell* at ¶ 14. The most immediate authority for these statements that was cited by Lord Nicholls was *Attorney General v. Guardian Newspapers Ltd (No. 2)*, [1990] 1 A.C. 109, 281 (per Lord Goff). That case arose from the publication of a book in Australia by a former member of MI5, the British Secret Service, who was then living in Australia. The attempt by the British government to prevent publication in Australia eventually failed on the ground that, as described by the House of Lords, "an Australian court should not accept jurisdiction to enforce obligations of confidence owed to a foreign government so as to protect that government's intelligence secrets and confidential political information." *Id.* at 254 (Lord Keith). The origins of an expanded duty of confidentiality was principally traced by Lord Keith (*id.* at 255) and Lord Griffiths (*id.* at 268) to *Margaret, Duchess of Argyll v. Duke of Argyll*, [1967] Ch. 302 (1965). In that case, the Duke was enjoined, *inter alia*, from publishing, in a newspaper, intimate matters that he had learned from conversations with the plaintiff, his former wife, during the course of their marriage, as well as the details, which he had agreed to keep confidential, of the settlement of prior legal proceedings involving the plaintiff and some of the Duke's relations. In the course of his judgment, the judge took it as an established principle of English law that an injunction may be granted not only to enjoin the publication of confidential information by someone who was "a party to the confidence but also by other persons into whose possession that information has improperly come." That the Duke was a party to confidences is clear, and it is not too much of a stretch to include the newspaper as a party to the confidence, particularly if it paid him anything for his disclosure and/or because it obviously knew that the Duke was using the newspaper to injure his former wife out of sheer spite and possibly even encouraged him in that endeavor.

described as the 'misuse of private information'."[9] According to him, it was in this guise that the values of Articles 8 and 10 became "part of the cause of action for breach of confidence."[10] This view of the governing law was accepted by all of their lordships. It was also accepted by all their lordships that even private information might be disclosed if there were a sufficient public interest. The issue at hand therefore was the application of that general legal doctrine to the facts of the case before them. The case thus required their lordships to first determine what was the private information involved in the case and then, if private information was in fact present, whether a sufficient public interest justified disclosure of that information. The answer to this second inquiry would also raise further questions about the extent of the disclosure that could thereby be justified as being in the public interest. For some of their lordships, this latter issue seems to have merged with the question of whether the disclosure of the private information at issue in the case was so *de minimis* as to not deserve any legal remedy at all.

As the House of Lords viewed the case, there were five main features about the articles that needed to be considered. These were: 1) the revelation that Campbell was a drug addict; 2) the revelation that she was seeking treatment; 3) the revelation that she was seeking treatment from Narcotics Anonymous; 4) the revelation of some details about that treatment; and 5) the publication of photographs taken outside the place of treatment. All five law lords agreed that the first and second revelations were permissible. Campbell, who was clearly a public figure, had herself raised the issue in a public arena and the revelation that, contrary to her public assertions, she was in fact addicted to drugs and receiving treatment was within the scope of the defendant's freedom of expression. The differences among the law lords concerned the other three matters. For Lord Nicholls and Lord Hoffman, as well as for the Court of Appeal, the revelation that Campbell was attending Narcotics Anonymous was not a particularly damaging revelation, given that it was permissible to reveal Campbell's drug addiction. That drug addicts seek help from Narcotics Anonymous was well known to the public, as was the type of treatment that such persons would receive there. It was not the equivalent of treatment at a medical clinic. Lord Hope, Lady Hale, and Lord Carswell thought otherwise, although for Lord Carswell it was more the revelation of the "details" of Campbell's treatment at Narcotics Anonymous— information about where she obtained the treatment and statements about the frequency and duration of her attendance—that bothered him rather than the mere statement that she attended Narcotics Anonymous.[11] All three emphasized the importance of the photographs. Indeed, Lord Hope expressly declared that, were it not for the photographs, he would have found the balance equal and

---

9. *Campbell* at ¶ 14.
10. *Id.* at ¶ 17.
11. *Id.* at ¶ 165.

would accordingly have given the journalists the benefit of a margin of appreciation in order not to interfere with their editorial discretion.[12]

For the two dissenters, Lord Nicholls and Lord Hoffman, however, the photographs were not unflattering and not a source of embarrassment to her. Lady Hale conceded that it would have been perfectly legitimate for the *Daily Mirror* to have used a file photograph of Campbell to accompany the story, but she stressed that the actual photographs were taken outside the Narcotics Anonymous meeting place.[13] If examined closely, they would enable someone with sufficient knowledge of London to identify the exact place where the meetings were held. For Lord Carswell, the third member of the majority, the importance of the photograph was demonstrated by the fact that photographs, such as the ones in question, are "a powerful prop . . . and a much valued part of newspaper reporting, especially in the tabloid or popular press (hence the enthusiasm of paparazzi to obtain pictures of celebrities for publication in the newspapers)."[14] Finally, it must be noted that in the course of the speeches of their lordships, statements were made about the hierarchy of speech. Political speech was mentioned by Lord Nicholls as particularly deserving of protection.[15] Lady Hale described a more complex hierarchy—at the top was political speech, followed by intellectual and educational speech, which in turn was followed by artistic speech.[16] The speech (or expression) in question, however, fell into none of these categories but rather into what might be called the "other" category.

We shall examine at greater length the attempts by the English courts to give more specific content to what sort of challenged expression might be entitled to a public interest defense when we discuss how a case-by-case approach to these sorts of cases might possibly produce a means for deciding conflicts between privacy concerns and expression that is both relatively clear and politically and socially acceptable. In that regard, we might note that, in recognizing a "public interest" defense in privacy cases, their lordships were imposing on true speech the same burdens that are imposed on the claim of privilege for the publication of false speech under the law of defamation, which seems odd indeed. This point is mentioned now because it will be a consideration that we shall confront when we attempt to construct what an appropriate decision-making process for these sorts of cases might look like. Indeed, in that later discussion we may even need to discuss why true expression about what is seen in public needs to serve any public interest at all in order to be given any privileged position among competing values. Is it not possible that expression is a good in itself or are we forced to conclude that, from the legal perspective, silence is the preferred human

---

12. *Id.* at ¶ 121.
13. *Id.* at ¶ 154–56.
14. *Id.* at ¶ 165.
15. *Id.* at ¶ 29.
16. *Id.* at ¶ 148–49.

condition? When we return to these cases again as we try to construct an acceptable model of what might plausibly be considered an acceptable judicial decision-making procedure for deciding these sorts of controversies, we shall have to note that, while Campbell only recovered a total of £3,500 in compensatory and aggravated damages in the English courts, she was awarded £1,086,295.47 in costs including attorneys' fees.[17]

The second case, von Hannover v. Germany,[18] decided by the European Court of Human Rights seven weeks after the Campbell case, involved, as the claimant, Princess Caroline of Monaco, the daughter of the late Princess of Monaco, née Grace Kelly. The claimant had sought relief in the German courts for the publication of photographs of her that had been taken from what might be called public places. Some of these photographs, including some with her children, were taken while she was shopping or riding on horseback or skiing or otherwise in public areas. Others showed her with a male companion in the far corner of the courtyard of a restaurant that was nevertheless visible from outside the restaurant. And still others showed her in an open air private bathing compound in which she was likewise visible from outside of that facility. After a very protracted course of litigation, the German courts had eventually ruled in the claimant's favor as to the photographs that included the children and as to those taken of her in the restaurant, but not as to the other photographs on the ground that, as a "figure of contemporary society, 'par excellence,'" she could not complain about pictures taken of her in a public space where she had no reasonable expectation of being in what could be called a "secluded place."[19] Princess Caroline then applied to the European Court of Human Rights.

The European Court, ruling in Princess Caroline's favor, found all these other photographs likewise objectionable, but reserved for further consideration a decision as to the appropriate remedy.[20] In deciding for the applicant on the merits, the Court conceded that none of the photographs had been unlawfully taken since they were taken from a public place. It felt, however, that publishing the photographs was more egregious than publishing an article, and it is more than merely plausible to conclude from reading the decision that the Court felt that punishing the publication of the photographs would discourage the

---

17. Campbell v. MGN Ltd (No. 2), [2005] 1 W. L. R. 3394 (H.L. 2004). Lord Hoffman noted the irony of such a huge disproportion between the amount recovered and the costs awarded in a case where five of the nine judges who heard the case thought she should recover nothing at all. Id. at ¶ 3. This latter decision is now on appeal to the European Court of Human Rights, Application No. 39401/04.

18. Von Hannover v. Germany, Application No. 59320/00, Judgment of June 24, 2004, 40 Eur. H.R. Rep. 1 (2005) (hereafter von Hannover).

19. Id. at ¶¶ 8–38.

20. See von Hannover v. Germany, Application No. 59320/00, Judgment of the Third Section (Just-Satisfaction-Friendly Settlement), July 28, 2005.

paparazzi. The decision is long but much of it is a description of the process followed, the judgments delivered by the German courts, and the submissions of the parties to the case and the interveners. Following the practice usually adhered to in civil law jurisdictions, the operative parts of the decision are much more conclusory, and more directly based on certain underlying principles of social justice, than are the speeches of the individual law lords in the *Campbell* case.

In reaching its decision, the European Court of Human Rights started from the position that its task was striking a "fair balance . . . between the competing interests of the individual and of the community as a whole."[21] The Court stressed that the case did not "concern the dissemination of 'ideas,' but of images concerning very personal or even intimate 'information' about an individual."[22] Furthermore, the Court noted that "photos appearing in the tabloid press are often taken in a climate of continual harassment which induces in the person concerned a very strong sense of intrusion into their private life."[23] The case was not like a recent case in which the Court had held that "the more time that elapsed, the more the public interest in the discussion of the history of the late President Mitterand's two terms of office prevailed over the requirement of protecting the President's rights with regard to medical confidentiality."[24] For the Court, the photographs of scenes from Princess Caroline's daily life involved "activities of a purely private nature."[25] Although the Court acknowledged that, as a member of the ruling family of Monaco, she represented that family "at certain cultural or charitable functions," she did not, however, exercise any "function within or on behalf of the State of Monaco."[26] There was, in short, "a fundamental distinction . . . between reporting facts . . . capable of contributing to a debate in a democratic society relating to politicians in the exercise of their functions, and reporting details of the private life of an individual," especially one such as Princess Caroline, who did not exercise official functions. The press served no "watchdog" function in this latter case.[27] The Court accepted that the public had a right to be informed and this right might extend "in certain special circumstances . . . to aspects of the private life of public figures, particularly where politicians are concerned" but that was not the instant case. Satisfying "the

---

21. *See von Hannover, supra* note 18, at ¶ 57.
22. *Id.* at ¶ 59. *See also id.* at ¶¶ 61–68.
23. *Id.* at ¶ 59. *See also id.* at ¶ 68.
24. *Id.* at ¶ 60, citing *Editions Plon v. France*, Application No. 58148/00, Judgment of May 18, 2004, at ¶ 53.
25. *Von Hannover* at ¶ 61.
26. *Id.* at ¶ 62.
27. *Id.* at ¶ 63. On August 20, 2009 the *Media Law Prof Blog* reported that a Dutch court had ruled against the Associated Press in a proceeding brought by the Crown Prince of the Netherlands for publishing pictures of him and his family while they were vacationing in Argentina. The court noted that, while the Crown Prince often did perform official duties, at the time the pictures were taken he was not.

curiosity of a particular readership regarding the details of the applicant's private life cannot be deemed to contribute to any debate of general interest to society despite the applicant being known to the public."[28] While the Court was prepared to accept that photographs can sometimes contribute to a debate of general interest, it ruled that the photographs in question did not. The Court also noted that, although taken from a public place, the photographs were taken without Princess Caroline's knowledge or consent. This was especially true of the photographs taken of her at the Monte Carlo Beach Club which, it appeared, were taken secretly, at a distance of several hundred yards. There was no suggestion that taking a person's photograph in or from a public place was actionable. It was the publication, at least in the media involved, that was subject to legal liability.

The European Court of Human Rights stressed "the fundamental importance of protecting private life from the point of view of the development of every human being's personality. That protection . . . [it declared] extends beyond the private family circle and also includes a social dimension."[29] Even people known to the general public "must be able to enjoy a 'legitimate expectation' of protection of and respect for their private life."[30] It did not consider that what level of privacy a person may *legitimately* expect is in turn largely based on the level of protection that the law will extend to him. Certainly after the *von Hannover* case, those expectations will be high. The European Court pointedly disagreed with the German courts' description of Princess Caroline as "a figure of contemporary society, 'par excellence.'" The distinction between figures of "contemporary society, 'par excellence'" and "'relatively' public figures" has to be precise and "clear and obvious so that, in a State governed by the rule of law, the individual has precise indications" about what he might do. "Above all," the Court concluded, people "need to know exactly when and where they are in a protected sphere or . . . in a sphere in which they must expect interference from others, especially the tabloid press."[31] The criterion of "spatial isolation," enunciated by the German courts, "although apposite in theory, is in reality too vague and difficult for the person concerned to determine in advance."[32] How a system dependent on ad hoc balancing of conflicting rights can produce this kind of certainty is another matter that will be addressed later when we discuss the possible conditions that would

---

28. *Von Hannover* at ¶ 65.
29. *Id.* at ¶ 69.
30. *Ibid.*
31. *Id.* at ¶ 73.
32. *Id.* at ¶ 75. No one would disagree with the value of providing people with a high degree of certainty when they are involved in matters of great concern to them. As was stated in the joint opinion of Justices O'Connor, Kennedy, and Souter in *Planned Parenthood of S.E. Pa. v. Casey*, 505 U.S. 883, 844 (1992), "Liberty finds no refuge in a jurisprudence of doubt." The question is whether the strongly worded assertions in *von Hannover* are able to provide that level of certainty.

be necessary for the decision-making process to produce this outcome. It certainly is not immediately obvious why the notion of legitimate expectation of privacy will provide greater certainty than the notion of spatial isolation. Surely the supposed defense of "public interest" is by no means self-defining if one accepts that the speaker is also entitled to a sufficient level of certainty as to what he may safely communicate to others. Spatial isolation is at least a fairly objective and empirically determined criterion. "Legitimate expectation of privacy" is clearly a social construct as is the notion of "public interest." Setting that issue aside for the moment, we may conclude this short examination of the Court's judgment by noting the Court's ultimate conclusion "that the decisive factor in balancing the protection of private life against freedom of expression should lie in the contribution that the published photos and articles make to a debate of general interest."[33] Here again is the same suggestion that was made in the *Campbell* case, namely that the pre-eminent value of expression is its contribution to certain important social activities and purposes.

Although the judgment of the Court awarding Princess Caroline the relief she sought was unanimous, two of the seven judges in the panel had some reservations about the Court's line of reasoning. Judge Cabral Barreto of Portugal in his brief separate opinion emphasized that Princess Caroline was a public figure who, it was "well known," had "for years played a role in European public life" and that, in his opinion, "information about her life contributes to a debate of public interest." Furthermore, the general interest did not have to be limited to political debate. He did agree with the Court's conclusion that the private life of a public figure does not "stop at their front door" and "that the criterion of spatial isolation used by the German courts" was too restrictive. The task of finding the right balance would, in his view, nevertheless be difficult. He concluded that it would "never be easy to define in concrete terms the situations that correspond to this 'legitimate expectation' and a case-by-case approach [was] therefore justified," but he cautioned, as did Lord Carswell in the *Campbell* case, that "[t]his casuistic approach may also give rise to differences of opinion." Although, as noted, he had joined in the Court's judgment, he nevertheless also expressed some doubts about whether some of the photographs that the Court found to be objectionable intrusions into Princess Caroline's private life really were so. Judge Zupančič of Slovenia wrote an even briefer separate opinion to express his adherence to "the hesitations" of Judge Cabral Barreto and explained his view that in this difficult balancing exercise something like a notion of a "reasonable expectation of privacy" should be the applicable criterion, a criterion that includes "an allusion to informed common sense." He noted that it was impossible "to separate by an iron curtain private life from public performance."

---

33. *Von Hannover* at ¶ 76.

We have here then two cases, both of which involve a claimant seeking protection of her "right to respect for her private life" and another party objecting that the granting of a judicial remedy would interfere with its "right to freedom of expression." In resolving that conflict under the approach taken in the *Campbell* case, courts will have to determine what is the information that a reasonable person would recognize as in some way "confidential" although it was not obtained by any intrusion on someone's private property nor subject to any contractual obligation of confidentiality and may even be generally already known by a small group of people. Having identified that information, they would then have to determine the public interest in the broader public dissemination of that information. Finally, in making those determinations, a court would have to factor in the social importance of the speech and the medium through which the information was disseminated. Was the information relevant to political discussion, or possibly also to educational or scientific discourse or artistic expression? Was it published in a serious newspaper or book or was it published in a tabloid or some other publication or medium of communication directed to what might be called a "popular audience"? If we were to follow the approach taken in the *von Hannover* case, we would have to confront the issue of whether it is really true that the public acts of non-officials are normally exclusively part of their private lives with no relevance to their public lives. Must expression dealing with such matters really contribute to a debate of general interest,[34] and is it really for courts to determine what is a debate and what is a matter of general interest? And how would they determine that? As has already been indicated, we shall be obliged to discuss these subjects later in this book. For the moment, it suffices to note that the positions of Ms. Campbell and Princess Caroline, in seeking protection for their private lives, and the position of the *Daily Mirror* and the publishers of the pictures of which Princess Caroline complained, in seeking protection for their freedom of expression, were certainly premised on some notion of justice or other moral entitlement incorporated in the law, although there is a difference between them both as to the content of that moral entitlement and an even greater difference about the perspective from which that entitlement should be viewed.

As this book is going to press, a Grand Chamber of the European Court of Human Rights is considering a second proceeding brought by Princess Caroline for the invasion of her privacy by the publication of photographs of her.[35] While we await whatever clarification of the law governing this sensitive area might be provided by the eventual decision of this second *von Hannover* case, we might consider whether, given the reliance on basic moral values in the cases thus far decided, we might even now reach some tentative conclusions, based solely on

---

34. *See id.* at ¶ 76.
35. *See* p. 156, *infra*.

some abstract principle of justice, as to what might be the appropriate solution of these controversies in an ideal world and what should be the role of the courts in arriving at that solution. For example, we might ask, what does justice require? One might want to say that, as an abstract matter, it would have been more just if the articles and photographs published in the *Daily Mirror* in the *Campbell* case and the photographs involved in the *von Hannover* case had never been published, but even such a wishing away of the problem is not without its difficulties. Suppose *The New York Times* or *The Washington Post* or some similarly reputable European newspaper, rather than a mass-circulation tabloid, had published an article on drug use by world-class fashion models and mentioned Ms. Campbell's seeking treatment for drug addiction despite her previous somewhat self-righteous contention that she herself never used drugs, and published, along with the article, a photograph of her in a public street outside the treatment center? Or suppose *The New York Times* or *The Washington Post* or a similarly reputable European newspaper, in their style sections, ran pictures of Princess Caroline of Monaco and pictures of her with her children and male companions? There are other variants of these scenarios that we shall have occasion to examine as the discussion proceeds and we endeavor to come up with a regime that produces something like a set of fairly clear Hohfeldian rights while, at the same time, recognizing the equal value of the conflicting rights in question.

In the United States, neither *The New York Times* nor *The Washington Post* could possibly be held liable, or restrained from publication pending trial, in the circumstances presented in the *Campbell* and *von Hannover* cases. While injunctions can be obtained to restrain publication of information obtained in the course of a confidential relationship, the *Pentagon Papers*[36] case clearly shows how difficult it is in the United States to restrain publication by someone who has received information improperly obtained by a third person when the publisher had neither instigated nor collaborated in any way in the improper obtaining of the information. As for successfully maintaining an action for damages after publication, *The Florida Star v. B.J.F.*[37] is instructive. In that case, a reporter saw the name of a woman who had been robbed and sexually assaulted in a report posted in the press room of the sheriff's office. There was also a sign posted in the press room that the names of victims of sexual assault were not matters of public record and were not to be published. There was, in addition, a Florida statute making it unlawful "to print, publish, or broadcast . . . in any instrument of mass communication the name, address or other identifying fact or information of the victim of any sexual offense."[38] The defendant newspaper published a one-paragraph article on the incident described in the sheriff department's report that included the plaintiff's full name. The plaintiff then brought

---

36. New York Times v. United States, 403 U.S. 713 (1971).
37. 491 U.S. 524 (1989).
38. *Id.* at 526 (the statute was FLA. STAT. § 794.03 (1987)).

an action in the Florida state courts against the newspaper and recovered a judgment of $75,000 in compensatory damages and $25,000 in punitive damages, a judgment that was affirmed on appeal. This judgment was in turn reversed by the Supreme Court of the United States. While the Court was not prepared to hold that "truthful publication is automatically constitutionally protected . . . or even that a State may never punish publication of the name of a victim of sexual offense," it nevertheless expressly declared that "punishment may lawfully be imposed, if at all," on a newspaper that "publishes truthful information which it has lawfully obtained only when narrowly tailored to a state interest of the highest order."[39] The Court found no such interest in the case before it. Since the Court was prepared to accept a fairly literal interpretation of the First Amendment's express denial of governmental power to restrict the freedom of speech, the decision was not all that difficult because freedom of expression is the preferred value. The Court was, of course, realistic enough to accept that such prohibitions might not be completely absolute, but nevertheless stressed that only the most compelling government interest could possibly justify restrictions on the publication of what in fact is true by someone like the reporter who was lawfully in the press room and had not illegally obtained the information. No one disputed the propriety of holding the sheriff's office itself liable for failure to fulfill its statutory duty not to disclose her name; and in fact the plaintiff had received a settlement from the sheriff's office that had been set off by the trial judge against the compensatory damages awarded her by the jury.

It is curious that *The Florida Star v. B.J.F.* was described by the three-judge Trial Chamber of the International Tribunal for the Prosecution of Persons Responsible for Serious Violations of International Humanitarian Law in the Territory of the Former Yugoslavia (commonly called the International Criminal Court for the former Yugoslavia (ICTY)) as having "held that state sanctions imposed on the press for disclosing the identities of sexual assault victims may be constitutional."[40] A person trained in the common law tradition would certainly find that description of the holding in the *B.J.F.* case rather odd to say the least. The failure to completely foreclose that possibility is not a holding that it might be constitutional.[41] Obviously, if the newspaper had itself been complicit

---

39. *Id.* at 541.

40. Prosecutor v. Duško Tadić, Case No. It-94-1-T, ruling of August 10, 1995 on Prosecutor's Motion for Protective Measures for Victims and Witnesses, ¶ 40, reported in 7 CRIMINAL LAW FORUM 139, 157–58.

41. It should be noted that in its opinion in *B.J.F.* the Court noted that, at trial, B.J.F. had testified that, after her name was published in the paper, *B.J.F.* at 528, her mother had received phone calls from a man who said he would rape B.J.F. again. *See also* Hood v. Naeter Brothers Publishing Co., 562 S.W.2d 770 (Mo. App. 1978), refusing to permit a man, who had observed a murder in the course of an armed robbery and whose name and address were reprinted in a newspaper report of the crime, to recover for emotional

in the sheriff's office violation of its statutory duty, the result would likely have been different. Perhaps because the United States Supreme Court did not declare that any such restrictions were never constitutional, a form of statement that rarely appears in common law adjudication, a person trained in the civil law tradition, who was looking for some general principle governing all such cases, might find the Trial Chamber's description of the *B.J.F.* case useful. At the same time, however, it also accentuates the significance of recognizing that different legal traditions, reflecting the differing procedures and styles of argumentation that exist even in the developed Western world, will make uniform treatment of similar human rights cases across different legal cultures difficult to achieve, even if there is a relatively complete agreement as to what is the scope of the human rights at issue. Be that as it may, a person trained in the common law tradition of the United States would treat the *B.J.F.* case as one in which there was no real need to balance rights; the right generated by the constitutional protection of speech would almost always trump assertions of a common law or statutory right of privacy. That is how the *B.J.F.* case was construed by the Supreme Court of California,[42] which as a consequence overruled prior California precedents that were more in tune with the House of Lords decision in the *Campbell* case and indeed were based on the same view of the American law of privacy that was taken by the law lords.[43]

The gap between the approach taken in Europe and that taken in the United States to conflicts between rights of privacy and rights to freedom of expression gives every indication of widening if current trends are maintained. That indeed would be regrettable, particularly in a world that purports to maintain that there are in fact universal human rights. The possibly widening gap is most concretely seen in the English courts' considerable expansion of the notion of "confidentiality." There are recent cases in England in which, in one case, a close friend revealed to the media information about a "renowned musician" who carefully guarded her privacy including "personal and private information" about herself;[44] and in another, a former sexual partner disclosed to a newspaper information about the personal and professional life of the chief executive of a major international company.[45] The musician won her suit to enjoin further publication of the

---

distress caused by his fear that he might be murdered by the criminals who apparently were still at large.

42. Gates v. Discovery Communications, Inc., 34 Cal. 4th 679 (2004), *overruling* Briscoe v. Readers Digest Ass'n, 4 Cal. 3d 529 (1971).

43. *See* note 7, *supra*, where we discussed their lordships' discussion of the help that might be gleaned from § 652D of the *Restatement (Second) of Torts*.

44. McKennit v. Ash, [2008] Q.B. 73 (C.A. 2006).

45. Lord Browne of Madingley v. Associated Newspapers Ltd, [2008] Q.B. 103 (2007). For a more detailed discussion of the evolution of the British law of confidentiality, *see* PAUL STANLY, THE LAW OF CONFIDENTIALITY: A RESTATEMENT (2008).

offending material; the chief executive of the major company succeeded in securing a temporary injunction pending trial on the publication of some material about his private life but not on the information concerning his business activities. The Supreme Court of the United States has not ruled on cases substantially similar to these. In the federal courts of appeal, however, there is authority that information passed on by close friends, and even an ex-wife, to an inquiring magazine reporter enjoys no privacy protection.[46] On the other hand, in Europe, the *Campbell* and *von Hannover* cases have, as we have seen, indicated that, if one publishes any information about a person, even a public figure or official, that is not generally known and is claimed to be intimate, the burden is on the publisher to show either that there is a significant public interest in publishing the information, or that the person in question did not have a legitimate expectation of privacy.

The strongest case for imposing a somewhat extended duty of confidentiality is when someone actually entices a person, under an assurance of confidentiality, to reveal intimate facts about himself, particularly where the recipient intends to pass on that information to a third party possibly even for a fee.[47] Much of the information that we learn about others, however, is voluntarily supplied. It is certainly common knowledge that people often pass on intimate details of their friends. This is a large part of what gossip is made of, and surely, however regrettable that might be, one would not want to live in a world organized around a legal regime determined to suppress a practice that has always existed so long as people have lived in groups, namely as long as there have been human beings. That would be a very intrusive regime indeed. In the *Campbell* case, the House of Lords relied on prior cases that suggested that not only may publication of confidential information by someone who might be said to be a party to that confidence, however broadly that term is defined, be enjoined; but so too may publication by any "other persons" into whose possession that information has

---

46. Virgil v. Time, Inc., 527 F.2d 1122 (9th Cir. 1975), *cert. denied*, 425 U.S. 998 (1976).

47. Indeed, the establishment of an extended duty of confidentiality subject to exceptions on the basis of a range of reasons based on the public interest could in some instances actually be destructive of confidentiality. In *Cohen v. Cowles Media Co.*, 501 U.S. 663 (1991), during the closing days of the 1982 gubernatorial election campaign, the plaintiff, who was associated with the Republican gubernatorial campaign, after receiving a promise that his identity would not be revealed, gave the newspaper reporters copies of publicly available court records that showed that the Democratic candidate for Lieutenant Governor had a minor criminal record. In their story revealing this information, they identified the plaintiff as the source. In consequence he lost his job. In a five-to-four decision, the Supreme Court of the United States held that the First Amendment did not preclude the plaintiff's actions to recover compensatory damages for the breach by the reporters of their promise of anonymity. One might maintain that the public interest is irrelevant here.

improperly come. That just begs the real question: What does it mean for information to come *improperly* into the possession of a person?

Prohibiting someone from taking advantage of information that he acquires as an "insider" to a set of financial dealings is a common and expected feature of securities law. Prohibiting someone from trading on information inadvertently obtained that he knows or should know is insider information is also not uncommon. It should, however, be noted that, in the United States at least, if a person accidentally overhears a conversation that includes insider information, the accidental listener is under no obligation not to profit from that information.[48] But regardless of what might be the correct resolution of the issue of whether such an accidental listener may trade on that information, it seems to be universally accepted in securities litigation that someone who accidentally overhears such a conversation can publish it to the world.[49] To say that a person who learns of what seems to be embarrassing private information about another is generally forbidden from disclosing it to third parties seems to be a stretch. One appreciates that Narcotics Anonymous does indeed try to preserve the anonymity of those who attend its meetings and of what is discussed at those meetings,[50] but it is unrealistic to expect that there will be no divulging of that information to family and close friends. How would controversies involving these sorts of facts be decided when the information is passed on by friends or family to third parties, including even the media, as it well might? And what if the person publishing the information had not attended the Narcotics Anonymous meeting but saw the person in question emerging from a place that the publisher knew to be a Narcotics Anonymous meeting place? Should even such an individual also really be under a duty of confidentiality?

One appreciates that in the United Kingdom, and perhaps in other European countries and in the United States as well, it is not uncommon for newspapers

---

48. *See,* e.g., SEC v. Falbo, 14 F. Supp. 2d 508 (S.D.N.Y. 1998); SEC v. Switzer, 590 F. Supp. 756 (W.D. Okla. 1984). The same may be true in New Zealand. *See* Peter Fitzsimons, *Insider Trading in New Zealand in* SECURITIES REGULATION IN AUSTRALIA AND NEW ZEALAND (G. Walker and B. Fisse eds., 1998), at 595, 611–12.

49. *See* Dirks v. SEC, 463 U.S. 646, 661–64 (1983). In the United Kingdom, which has adopted the European Directive on Insider Trading, such a person might be considered a "secondary insider" but he only incurs liability if he himself trades on the information. *See* Barry A. K. Rider, *Insider Trading: An English Comment in New Zealand, in* ESSAYS ON INSIDER TRADING AND SECURITIES LITIGATION (C. Richett and R. Grantham eds., 1997), at 60, 97–106. Once the information is disclosed to the world, it is of course no longer confidential, i.e., inside information, and anyone can trade on it.

50. In a publication entitled *Frequently Asked Questions Media* (FAQ of March 2007, for responding to media inquiries), Narcotics Anonymous emphasizes its policy of anonymity and declares that it will not confirm whether someone has attended meetings or is a member (Q&A 12), and that "typically" there should be no photographs of members at meetings (Q&A 11). These are certainly reasonable policies.

and television broadcasters to pay people for information that they have obtained as a result of a confidential relationship. That is a factor which we shall have to consider when we actually try to construct a decision-making procedure for handling these types of cases in the final chapters of this book. But what if there is no such payment, so that it cannot be said that the eventual disseminator of the information either instigated or facilitated or even encouraged the breach of confidence? None of the British cases I have cited discusses that possible scenario, nor is it discussed in any of the cases cited in the *Campbell* case itself. There are, however, cases in the United States in which dissemination of information known to be both confidential and improperly obtained or revealed was not subject to legal sanction, because the disseminator neither encouraged nor instigated the improper obtaining or revealing of such information. The most famous of these is the *Pentagon Papers* case, to which we have already alluded, where classified government documents were given to *The New York Times* and *The Washington Post*.[51] As noted earlier, the United States Supreme Court vacated a preliminary injunction pending trial against publication of that information on the ground that it was a forbidden prior restraint on speech. More recently and even more germane to the issue we are discussing, in *Bartnicki v. Vopper*,[52] the United States Supreme Court affirmed a lower court dismissal of an action against media defendants and the individual who gave them copies of recordings of illegal wiretaps of conversations of a local politician made by an unknown third party.

It certainly would be ridiculous to try to make punishable the exchange of information by neighbors about other people in their neighborhood. Why should the press not be able to republish the same information if it is true? It would be an odd governing "principle" that a person of leisure who is curious about someone, even an insignificant someone, may lawfully go around and question that individual's friends and neighbors, but a reporter who does the same thing because he too is curious about the rich or famous or powerful is acting unlawfully if he then publishes the information in a newspaper or on television to satisfy the curiosity of the less rich. It is not entirely clear that the House of Lords in the *Campbell* case actually meant to move British law that far in that direction. Nevertheless, because of the more general statements in the *von Hannover* case and the fact that the information in that case was not even arguably confidential, it is clear that, whatever was the intention of the law lords in the *Campbell* case, the European Court of Human Rights envisaged and seems to have been endorsing fairly broad restrictions of expression in order to protect its general notion of individual privacy, even when such a person appears in areas physically open to or observable by the public. As odd as it might sound, the broad language of the

---

51. New York Times v. United States, 403 U.S. 713 (1971).
52. 532 U.S. 514 (2001). This publication would probably be illegal in France. *See* French Penal Code, Article 226-2.

Court suggests that someone who saw Princess Caroline holding hands with a male companion on a public street would be breaching her right of privacy if he published a photograph he had taken of this scene on an Internet blog. And there is in fact recent authority in England suggesting that this is indeed the law.[53] The fact that it might in practice often be almost impossible to punish such a person raises doubts about the wisdom of any such judicial intimations of what might be "punishable" behavior. Western nations have heralded the ability of the Internet to circumvent attempts in autocratic nations to suppress the flow of information. Why should it be surprising if the Internet should be used to make attempts to suppress the exchange of information deemed private equally ineffective?[54]

Because of the enormous range of possible situations to which these doctrinal statements might be applied, it is unsurprising that the European Court of Human Rights and the House of Lords expressly and readily conceded that the appropriate decision in these sorts of cases can only be reached on a case-by-case basis by weighing or balancing the factors at play in each case. As both of these courts recognized, relatively small factual differences can tilt the eventual decision one way or another. In later chapters of this book we shall discuss in some detail, using as illustrations the conflict between expression and privacy as well as the conflict between expression and other important public values, how we might attempt to resolve these sorts of controversies by courts through a method of case-by-case decision making in ways that most people would consider at least acceptable, even if not ideal. If it were possible to construct such a method, it might be a reason to consider recommending the European model for universal adoption.

In the course of illustrating the difficulties involved in satisfactorily resolving conflicts of defeasible human rights, each of which is stated to be of great value,

---

53. *See* Murray v. Express Newspapers LLC, [2008] 3 W.L.R. 1360 (C.A.). The case involved photographs of the 19-month-old son of J.K. Rowling while being pushed by his father in a "buggy" as he accompanied his parents to and from a café. In a New Zealand case involving practically identical facts, the Court of Appeal unanimously ruled that no action would lie even though, in a three-to-two decision, the majority declared that New Zealand recognized the action for breach of confidence along the lines adopted by the United Kingdom. Hosking v. Runting, [2005] 1 N.Z.L.R. 1 (2004) (C.A.).

54. *See* Jane Croft and Jim Pickard, *Gagging Order Eased*, FT.COM, October 13, 2009, reporting the lifting of a "super injunction" enjoining reports of a Member of Parliament's question about legislation to protect whistleblowers that apparently was occasioned by an inquiry into the conduct of the company that had obtained the gag order. The reason for lifting the order was the flood of postings about the matter. A super injunction forbids even mention in the press that the injunction has been issued. *See also* the defeat of the attempt to enjoin the publication of the book discussed in note 8, *supra*. With the rise of the "Twitter" phenomenon, the attempt to suppress the dissemination of such information is bound to fail.

we have once more seen that the assumption of a set of supposedly universal human rights in a concrete meaningful sense is, even in the Western world, not as firmly anchored in reality as is generally thought. The contrasting approaches taken in Europe and in the United States highlight that issue and show that it is not solely the effect of the different procedural traditions in the Western world, that we have already noted, but reflect also many basic substantive differences among the basic values of the various Western societies. These differences among the democracies of the developed world are already having significant practical consequences. For example, some European judgments in defamation cases and other sorts of cases in which expression either has been punished or restricted have been denied enforcement in the United States on the ground that it would be contrary to the public policy of the United States, which assigns priority to freedom of expression.[55]

There is no reason to think that these instances will not multiply in the future. That increasing dissonance is particularly likely if one takes into account an important factor that was not considered by either the House of Lords in the *Campbell* case or by the European Court of Human Rights in the *von Hannover* case. It is a factor that undoubtedly figured in the adoption of the First Amendment to the American Constitution, and which, I submit, requires some serious consideration and discussion. Although we speak of courts of justice, it is recognized that the courts cannot render perfect justice, not only because it is impractical for them to do so but also because, in a free society, there is also a strong interest in protecting the individual from the overwhelming coercive power of the state, even if the individual has acted unjustly or in some other socially undesirable way. To take an extreme example, the countries of the European Community and many other countries, as well as many of the several states of the United States, have abolished capital punishment no matter how heinous the conduct of the criminal. There are a number of good reasons to abolish the death penalty. Some of these are to varying degrees practical. As it currently operates in the United States, it is extremely expensive to administer. Moreover, despite the additional judicial attention devoted to death penalty cases—which might very likely not be available for poorer people were the death penalty to be completely abolished—there is always the possibility of condemning an innocent person to death. From the moral perspective, however, which for

---

55. *See,* e.g., SARL Louis Feraud Int'l v. Viewfinder Inc., 406 F. Supp. 2d 274 (S.D.N.Y. 2005). For those seeking a declaratory judgment that a foreign defamation or privacy award is unenforceable in the United States the difficulty is to obtain jurisdiction over the person who secured the foreign judgment. *See* Ehrenfeld v. Mahfouz, 518 F. 3d 102 (2d Cir. 2008), and N.Y. CIV. PRAC. LAW § 302, as amended 2008. There may also be the need to show that an attempt will actually be made to enforce the judgment in the United States. *See* Yahoo! Inc. v. La Ligue Contre Le Racisme, 433 F. 3d 1199 (9th Cir. 2006) (involving French judgment ordering website to block sales of Nazi paraphernalia).

many people is the most important, one who has killed a number of innocent people in a particularly heinous way is not spared the death penalty because, in a Kantian sense, he does not deserve it. He is spared rather because it has been concluded that the state should not be in the business of putting even convicted criminals to death, no matter how much they may be said to deserve that penalty.[56] This of course is not to deny that some notion of human dignity also seems to underlie opposition to the death penalty and generate sympathy for those who are exposed to its infliction. Indeed, any state-sanctioned punishment, no matter how well deserved, impacts the dignity of those upon whom it is inflicted, but the judicially expressed contempt for paparazzi indicates that this notion has not figured in courts' attempts to punish those who have used their freedom of expression in ways that others claim disturbs their emotional tranquility. That lack of concern for the paparazzi reflects the failure to recognize fully the implications of a more general political factor, to which we shall now turn, that figures in all political societies and particularly in a free and democratic society.

The law, for example, *normally* does not punish those who break gratuitous promises or those who are rude to others or who are disloyal to their friends or spouses, or who deny what are accepted as historical facts or even who lie, not because it does not consider these actions as unjust or because it always considers these injustices trivial, but because it recognizes that, in a free society, the use of force, even to achieve justice, is itself also an evil to which resort should not too frequently be made. Like the *ne bis in idem* provisions of the United States and other constitutions and charters of fundamental rights, the First Amendment of the United States Constitution was designed to give effect to this factor in the daily life of a free society. Its wording was certainly not based on the assumption that speech is incapable of causing injustice, often even grave injustice, just as a *ne bis in idem* provision is not based on the assumption that those guilty of heinous crimes who have escaped conviction because of technical errors in their trials do not deserve to be punished. The government is forbidden from abridging freedom of speech despite the injustices such speech could create, although inevitably in practice, there will be exceptions. False speech can be punished if it is likely to damage another's reputation, but even then not in all circumstances. Traditional confidential relationships will also be protected, but the prohibition against governmental interference has come to be as near to absolute as it could be and represents an important value in itself. It was certainly at least thought to have been so in the eighteenth century when people took a less benign view of

---

56. Even in the more emotionally charged situation of torture, Lord Phillips has declared: "As Buxton LJ [in the Court of Appeal] observed, the prohibition on receiving evidence obtained by torture is not primarily because such evidence is unreliable or because the reception of evidence will make the trial unfair. Rather it is because 'the state must stand firm against the conduct that produced the evidence.'" RB (Algeria) v. Secretary of State for the Home Dep't, [2009] 4 W.L.R. 1045 (H.L.) at ¶ 153.

the motives of those who exercised the authority and power of the state. Indeed, it has been asserted with great historical support that the purpose of the First Amendment of the United States Constitution was not so much to recognize the rights of citizens but rather to deny the government of the United States all power to regulate speech.[57] Unlike the European Convention and modern national constitutional documents, the United States Constitution was an eighteenth-century document which, in addition to providing the structure for an effective government, was also, as Justice William O. Douglas was wont to stress, designed to get government "off the backs of the people and keep it off."[58] Even in the twenty-first century, that view surely retains some validity. Is it presumptuous to suggest that it would have been preferable if the House of Lords and the European Court of Human Rights had at least given more attention to the desirability of introducing state coercion into these disputes between individuals? We shall have more to say about these issues in the final chapter of this book.

For the moment we can conclude that, unless a satisfactory and reasonably objective method of case-by-case decision making can be devised after *Campbell* and *von Hannover*, there will undoubtedly be many more such cases in which the courts will be asked to punish speech claimed to interfere with their private life. Because the cases will be so fact-dependent, people will be called upon to bear the expense and inconvenience of appearing in court to justify their speech, as the court decides whether there is a sufficient public interest to justify permitting their speech to go unpunished. It seems clear then that, if a robust freedom of expression is to survive in a world of conflicting rights of equal value, the factors that need to be balanced are more numerous, more complex, and more difficult to reconcile than was recognized in the *Campbell* and *von Hannover* cases. The task before us, as the discussion proceeds, will be to attempt to construct, in an intellectually satisfying way, a method for judicial resolution of cases involving these difficult balancing exercises. It would be ironic if the broad recognition of a variety of human rights should lead not only to a degree of state regulation of the discourse of citizens that many might consider intolerable, but also, and perhaps even more regrettably, eventually to an institutionalized form of political correctness. One appreciates that the European Court of Human Rights has declared that freedom of expression protects speech that shocks or offends others.[59] But at

---

57. *See* DAVID L. LANGE AND H. JEFFERSON POWELL, NO LAW 225–60 (2009).

58. W.E.B. DuBois Clubs of America v. Clark 389 U.S. 309, 318 (1967). *See also* his dissenting opinion, joined by Justice Marshall, in *Laird v. Tatum*, 408 U.S. 1, 28 (1972): "The Constitution was designed to keep government off the backs of the people." The majority had ruled that the plaintiffs, who had brought the case to challenge certain government regulations by means of a class action, did not have the requisite standing to do so because they themselves were not yet in danger of being affected by the regulations.

59. *See* Handyside v. United Kingdom, Application No. 5493/72, Judgment of December 7, 1976, ¶ 49, 1 Eur. H.R. Rep. 737, 754 (1979–80). The Court nevertheless upheld the

the same time it has, as we have seen, conditioned that privilege on the speech in question serving some important judicially determined social purpose.

Officially administered regulation of speech, though ostensibly prompted by the desire to secure a regime of social justice for the benefit of the individual members of the body politic, runs the risk of forcing the courts to play the role of a *pater familias* resolving a quarrel between squabbling children that they might best be left to sort out themselves.[60] This is another reason for trying, if possible, to come up with a satisfactory outline of an acceptable and workable method of case-by-case adjudication that will allow us to avoid such an undesirable result. Finally, there is the underlying question of when national authorities have the benefit of the margin of appreciation and how, if at all, it can be handled case by case. If, as discussed in Chapter 4, the benefit of a margin of appreciation is given to the Turkish government regarding a woman's ability to wear a headscarf in medical school or to the Swiss authorities' declaration that a painting is obscene in one canton, but not in another, on the ground there is no European consensus on these issues, why is Germany prevented from deciding that what a well-known person does in public is fair game. It should be noted that, as a private lawyer, the much-criticized Justice Eady, as part of an officially commissioned report, had included a proposed statute recognizing the action for invasion of privacy that exempted activities conducted in public.[61] Was *von Hannover* declaring that it was enforcing a European consensus? Or was it imposing one? Or was it possibly deciding that Princess Caroline's right to be protected from paparazzi was more important than Leyla Sahin's right to go to medical school wearing a headscarf?

---

successful prosecution of a person who had published a handbook for teenagers including advice on subjects such as masturbation and homosexuality. The case is discussed in Chapter 4, note 41, *supra*.

60. One might note that the very expanded notions of standing permitting groups and persons not directly affected by the speech of the defendant to initiate actions or prosecutions against him, as in the Holocaust denial cases cited in note 13 of Chapter 4, *supra*, and in related cases, such as *La Ligue Contre Le Racisme* cited earlier in this chapter at note 55, *supra*, brings to mind Lord Macaulay's words in his essay on Frederick the Great that: "We could make shift to live under a debauchee or a tyrant; but to be ruled by a busybody is more than human nature can bear." V Thomas Babington Macaulay, Critical & Historical Essays 41 (Rev. ed. 1850).

61. In a speech delivered by Mr. Justice Eady on December 1, 2009, at the "Justice" conference entitled "Privacy and the Press–Where Are We Now?" that is available on the official website of the Judiciary of England and Wales, he noted that, in the period 1989–90, as a member of the Calcutt Commission, he had helped draft a proposed statute which would recognize an action for invasion of privacy, but which excluded from its coverage "anything occurring in a public place." *Id.* at p. 2. Presumably such a statute would now run afoul of the Convention.

PART III
THE LIMITED HELP FROM PHILOSOPHY AND THE SOCIAL SCIENCES

6. THE EPISTEMOLOGY OF JUDICIAL DECISION MAKING

By subjecting conflicts between competing "human rights" to judicial resolution, we are committed to at least two basic assumptions as to what the judicial process can deliver. The first is that the judicial process is structured so that it is both fair and impartial and that it is furthermore staffed by fair-minded and intelligent people who are capable of making the aspiration to fairness and impartiality a reality. This is a *sine qua non* of all legal systems and is assumed by all discussions of the role of the judiciary in modern times. There is a second assumption, which is also taken for granted but which is more problematic, namely that the law, and that of course also includes human rights law, is something known by the people who are to apply it or, at the very least, knowable by those applying the law because of something that takes place during the process of adjudication. Certainly, for most people, especially non-lawyers, the reason for entrusting courts with the responsibility for resolving conflicts between basic human rights and important state interests and between conflicting basic human rights is more than an attempt to bring these difficult conflicts to an impartial arbiter. The referral to the courts is, rather, premised in very large part on the assumption that the courts will be able to settle these disputes in a socially acceptable way by applying a known body of law that dictates the appropriate resolution of those disputes. For this assumption to be plausible, it must be the case that, for the most part, the law is just out there waiting to be discovered by a trained judiciary and furthermore that its application to concrete cases is a quasi-mechanical operation, a ministerial task if you will, that involves little of the sort of consequential reasoning that is inevitably involved in the exercise of practical wisdom. Certainly this was the shared assumption in the famous controversy between H.L.A. Hart and Ronald Dworkin.[1] For Hart, in a mature legal system like that of the United Kingdom, there was a sufficiently rich body of judicial precedents and statutes to make it possible for the judiciary to discover the relevant law and apply it to concrete cases without having to exercise much discretion. That is to

---

1. *See* H.L.A. Hart, The Concept of Law (1961) [hereafter The Concept of Law]. For Dworkin's initial sally against Hart, *see* Ronald Dworkin, *The Model of Rules*, 35 U. Chi. L. Rev. 14 (1967). It is among his essays reprinted in Ronald Dworkin, Taking Rights Seriously (1977). The next chapter will contain much more extensive discussion of Dworkin's work and his criticism of "positivism" and "pragmatism." For a contemporaneous criticism of that article, *see* George C. Christie, *The Model of Principles*, 1968 Duke L.J. 649.

say, most cases had a clearly discoverable "right" answer. Hart nevertheless acknowledged that when a new case fell at the margin of the previously decided cases and existing statutes, at the penumbra so to speak of existing doctrine, the judge would be required to exercise his discretion, and in doing so would be forced to rely on considerations of public policy. This allowance for what Dworkin called pragmatic considerations, and the judicial discretion which it presupposed, formed the basis of Dworkin's critique of Hart.

Dworkin's argument was that, even in those cases that Hart would place at the margins of established legal doctrine, there were more basic norms, which Dworkin called principles, embedded in the legal system. Furthermore, he maintained, these principles confined the so-called discretion of judges so that whatever discretion judges might be said to have in deciding such cases was a very weak discretion indeed. The mantra underlying Dworkin's theory was that there were indeed right answers in (almost) all cases litigated in the developed legal systems prevailing in the United Kingdom, the United States, and the rest of the common law world. Dworkin was adamant that the strong discretionary role implied by policy-oriented judicial decision making was totally inappropriate in a society governed by the rule of law. In the next chapter, we shall explore how Dworkin's principle-driven theory of adjudication, which he expanded to include the basic moral principles underlying a particular society, has fared in the few instances in which courts could be said to have rigorously tried to apply it. For the present we shall confine ourselves to whether the presupposed baseline of a known body of law that enables the judiciary to apply it to concrete cases without having to exercise much "discretion" is a useful assumption in a world undergoing rapid economic and social change and particularly when the courts are trying to resolve the hotly contested and emotionally charged cases with which we are concerned.

In all fairness to Hart, we must recognize that he was writing at a time when social and economic change was less visible. He was also writing at a time when the United Kingdom had not entered the European Community and it was taken as a given that the House of Lords was bound by its own decisions. Furthermore, although the United Kingdom was then a member of the Council of Europe, the provisions of the European Convention for the Protection of Human Rights and Fundamental Freedoms with which we are concerned had not yet been incorporated into its domestic law.[2] Nevertheless, even in what are thought to be stable times, as in retrospect we might believe to have been the case in 1961 when Hart's *The Concept of Law* was published, and particularly with regard to matters that are even now not considered controversial, it is hard to deny that the application of law inevitably works some change in legal doctrine. In a common law system, some of that change may be unnoticed and even unintended. For example,

---

2. That incorporation was done by Human Rights Act 1998.

language in a prior case may be misunderstood, or unconsciously or perhaps even consciously misinterpreted when supposedly clear doctrinal statements must be adapted to provide answers to situations unanticipated when these doctrinal statements were formulated. Moreover, when results ostensibly dictated by accepted doctrine contradict common sense or basic notions of justice, it is inevitable that courts will, as Llewellyn so passionately emphasized,[3] find ways to stretch "established" doctrine.

In this chapter, therefore, there is no better way to start than to ask: What is the law, particularly the law of human rights; how is it known; and how can that knowledge of the content or meaning of the law be separated from the process of its application? In the areas with which we are concerned, only if "the law" is a set of general maxims, even clichés if you will, can the law be said to be easily "discovered" and studied apart from its actual and potential applications. This might at first glance be a superficially plausible view of the law in a code system in which there is an official verbal formulation of the law, but the generality in which most such legal provisions are worded often makes the application of these provisions anything but a ministerial task. Rather, these provisions serve only as the starting point for the decision of concrete cases, a process that in any hotly contested case clearly involves the exercise of practical wisdom. It is scant consolation to tell a person that the law applied in his case has been the very same law that was applied in substantially similar previous cases when his case was admittedly decided differently. Even in the common law world, where statutes are typically more detailed and narrowly worded, the "meaning" of a statute has to be teased out from the decisions and statements of the judges called upon to interpret and apply the statutory provision in question. However intellectually comforting it might be to insist on the purity and knowability of the law regardless of its possibly inconsistent applications, that is hardly an intellectually satisfying option when it is accepted, *ab initio*, that a particular body of law is to be developed case by case.

The problem is that the very notion of legal development by case-by-case adjudication presupposes that the courts are making the law at the same time as they are finding the law. Indeed, in turning to case-by-case adjudication to produce a

---

3. *See* KARL N. LLEWELLYN, THE COMMON LAW TRADITION: DECIDING APPEALS 219–22 (1960) [hereafter THE COMMON LAW TRADITION]. He cautioned that if "appellate courts should ever take to doing daily what they have absolute and unchallenged power to do sometimes, we should have to get rid of the guilty judges; we might in the process and for a while get rid even of the courts." *Id.* at 219–20. There is an interesting discussion of the Supreme Court of the United States in the "school desegregation" case in Mark Tushnet and Katya Lezin, *What Really Happened in* Brown v. Board of Education, 91 COLUM. L. REV. 1867 (1991). Especially relevant is the attribution to Justice Jackson of the view that one had to understand one thing about the Court, namely that "sometimes it acted 'politically' and sometimes it acted 'legally.'" *Id.* at 1894.

consistent and coherent body of law from broad declarations of human rights, which often come in conflict, we are clearly accepting a vision of the law as "a process of becoming."[4] Whether that process will ever be able to produce a level of clarity and detail that permits one to conclude that, for a time at least, the law has ceased "becoming" and actually has "become" is something that we shall explore when we consider how a process of case-by-case adjudication might help clarify the human rights law that we are discussing. For the moment, we might conclude that Hart's assumption that, in most cases, there was a law out there waiting to be discovered by trained observers, is not only belied by the increased number of three-to-two decisions in the House of Lords noted earlier in Chapter 1,[5] but is made logically untenable by the House of Lords' joining other common law courts in rejecting the doctrine of absolutely binding precedent, as well as by Hart's own admission that the core of his theory of law, the so-called "rule of recognition," is itself created by the final appellate courts whose activities are in turn directed by it.[6] One might say that Dworkin's notion of principles as even more basic than legal rules is an attempt to save the day by finding the desired certainty and stability at a deeper social level. How successful that attempt might be is something we shall, as already noted, explore in the next chapter.

Given that, certainly for the moment, case-by-case adjudication of the controversial and highly contested human rights controversies that we have described involves a process in which the courts are making law in the process of finding the law, it seems self-evident that they must engage in some amount of policy-based consequential reasoning. For example, in the *Sahin* case discussed in Chapter 4, it was decided that the Turkish authorities could conclude that Sahin's wearing a head-scarf threatened Turkey's secularism. In the *Campbell* case, discussed in Chapter 5, a major assumption of the majority was that knowing that Campbell was seeking help from Narcotics Anonymous and particularly knowing the place where she was receiving that treatment would adversely affect her recovery from her addiction. Finally, in the *von Hannover* case, which was also discussed in Chapter 5, stress was laid on the fact that upholding Princess Caroline's claims in their entirety would facilitate the social objective of discouraging paparazzi. It is obvious that all these instances involve the use of some sort of policy-based consequential reasoning. Indeed, for those who adhere to a law and economics approach to judicial reasoning, a decision-making process involving consequential reasoning is presupposed because the insistence that economic efficiency is the appropriate criterion for evaluating judicial outcomes requires courts to predict the anticipated economic consequence of their decisions. One might say of course that the law and economics approach, by

---

4. This now commonplace expression is usually attributed to LON L. FULLER, THE LAW IN QUEST OF ITSELF 10 (1940).
5. *See* Chapter 1, note 18, *supra*.
6. THE CONCEPT OF LAW, *supra* note 1, at 144–50.

focusing on the predicted economic consequences of particular resolutions to legal disputes, is in theory a more objective process and less subject to the criticism that the courts are exercising the legislative function that Dworkin and countless observers before him have declared is inappropriate for the judiciary. One might further wish to say that the law and economics approach is actually only the application of a basic norm of tort law that directs courts to decide cases in a way that promotes economic efficiency throughout society. Likewise, Dworkin could and undoubtedly would maintain that judges under his theory would only be engaged in the administrative task of implementing well-known and universally accepted moral principles. The persuasiveness of all these contentions is more than debatable.

It can be readily acknowledged that what we accept as a legal norm may direct the courts to engage in consequential reasoning in the application of that norm. For example, an important American anti-trust law, the Clayton Act of 1914, proscribes conduct that "might substantially lessen competition . . . in any line of commerce."[7] Whether even such not uncommon provisions, which ostensibly suggest that the correct legal decision can be determined by a fairly limited examination of relatively concrete economic statistics, actually remove a substantial law-making element from judicial decision making is another matter. Be that as it may, and even accepting the supposed objective nature of the even broader general law and economic tests, they are all too simplistic to capture the complexity of economic and social life.[8] But, regardless of one's views on these matters, it stretches credulity to say that a supposed broad legal goal or principle like "promote economic efficiency" or, on the moral level, an injunction to "promote the good" or "human dignity" turns the instantiation of these imperatives into simply an administrative application of a *known* norm. That is why people turn to case-by-case adjudication. It is seen as a potential way of protecting judges from the charge that they are not merely inevitably making some law in the process of applying it but rather are also acting as super-legislators undertaking to decide fundamental issues of social policy. In noting that, in making their decisions, courts will inevitably consider not only the consequences of their decisions for the parties before them but often also the more general economic, social, and moral consequences of those decisions, we have not exhausted the extent to which courts must engage in some type of predictive exercises. As we explore these additional ways in which predictive processes figure in judicial

---

7. Various versions of this language appear in §§ 2, 3, and 7 of the Clayton Act which have been codified as 15 U.S.C. §§ 13, 14, and 18.

8. Obviously, even if one could identify all the relevant considerations, quantifying the costs and benefits would be a daunting task and, to the extent the costs and benefits consist of intangible values, impossible. It is undoubtedly for this reason that people are driven to oversimplify problems and to rely on abstractions for achieving solutions to complex economic problems.

decision making, we shall see that, although they make the process more complicated, they also may sometimes, but not always, make it more circumscribed and predictable.

We might begin by noting that, in the hierarchically organized judicial systems that characterize the modern world, a lower court must always take into account the likely reaction of the judges sitting on the courts to which its judgments might be appealed. Even the highest appellate courts must take some note of the possibility of legislative or possibly even constitutional override. In politically controversial areas, the possibility of such an override will vary from jurisdiction to jurisdiction, but the greater the possibility of such an override, the more a final appellate court will take that possibility into account. To put the matter more succinctly, there is some truth to Mr. Dooley's cynical observation about the United States Supreme Court's following the election returns.[9] Extending our focus to include these features of the legal structure, however, does not begin to exhaust the range of predictions of other people's reactions that may play a role in a judge's decision-making processes. A judge, particularly a judge on a multi-member court, would surely consider the reactions of his colleagues on his court as well as the reactions of his fellow members of the legal profession, both those in active practice and those in academia. These features of judicial decision making are also part of what Llewellyn described as steadying factors.[10]

While some sort of predictive process plays an important role in empirical studies of the day-to-day operation of a legal system, the use of predictive models has not received as much attention in jurisprudential writing as it might deserve. Some of this lack of attention is undoubtedly owing to some assertions of H.L.A. Hart[11] in a sharp criticism of Scandinavian legal realism, particularly as set forth by the Dane Alf Ross in his book *On Law and Justice,* the English language edition of which appeared in 1958.[12] Since one of the common features of both American and Scandinavian legal realism was treating what people called law as the predictions of what officials would do under certain factual circumstances, its proponents were taking what Hart called the external point of view of observers of the judicial process, a group that could also include lawyers advising clients or litigating contested issues before courts. For Hart, this missed the essential point of what law was because it failed to take into account the internal point of view of the judge who was charged with deciding a case. It was this

---

9. "'But there's wan thing I'm sure about.' 'What's that?' asked Mr. Hennessy. 'That is,' said Mr. Dooley, 'no matther whether th' constitution follows th' flag or not, th' supreme court follows th' iliction returns.'" FINLEY PETER DUNNE, MR. DOOLEY'S OPINIONS 26 (1901).

10. *See* THE COMMON LAW TRADITION, *supra* note 3, at 14, 190–91, 337, 342 and *passim.*

11. H.L.A. HART, *Scandinavian Realism,* [1959] CAMB. L.J. 233.

12. ALF ROSS, ON LAW AND JUSTICE (1958). The book was originally published in Danish in 1953.

internal perspective that supplied the normative element of law, namely the sense of an obligation to engage in a certain type of behavior which, in the case of a judge, would be to decide a case in a certain way. Ross had tried to allow for this normative feature of law by defining a legal norm as a combination of two predictions. The first was a prediction that, if a certain hypothetical factual situation arose, the judge would rule in a certain way, and the second was a prediction that the judge would do so because he felt under an obligation to do so.[13] This did not satisfy Hart. For Hart, it seemed clear that Ross was making a logical blunder. The judge, in the situations posited by Ross, was engaged in deciding a case, not in predicting what he would do. Hart did not explain what mental processes a judge engaged in when he decided a case or stated the governing law; whatever it was, it was not predicting his own behavior.

Much has been made of this claim of Hart's. In the words of a thoughtful legal scholar:

> Predictivism provides the judge with few justificatory resources. The deciding judge is not trying to predict anything. He is trying to decide, and doing so in light of any relevant reasons of authority and reasons of substance.[14]

---

13. I have stated the two prongs of Ross' thesis somewhat succinctly because that is all that is required for purposes of the present discussion. In fact, in the course of his discussion, Ross refined the second prong of the predictive process as consisting of a prediction that the postulated legal norm "will form an integral part of the reasoning underlying the judgment" that would be rendered in the circumstances envisioned. Ross, *supra* note 12, at 42. Ross, in doing so, wanted to anticipate a situation in which a judge, while recognizing an obligation to rule in a certain way, nevertheless ruled in another way because the "ideas which the judge holds as to what is valid law do not constitute the only factor by which he is motivated." *Id.* at 43. By so doing Ross might be said to have anticipated an objection made by Hart to all predictive theories of law when Hart revisited the subject in THE CONCEPT OF LAW, *supra* note 1, at 79–88. There, Hart insisted that, under a predicative approach to law, to say that a person was likely to suffer a penalty if he behaved in a certain way could not possibly indicate that the person had a legal obligation to behave in that way if he did not behave as it was predicted he would. Hart gave as an example a person who "had escaped from the jurisdiction or had successfully escaped from the jurisdiction or bribed the police or the court." *Id.* at 82. But even a judge could recognize an obligation to have ruled in a certain way, even if he had not in fact done so. His failure to have so ruled by no means negates his acceptance of that obligation nor does it falsify the prediction that the judge had felt a legal obligation to have acted in a way other than he did. It only indicates that he might have had reasons not to do so, either good ones such as overriding moral obligations or less good ones, such as his family being threatened with death by drug dealers or because he was bribed. In the jury nullification situations we discussed in Chapter 3, the fact that a jury acquits in the face of the evidence does not necessarily mean that they felt no obligation to convict. Actually the whole notion of conflicting human rights envisages judges experiencing just such conflicting obligations.

14. ROBERT S. SUMMERS, INSTRUMENTALISM AND AMERICAN LEGAL THEORY 132 (1982).

This assertion is obviously not totally true. First of all, as we have seen, it is clear that lower court judges are always predicting what an appellate court would do when deciding appeals from their decisions; and that means, in cases of doubt, they must imagine, to at least some extent, what they would do if they were to assume the personae of the actual judges who would decide the appeal. More germanely, there are situations in which judges, even judges on final appellate courts, are in fact directed to decide the case in the way the courts of some other jurisdiction would decide the case. That is a common situation for federal judges in the United States who, when exercising the diversity jurisdiction of the federal courts, are obliged to decide the case according to the law of the state in which the federal trial court is located. It is also becoming increasingly common, with the expansion of international trade and the other consequences of globalization, that the courts of one nation are obliged to decide a case on the basis of the law of another. Surely in deciding a case in which the law in that other jurisdiction was unclear, a judge would consider what he would do if he were a judge on the highest court of the jurisdiction in question.[15] That again is clearly an instance of a judge deciding a case on the basis of what he would do in certain situations. Indeed, as a former colleague of mine (H. Jefferson Powell) has perceptively noted in commenting on a draft of this book, an essential starting point in all cases for a common law appellate judge, even if not consciously recognized, is to ask himself: "How would I decide this case if I were one of the judges below bound to give effect in good faith to the law as stated by the court on which I sit?" Surely the integrity of the judicial process as a whole, in a common law system, requires at least that much.

These observations point to a more basic objection to the blanket condemnation of "predictivism." The issue is worth exploring not to make an academic point about what many might believe is a very arcane issue but to bring out a feature of human discourse that is particularly present, even if unobserved, in the types of judicial decision making that we have been discussing and which cannot be ignored if we are seriously to examine what judges are asked to do in the types of litigation that is our focus. The cases we have been examining are clearly among those cases where the quasi-deductive methods of judicial reasoning pre-supposed by Hart and other scholars do not provide sufficiently clear direction. If that lack of direction cannot be remedied by the philosophical or other approaches that we shall examine in the next chapters, what is a judge doing when he has to decide one of these difficult cases? Is it a question of a

---

15. Article 1 of the Swiss Civil Code expressly directs the judge to engage in this sort of mental exercise when he finds no applicable provision in the Code and no sufficient guidance in "customary law." It directs him to decide the case under "the rules he would lay down if he had himself to act as legislator." In this circumstance it adds that, in performing that task, the judge "must be guided by approved legal doctrine and case law," which is of course to state the obvious.

judge immersing himself in the "facts" of a particular case and producing a decision in reliance on a hunch, as was maintained by Judge Hutcheson?[16] If a judge is unprepared to accept that description of what the judicial role consists of, must he accept that, whether he enjoys the endeavor or not, he is exercising a legislative role?

Perhaps we can see a way out of this dilemma if we pursue our inquiry a bit further. Let us assume that a conscientious judge has examined what he accepts is the applicable law governing his case and has considered so far as he can the social and economic consequences of a decision one way or another, but he is still uncertain of what the correct decision would be. It is at times like this that people start looking at basic values, such as justice, fairness, etc., for assistance. As we pointed out in the first chapter,[17] it is at this point in their thought processes and arguments that people start to fall back on some notion of an ideal audience as described by Chaïm Perelman, Jürgen Habermas, George Herbert Mead, and Adam Smith. If one further accepts that, when people are appealing to an ideal audience to justify a decision to act in one way or another, and thus using this ideal audience as a proxy for their better selves, are they not in a sense predicting how their better selves would want them to act? This comes out more clearly in Adam Smith's reference to the "impartial" and "dispassionate spectator" to whom we turn for moral approbation.[18] As Bernard Williams has said, "what anyone truly believes must be consistent with what others truly believe, and anyone deliberating about the truth"—we could substitute here, the correct decision of a case—"is committed, by the nature of the process, to the aim of a consistent set of beliefs, one's own and others."[19] Indeed, the essence of the "internal point of view" may be said to be engaging in and feeling bound by the results of these predictive processes.

Unless one is an all-powerful God, there is thus no necessary incompatibility between the internal point of view and the reliance on a predictive methodology. Surely, in the contested human rights cases with which we are concerned, when judges are deciding what the public has a genuine interest in knowing or what decision is required in order to uphold "human dignity," judges must be assum-

---

16. Joseph C. Hutcheson, *The Judgment Intuitive: The Function of the "Hunch" in Judicial Decision*, 14 CORNELL L.Q. 274 (1929).

17. *See* pp. 4–6, *supra*.

18. For references to Smith's discussion *see* Chapter 1, note 12, *supra*.

19. BERNARD WILLIAMS, ETHICS AND THE LIMITS OF PHILOSOPHY 68 (1985). Indeed, in deciding a difficult case, a judge will certainly be considering whether he can construct a reasoned justification of his decision that will satisfy the actual and ideal audiences he is addressing. If he feels that his reasoning would not be found convincing to either of these audiences, he might change his mind or, in the alternative, consider how he might handle any criticism he might receive. He might even consider whether in retrospect he will feel proud of both his decision and the reasons with which he supported it. Here an appeal to the predicted reactions of an ideal audience will be of great comfort to him.

ing that their decisions on these questions are not purely idiosyncratic, but rather should accord with the decisions that other rational and impartial observers would have arrived at. This appeal to an ideal universal audience is also implicit in the work of Ronald Dworkin and of John Rawls, which we shall examine in the next chapter. Dworkin's thesis is that we should conjure up an ideal judge whom he calls Hercules, and he argues that human judges should decide difficult cases in the way that they imagined Hercules would, that is to imagine how they would behave if they were Hercules. Likewise Rawls urges us to approach the basic moral questions that confront society by imagining what a rational, self-interested person would choose in an ideal situation in which personal biases are eliminated. These are obviously helpful suggestions and they clearly require us to engage in a type of predictive endeavor. The question that we shall discuss in the next chapter is whether these suggestions are adequate to provide the guidance we are seeking. On a less abstract level, one might consider a Justice of the United States Supreme Court who considers that he is bound, in the final analysis, by the "original intent" of the framers of the American Constitution. For many, this would be a cramped version of an "ideal audience" but it is nevertheless his conception of that audience. Such a Justice certainly takes what Hart calls an internal point of view. In deciding the case before him, such a Justice is engaging in a thought experiment in which he imagines he is behaving as the framers of the Constitution would. Although this approach is not without its attractions, it would seem to be hard to maintain that, after over 200 years of enormous social, political, and legal change, such an approach is rich enough to meet the demands placed on it, even assuming that it is possible to imagine how the framers would have responded to the vastly changed circumstances of the present. Nevertheless, it is a position that many find attractive.[20]

We can close the present chapter by emphasizing that the prediction of the reaction of an ideal audience, accepted as such by the judge, is an essential feature of the judicial exercise of discretion. This is particularly true in case-by-case adjudication which presupposes that the facts involved in each particular case are of paramount importance in arriving at the proper decision. What we are searching for in human rights adjudication is a methodology for directing that appeal to an ideal audience that is both sufficiently universal and at the same time sufficiently concrete to be plausibly regarded as a credible means of controlling the discretional authority of judges, particularly of judges sitting on the highest appellate courts. This, as we have seen, is a difficult task that is not made any easier by the indisputable fact that there are sharp differences among different legal cultures' visions of both the substantive content of many purported universal human rights and also of the appropriate resolution when

---

20. For a very recent review and critique of this literature, *see* Thomas B. Colby and Peter J. Smith, *Living Originalism*, 59 DUKE L.J. 239 (2009).

accepted human rights come into conflict. For example, the ideal audience to which some people appeal believes that secularism is a paramount social value. For others, the audience to which they appeal takes a dim view of paparazzi. Others still, as we shall see in the closing chapters, have strong views on what is truly "artistic expression" and thus what would be entitled to some heightened legal protection. The purpose of this book is to determine whether, despite these divergent views, we can develop a process of case-by-case adjudication that is capable of resolving conflicts between competing views in a way that gives sufficiently clear guidance to insure that the appeal to rights is not merely a rhetorical flourish but part of a process that citizens of the developed world can accept as appropriate for the judicial role. If it turns out that we cannot produce a completely acceptable process, we must then also consider what might possibly be a plausible and acceptable second best decision-making process.

7. THE UNSUCCESSFUL ATTEMPT TO FIND A PHILOSOPHICAL "NORTH STAR" TO AID IN JUDICIAL DECISION MAKING

The prospect that conflicts between fundamental human rights of supposedly equal value may have to be decided by a diverse body of judges, each of whom may have his or her own vision of the relative value of the rights at issue in the case before the court is not a comforting one. It is understandable that people should attempt to alleviate that discomfort by resorting to some more basic philosophical principle or value that will enable us to resolve those conflicts in a way that even people with different ideas about the value of the rights in question are willing to accept as legitimate. General concepts like "human dignity" seem too vague and undefined to provide the guidance sought, particularly when talking about a world with different social as well as legal traditions. There are, however, two well-known recent attempts by Ronald Dworkin and John Rawls to provide more specific but still plausibly neutral and universally acceptable methods for providing that guidance. In this chapter we shall see if those proposals, however valuable and insightful they might be, are in fact capable of providing the guidance sought. In my judgment, they are not. In the discussion that follows, I shall undertake to justify that assertion.

As noted in the previous chapter, Dworkin started out from the proposition that even in difficult cases—the so-called hard cases—the decisional discretion of judges was sharply confined, if not totally eliminated, by the existence in a mature legal system of meta-norms, which he called "principles," that directed the discretion of judges in the hard cases.[1] He further maintained that these principles, unlike the more specific and detailed norms of a legal system (the so-called ordinary rules of law), did not operate in an all-or-nothing manner, but rather served to guide the judge in searching for the right answer in those cases where the ordinary rules of law provided either no clear answer—because they

---

1. As noted in Chapter 6, *supra* note 1, Dworkin's first major exposition of this thesis was in Ronald Dworkin, *The Model of Rules,* 35 U. CHI. L. REV. 14 (1967), later reprinted along with other essays in TAKING RIGHTS SERIOUSLY 14 (1977) [hereafter TAKING RIGHTS SERIOUSLY, to which all future citations will be made]. He had, however, sketched out his argument earlier in Ronald Dworkin, *Judicial Discretion,* 60 J. PHIL. 638 (1963). The most complete exposition of Dworkin's philosophical approach still seems to be RONALD DWORKIN, LAW'S EMPIRE (1986) [hereafter LAW'S EMPIRE]. It is extensively reviewed in George C. Christie, *Dworkin's Empire,* (1987) DUKE L.J. 157 [hereafter *Dworkin's Empire*], which contains numerous citations to his earlier work.

gave conflicting answers or because there were gaps in the law—or gave answers that the court felt were unjust. At the same time, since Dworkin also accepted that these meta-norms or principles might lead to different results if two or more principles were possibly applicable in some particular situation, he recognized from the beginning that he was obliged to come up with a means of weighting these principles in order to resolve those conflicts.[2]

However, neither Dworkin nor anyone else has thus far been able to accomplish that task. It was therefore necessary for him to try another tack to explain how judges might decide the cases in which principles came into conflict. Accordingly, in order to resolve those conflicts and thereby preserve the plausibility of his thesis, Dworkin eventually came to accept that, at bottom, all such conflicts were moral conflicts. This, in turn, almost inevitably led him to assert that, in the mature societies with which he was concerned, namely the United Kingdom and the United States, the moral foundations of society were sufficiently complex and developed to provide the necessary "right answers" to the moral and thus the legal issues involved, at least—and this was a big concession on his part—in "almost all" contested situations.[3] This evolution of Dworkin's theory to one that is ultimately based on basic moral principles is understandable in that his examples of how legal principles can override legal rules are somewhat compromised by the fact that the actual cases used by Dworkin to support his thesis were as much applications of precedent as they were of principle.[4] In trying to explain how the basic morality of the societies on which he had focused fulfilled that function, he set forth—obviously relying in part on Rawls—what he thought were the basic moral principles of those societies, and perhaps of any society. Among these were that, in a just society, each member

---

2. TAKING RIGHTS SERIOUSLY, *supra* note 1, at 22–31, 35–36.

3. This in no way controversial summary of the evolution of Dworkin's theory is based on the more detailed discussion in *Dworkin's Empire*, *supra* note 1. Dworkin's principal original discussion of the issues covered in this part of the text is contained in *Hard Cases*, originally published in 1972 in the *Harvard Law Review* and reprinted in TAKING RIGHTS SERIOUSLY, *supra* note 1, at 81, and *No Right Answer?*, originally published in the *N.Y.U. Law Review* in 1978 and reprinted in RONALD DWORKIN, A MATTER OF PRINCIPLE 119 (1985).

4. The most famous of Dworkin's examples was *Riggs v. Palmer*, 115 N.Y. 506 (1889), in which a young man who had killed his grandfather in order to inherit under the old man's will was refused recovery. *See* TAKING RIGHTS SERIOUSLY, *supra* note 1, at 29. There was however a clear legal basis for that decision because the United States Supreme Court had already held that the beneficiary of a life insurance policy who killed the insured could not receive the proceeds of the policy, and there were many cases holding that, notwithstanding the statute of wills, a will procured by fraud could be voided. There certainly was not a clear legal rule in place, prior to *Riggs v. Palmer*, that mandated enforcement of the will as written. The same may be said for Dworkin's other examples of principles overriding clear legal rules. *See* George C. Christie, *The Model of Principles*, 1968 DUKE L.J. 649, 660–67.

must have a "*concern* for the well-being of others in the group," and that the practices of the group must "show not only concern, but an *equal* concern for all [its] members."[5] It was against this moral background that the judge in a hard case, struggling to maintain the "integrity" of the judicial process, was to interpret the legal and social history of his society so as to reach a decision that would show that society in the best light. Insofar as judges were required to engage in some type of consequential reasoning to permit them to determine the "right" decision to a dispute, the only relevant considerations were the possible moral justifications for a decision, and presumably, since society is obliged to show equal concern for its members, the moral consequences of a decision one way or the other on the litigants. One might say that we are here again discussing the unavoidable need to engage in some sort of predictive endeavor but Dworkin seems to have proceeded on the assumption that the morally relevant consequences were so self-evident that the answer could be reached more by thought experiments than by careful examination of the minutia of everyday life. As we have already noted in the previous chapter, the essence of that experiment was to imagine how a super-judge called "Hercules" would decide the cases in question.

One may accept much of what Dworkin says as insightful and valuable. The question is how it helps the courts engaged in deciding cases, let alone the so-called hard cases, to avoid the consequential or policy-oriented considerations that he claims should not be relied on by judges. Furthermore, in addition to the observance of basic substantive moral principles, Dworkin insisted that the integrity of the judicial process required that whatever moral principles were relied on must also be general in application. Dworkin recognized that for his method of reasoning to be useful, relying as it does on resort to general principles, it must be applicable to the real-life activities of courts. Thus, in giving concrete expression to how principles incorporating these basic values functioned in tort law, Dworkin declared that, to meet the requirement of generality of application, if a government "appeals to the principle that people have the right to compensation from those who injure them carelessly, as its reason why manufacturers are liable for defective automobiles, it must give full effect to that principle in deciding whether accountants are liable for their mistakes as well."[6] Dworkin never gave any reason why the two situations were comparable, undoubtedly because for him their comparability was self-evident.

---

5. *See* LAW'S EMPIRE, *supra* note 1, at 200. For a fuller exposition of Dworkin's views on these matters, the reader is again referred to *Dworkin's Empire*, *supra* note 1.

6. LAW'S EMPIRE, *supra* note 1, at 165. This discussion of Dworkin's attempt in LAW'S EMPIRE to apply his theory to concrete legal situations is based in large part on GEORGE C. CHRISTIE, THE NOTION OF AN IDEAL AUDIENCE IN LEGAL ARGUMENT, Ch. 8 (2000) [hereafter THE NOTION OF AN IDEAL AUDIENCE].

At the risk of some oversimplification, which is not very germane to the point now under consideration, the accepted legal doctrine underlying recovery for physical injury for negligently manufactured automobiles provides for liability to all those who may reasonably be foreseen as suffering physical injury or as being threatened with physical injury owing to the negligence of the automobile manufacturer. That part of Dworkin's assertion was uncontroversial; it was the wholesale extension of that doctrine to the liability of accountants to meet the requirement of principled generality that was the issue. Indeed, a few American courts in the 1980s actually suggested extending the liability of accountants to all who might have been reasonably foreseen as likely to suffer monetary loss owing to an accountant's negligence rather than to the more limited class of potential victims who could seek legal relief under the traditional doctrine.[7] But all those impulses have since been almost entirely repudiated by the courts on grounds of public policy as well as the feeling that the situations are not that comparable after all.[8] One might also add that automobile manufacturers are also subject to strict liability for physical injuries in some situations, that is, to liability without proof of fault. Similar broad liability of accountants has never been suggested, undoubtedly because, for a large number of informed observers, the situations were indeed not self-evidently comparable.

Dworkin's insistence that principle required application of the modern, expanded version of the reasonable foreseeability test beyond physical-injury situations received a more extended examination in the context of a broader and more extensive controversy surrounding the recovery of "pure economic loss" that went well beyond the accountancy cases.[9] In that broader context, pure economic loss consists of monetary losses not directly connected to what might be called physical injury to person or property, such as the loss of profits that a bakery might suffer because its specially designed delivery truck had been destroyed by someone's negligent behavior. Traditionally, such losses were generally not recoverable in a negligence action and, in the situations where they were recoverable, the class of eligible plaintiffs was not extended to all reasonably foreseeable victims of the defendant's negligent conduct. Starting in 1977, however, the House of Lords decided a series of cases that reached its zenith in 1982 in which it seemed increasingly ready to adopt an expanded application of the reasonable foreseeability doctrine in all economic loss areas along the lines that Dworkin had advocated for accountants. As the decade advanced, however, their lordships came to have doubts about the wisdom of such an expansion, and cases decided just a few years previously were given a narrow interpretation.

---

7. *See*, e.g., Rosenblum v. Adler, 93 N.J. 324 (1983).

8. *See*, e.g., Bily v. Arthur Young & Co., 3 Cal. 4th 370 (1992); RESTATEMENT (SECOND) OF TORTS § 552 (1977).

9. These largely British cases decided by the House of Lords are discussed in THE NOTION OF AN IDEAL AUDIENCE, *supra* note 6, at 122–24.

Finally, in 1990,[10] the House of Lords held that its initial step in that journey, the 1977 case of *Anns v. Merton London Borough Council*,[11] had been wrongly decided, and it overruled all subsequent cases that had been decided on the basis of *Anns*. More importantly for our purposes, in those situations in which recovery of pure economic loss is allowed in a negligence action, such as in the accountancy cases to which Dworkin referred, the class of those who might be said to have suffered legally recognized damages from the defendant's negligent conduct continues to be much more narrowly circumscribed than if recovery for physical injury to person or property were at issue. This was a clear rejection of the one-size-fits-all theory that underlies Dworkin's search for broad governing principles of general application.

The larger philosophical issue underlying all these economic loss cases was most clearly judicially considered in *McLoughlin v. O'Brian*,[12] a case that involved serious emotional harm decided by the House of Lords in 1982, at the high-water mark of their lordships' flirtation with subsuming pure economic loss under the general principle that the extent of liability for all negligently inflicted loss should be judged under the reasonable foreseeability doctrine. The *McLoughlin* case involved a woman who sought damages against a driver whose negligence caused an accident that killed one of her children and injured her husband and other children. She herself had not witnessed the accident but first saw some of the survivors in the hospital over an hour later. Reversing the Court of Appeal, which had upheld the trial court's judgment for the defendant, their lordships held that the plaintiff could recover for her emotional trauma. That part of the decision was unanimous. What was not unanimous was agreement on the grounds given for this decision. On the one side, Lord Bridge of Harwich declared that "there are no policy considerations sufficient to justify limiting the liability of negligent tort-feasors by reference to some narrower criterion than that of reasonable foreseeability."[13] He was supported by Lord Scarman, who noted that the line between liability and no liability could not be drawn on policy grounds as the Court of Appeal had "manfully tried to do in this case [s]imply . . . because the policy issue as to where to draw the line is not justiciable."[14]

One could not have asked for a more explicit adoption of Dworkin's position. Whether a court that seriously adopted that position could decide the difficult human rights cases we have been considering is another matter. If the position were to be taken seriously, one could easily argue that all the cases which we have discussed presented "non-justiciable questions." They seem to involve primarily what their lordships described as questions of "policy." Be that as it may, in

---

10. Murphy v. Brentwood District Council, [1991] 1 A.C. 398 (1990).
11. [1978] 1 A.C. 410 (1977).
12. [1983] A.C. 410 (1982).
13. *Id*. at 443.
14. *Id*. at 431.

McLoughlin itself, all these pronouncements seemingly adopting Dworkin's whole approach were sharply criticized by Lord Edmund-Davies who, in particular, pointedly and vigorously replied to Lord Scarman's rejection of policy. Lord Edmund-Davies found that position "as novel as it is startling"; novel because it had not been mentioned in argument and "startling because in my respectful judgment it runs counter to well-established and wholly acceptable law."[15] In using the *McLoughlin* case to illustrate his theory, Dworkin was using his method of analysis merely to describe the appropriate justification for that decision. For him, the correctness of the decision was self-evident. In point of fact however, in subsequent cases, their lordships took a markedly more restrictive view of the extent of liability in these types of cases. Liability for emotional injuries to bystanders, who were not themselves threatened with physical injury and who were described as secondary victims, was limited to those who, in some sense, had directly perceived the injury to the primary victim, that is the person killed, injured, or imperiled, and who, in addition, also had a close tie of affection with the primary victim.[16] Under this narrower view of the governing legal doctrine, it is questionable whether the *McLoughlin* case would now be decided the same way. So much again for the triumph of general principle. Moreover, in his attempt to use the *McLoughlin* case to illustrate how his theory might be made concrete enough to be applied to an increasingly important current legal issue, Dworkin opened himself up to the criticism that, in the actual legal world, "principles" were largely just more generally worded "legal rules"[17] and, perhaps more importantly, especially for our purposes, subject to the criticism that the distinction between so-called policy and principle often lies in the eye of the beholder.[18]

---

15. *Id.* at 427.

16. These developments in both the United States and Great Britain are described more fully in THE NOTION OF AN IDEAL AUDIENCE, *supra* note 6, at 119–22. It is noteworthy that even the requirement of a close tie of affection with the primary victim has been further tightened because "the quality of brotherly love is well known to differ widely." Alcock v. Chief Constable of the South Yorks. Police, [1992] AC. 310, 406 (1991) (per Lord Ackner).

17. This point has been very well made in Kent Greenawalt, *Policy, Rights and Judicial Decisions*, 11 GA. L. REV. 991 (1977). *See also* his *Discretion and Judicial Decision*, 75 COLUM. L. REV. 359 (1975).

18. In LAW'S EMPIRE, *supra* note 1, at 240–41, Dworkin set forth six possible justifications for the decision. Three were classed as policy arguments, which were of course rejected; and three were classed as arguments of principle. Regarding the two better principle-based justifications, between which he was diffident about choosing, one was: "People have a moral right to compensation for reasonably foreseeable injury but not in circumstances when recognizing such a right would impose massive and destructive financial burdens on people who have been careless out of proportion to their moral fault." *Id.* at 241. How this proposition differs from what most people would call "policy" escapes me. More to the point, one of the justifications which Dworkin rejected, because it could plausibly be considered "a naked appeal to policy," was: "People should recover compensation

The failure of Dworkin's use of principle to answer definitively the question of the extent of liability for pure economic loss or the scope of liability for the negligent infliction of emotional distress is not due to the perverseness of judges who refuse to follow Dworkin's approach to legal decision making; nor is it due to the rejection of the relevance of moral considerations in legal argument; nor, finally, is it due to any disagreement on the value of integrity or of generality or of equal concern for all human beings in either legal or moral argumentation. Rather it is due to the fact that life and, consequently, the moral universe according to which we organize our lives are just too complex to be captured in any concise formula that sufficiently points us in one direction or the other. It is a dangerous illusion to believe that we can ever come up with a formula or set of formulas that can enable judges to decide concrete cases without being burdened with moral responsibility for their decisions. Responsibility and, in a democratic society, accountability are inseparable from the exercise of all power, even of judicial power, and nowhere more so than in the controversial fields with which we are concerned. If Dworkin's principle-based theory of legal argumentation is unable to produce clear right answers in comparatively mundane tort cases, it requires a huge leap of faith to believe that it could do better in solving a conflict between two basic human rights that are regarded as of equal value. It is not that anyone disputes the proposition that human rights adjudication must be principled. The problem is that, despite the universal call for the resort to principle in deciding highly contested human rights cases, no one has actually been able to come up with any set of substantive principles that are adequate to do the job. All we are left with is the formal requirement of all legal systems that like cases should be treated alike. Since no two cases are exactly alike, we are left with the issue of what does that mean in practice. The purpose of this book is to explore how far that formal principle can take us.

Accepting that popular theories about the nature of legal reasoning along the lines presented by Dworkin are unable to give us the necessary concrete assistance that we are seeking in deciding the controversial types of human rights cases that we have been examining, is it nevertheless possible that deeper contemporary philosophical inquiries into the substantive nature of justice might be of some help to judges actually trying to act like judges and not like legislators, or perhaps even like philosopher kings to whom the welfare of society has been delegated? The most important contemporary discussion of justice, certainly in the English-speaking world and very arguably in the entire developed world, is

---

for emotional injury when a practice of requiring compensation in their circumstances would diminish the overall costs of accidents or otherwise make the community richer in the long run." *Id.* at 240. Would not many people consider it as splitting hairs to maintain that one of the those two justifications is clearly principle and the other clearly policy?

that of John Rawls,[19] who asserted that the basis upon which justice in the modern nation-state may be achieved is the principle of equality as fleshed out in some detail in his work so that it is not a mere shibboleth but rather a concept that can direct major political decisions.

The core of Rawls' theory is premised on the assumption that, in a tolerant and diverse society, universal agreement on a comprehensive vision of the nature of the good is impossible. The most that people might universally accept would be that the basic social and economic goods of a society should be distributed by a method that all would consider fair. Hence, as he himself declared, his theory is based on the notion of "Justice as Fairness."[20] Accordingly, to satisfy that requirement, one should try to determine what the structure of an ideal society, or, at least, one with the level of social and economic development achieved in the developed world—that is, what Rawls calls a modern democratic society—would look like if chosen by representative people on the basis of their perception of their own self-interest under certain ideal conditions. These ideal conditions, described as the original position, include a veil of ignorance, that is to say a complete lack of knowledge on the part of the participants about their health, physical and mental abilities, and any other contingent features of actual existence that might influence their choice of the basic principles that are to govern their society.

As is well known, Rawls concludes that rational, self-interested people deliberating in the original position under such ideal conditions would insist on the lexical priority of personal liberty, including freedom of expression, although Rawls' view as to what those liberties are does not exactly track the liberties enshrined in constitutions such as that of the United States. It is, as we shall soon note, considerably more restrictive. These rational, self-interested people would also insist on a society characterized by fair equality of opportunity, premised on the assumption that no one has any moral claim to the advantages he obtains from his intellectual or moral or, presumably, his physical abilities. Having achieved these two desiderata, they would then insist that the distribution of social goods like wealth should be based on the system that would be chosen by these representative people through the application of the maximin principle which, although it operates most clearly at the level of the distribution of social goods, also informs both the discussion about the nature of the political liberty to be guaranteed in the ideal state and the discussion of what fair equality of opportunity means. Under these stipulated initial conditions, Rawls asserted

---

19. JOHN RAWLS, A THEORY OF JUSTICE (1971) [hereafter THEORY OF JUSTICE]. A revised edition [hereafter *rev. ed.*] was published in 1999. Since Rawls' theory is well known, page references will only be given when quotes are involved or some statement in the text is particularly crucial or could possibly be considered controversial.

20. *Id.* at 3. This is the title of Rawls' first chapter and is used in the book's first paragraph to explain the main theme of his book.

that rational, self-interested people, using the maximin principle, would insist that social goods be distributed equally unless an unequal distribution would lead to an improvement in the lot of the least advantaged. The end result of the exercise is to provide a model of how a diverse secular society could establish a political structure that would satisfy our basic notions of justice and which, despite the absence of a universally shared vision of the good, could be counted on to produce just, that is to say fair, solutions to the problems that any society faces over time.

As we turn to a discussion of whether or not Rawls' theory is of much help in giving guidance to courts in deciding the issues we have been considering, it is important to note at the outset some more general features of Rawls' work which will profoundly affect the ability to use his emphasis on equality in the types of human rights litigation that we have been considering. Like many moral philosophers, Rawls proceeded on the assumption of a relatively static social universe that, to the extent it evolves over time, changes very slowly. But could that ever be the case and, more to the point, is that the case in the modern world? Robert Nozick[21] long ago pointed out that a society organized in accordance with Rawls' principles that permitted any significant degree of free exchange among its members would sooner or later, and likely much sooner than later, find that its citizens had traded themselves into a situation in which increasing disparities of wealth could not easily, if at all, be justified by any improvement in the lot of the least advantaged. Nozick's point was that, in order to preserve Rawls' desired end state, namely a society in which economic inequalities are only permitted to the extent of their producing an improvement in the lot of the least advantaged members of society, an extensive degree of state intervention would be required to insure the continual redistribution of wealth that would be needed to maintain the desired equilibrium. Rawls has never really responded to this criticism, possibly because he was prepared to accept the confiscatory rates of taxation and the constant close surveillance of economic activity to prevent tax avoidance that would be necessary to maintain the equilibrium that he seeks. In such circumstances, the commitment to a relatively free society would be severely compromised. The required level of governmental intrusion into the lives of citizens might perhaps be sufficiently low to be tolerable in a static society; it might well escalate to intolerable levels in a dynamic society.

The problem of state intrusion into the lives of its citizens, particularly in a dynamic world, is highlighted in Rawls' later work which considers real life issues much more closely related to the sorts of human rights cases upon which we have focused. As everyone is aware, Rawls was vehement on the need to regulate and limit the amount anyone can spend on political campaigns.[22] The

---

21. ROBERT NOZICK, ANARCHY, STATE AND UTOPIA 183–231 (1974).
22. *See* JOHN RAWLS, POLITICAL LIBERALISM 356–63 (1993) [hereafter POLITICAL LIBERALISM].

rationale was that people are entitled not merely to the legal right to free political discussion but to the equal opportunity actually to exercise that right. Rawls never told us why people like Rupert Murdoch or the late Robert Maxwell should be able, in their all too partisan newspapers, to advocate the election of one candidate rather than another, but the attacked candidate should not be able to raise enough money to purchase television time or space in other news media to counteract that endorsement. If Rawls were consistent, he would have to admit that he really is not in favor of a largely unfettered and unregulated press. But, even leaving aside the Murdochs or the Maxwells or even *The New York Times*, if one takes seriously Rawls' assertion that no one has a moral entitlement to his greater talents and abilities or to his strength of character, since these are all the result either of genetics or of nurturing,[23] then it would follow that the state should intervene to insure that the more articulate and charismatic do not, by the exercise of those morally undeserved personal characteristics, prevent others, over time, from having a fair equality of opportunity to influence political debate. Rawls may in fact believe that a state as intrusive as the one preferred by Plato is a necessary feature of any society committed to justice as fairness. If so, he should have said it more directly, and not merely hinted at it in the campaign finance instance or, as we shall have occasion to discuss, in his suggestion that the tax laws and the antitrust laws should be used to hinder or restrict advertising that he characterized as "socially wasteful," which is hardly an endorsement of a robust right to freedom of expression

The principal issues on which serious attempts have been made to apply Rawls' body of thought to important fundamental legal issues have been the need for judicial recognition, on moral grounds, of what might be called "welfare rights" and the desire to provide some additional philosophically based justifications for affirmative action policies. In relying on Rawls' thought, all these attempts presuppose the validity and general acceptance of Rawls' difference principle for allocating social goods as applied through the use of the maximin principle. The application of the maximin principle is not without its problems, however. As originally applied by Rawls, neither the maximin principle itself nor any other principle establishes either the lexical priority of personal liberty or the special weight to be granted to the principle of fair equality of opportunity. That required, as Rawls came to recognize, the additional assumption that the participants in the discussions taking place in the original position, who know nothing about what the lottery of life will deliver to them in the way of health and physical and mental abilities, nonetheless know that they are creating a framework for a relatively advanced society.[24] Whether this is a significant piercing of Rawls' veil

---

23. THEORY OF JUSTICE, *supra* note 19, at 100–18 and *passim*. Rawls softened his language in the revised edition but not his position. *See rev. ed., supra* note 19, at 87.

24. *See* John Rawls, *Justice as Fairness: Political not Metaphysical*, 14 PHIL. & PUB. AFF. 223 (1985). This assumption underlies the discussion in JOHN RAWLS, JUSTICE AS FAIRNESS: A RESTATEMENT (2001) [hereafter JUSTICE AS FAIRNESS].

of ignorance or not, this extra bit of knowledge presumably would lead all rational, self-interested people to place basic liberty lexically prior to any other basic social goods and, among social goods, to place fair equality of opportunity above all the remaining social goods. Without it, rational, self-interested people living at a bare subsistence level might well choose material welfare over either liberty or equality of opportunity.

The inadequacy of the maximin principle to support Rawls' thesis is most evident, however, in the core area of its application, namely in the formulation of the difference principle which is to govern the distribution of most basic social goods. Under Rawls' notion of the requirements of distributive justice, as we have already noted, any deviations from the equal distribution of these social goods must be justified by showing that permitting an unequal distribution will enhance the lot of the least advantaged members of society. This is presumably what rational, self-interested people, who know nothing about what their eventual position in society will be, would choose if they found themselves in Rawls' original position. But, as the difference principle itself implicitly acknowledges and attempts to accommodate, social life is not static; it changes over time and those who choose the difference principle are obviously aware of this general fact of social life. Given this presumed knowledge about social development, what strategy would rational, self-interested people who are guided by the maximin principle in their deliberations choose to pursue, even if, despite their presumed preference for personal liberty above possession of material goods, the prospect of a rather intrusive state apparatus does not particularly concern them?

Before he died in November of 2002, Rawls himself gave a hint at the choices such a person would face in his last book, *Justice as Fairness: A Restatement*, published in 2001, in which he actually discussed the question of why a rational, self-interested person would choose the difference principle as the basic distributive principle of social goods rather than some version of a capitalist society with a state-guaranteed minimum level of welfare for all its citizens. His argument is not very convincing. From the position of a rational, self-interested person, the choice would seem to be clear. Such a person would realize that there is an absolute limit to the downside risk, even if he were one of the few who fall into the category of the least advantaged. Indeed, as Rawls himself recognized, the material welfare of the least advantaged might very well be higher in a guaranteed-minimum-welfare capitalist state than it would in the type of society that he envisaged.[25] Given, therefore, the very limited and probably non-existent risk of a downside outcome, why would a rational, self-interested individual, knowing that he is unlikely to be among the least advantaged members of society, not choose, as the preferable social scheme, one that would offer him a potentially greater material payoff than one organized under the difference principle? If one

---

25. *Id.* at 126–30.

now takes into account that such a rational, self-interested person would also know that there is a 50 percent probability that he would have an above-average endowment of physical and mental abilities and that, therefore, he would be highly likely to benefit from a system which would, because it is of necessity dynamic, allow him greater opportunity to reap over time the advantages that those above-average endowments would afford him, the rational choice becomes obvious to any self-interested person, even if he were to use the maximin principle to decide among possible alternatives.

Rawls gives two kinds of reasons why a rational, self-interested person would not choose a society that permitted the economic freedom and the resultant greater economic inequality that would be permitted in a guaranteed-minimum-welfare capitalist state organized on democratic principles. The first kind of reason relates to the administrative feasibility of the two alternatives under consideration. Rawls suggests that a guaranteed-minimum-welfare capitalist regime, which he believes should be characterized as an instance of a society organized on the principle of restricted utility, would suffer from indeterminacy.[26] Why it would be more difficult in practice to establish the guaranteed minimum than to establish who are the least advantaged, or to determine *ex ante* what proposed changes in distribution would or would not enhance the position of the least advantaged, is not immediately obvious. Moreover, as we already indicated, Rawls also argued that society should regulate and limit expenditures on "socially wasteful" advertising.[27] Rawls seems to have felt that a democratic society could easily determine what is advertising that appeals to consumers on the basis of "superficial and unimportant properties" or what should be forbidden or discouraged because it tries "to influence consumers' preferences by presenting the firm as trustworthy through the use of slogans, eye-catching photographs, and so on." The supposed greater ease of making these determinations escapes me, particularly if they have to be made by courts. Indeed, the apparent drabness of the type of society that Rawls sets forth as the optimal one is perhaps a good reason to believe that it is not a desirable one. Be that as it may, the success of guaranteed-minimum-welfare capitalist societies in Western Europe, Canada, Australia, and New Zealand is certainly very strong evidence that establishing such economic minimums through legislation and administrative agencies is not such an insurmountable problem. Many people might indeed prefer a Rawlsian world, but to posit the possibility of universal agreement on that point seems chimerical.

The second and, to him, more important objection put forth by Rawls against a guaranteed-minimum-welfare capitalist society is that the greater the inequality of condition permitted by society, the greater the resentment and the loss of

---

26. *Id.* at 127–29.
27. This and the other quoted statements that immediately follow can be found in POLITICAL LIBERALISM, *supra* note 22, at 365.

self-esteem and alienation of those who enjoy lesser advantages. Rawls suggests that a society with greater disparities of income and wealth than he believes optimal would be a less stable society,[28] which clearly must be one of the reasons he claims that rational, self-interested-and-risk-averse people would choose his system of political justice, even if it were considerably more likely that they would be materially better off under a guaranteed-minimum-welfare capitalist regime, in which basic material welfare was guaranteed and the chances of their being among the least advantaged were quite low and likely even non-existent. To prefer Rawls' proposal, because it promises greater social stability, involves the assumption that, in a dynamic world, a society which permits a greater degree of inequality than would be permitted in a society organized as Rawls wishes would necessarily generate greater alienation and resentment, even if, as Rawls himself at times seems to recognize, the maintenance of his preferred social structure would require a very intrusive and at times coercive state. There certainly seems no warrant for assuming that all rational, self-interested people would prefer to live in such a Rawlsian world.[29]

Despite his protestations that universal agreement about the content of the good is unobtainable, Rawls' position can only be maintained if one accepts that equality is an ultimate social good that all would accept. Moreover, it is not equality in the abstract but a specific vision of equality that must be universally accepted. One might secure as universal an agreement as is practically possible for the proposition that equality before the law is an ultimate good. General agreement that no one is entitled to the advantages obtainable by superior abilities or talents has never yet been attained, despite massive re-education schemes; and the history of the human race suggests that it never will be. Rawls himself admits that the family is the greatest single impediment to the achievement of equality in the real world.[30] The fact that he shrinks from proposing a solution to what some might consider an "unfortunate" social contingency speaks volumes. It is no answer to argue that Rawls is only talking about what the ideal structure

---

28. *See* JUSTICE AS FAIRNESS, *supra* note 24, at 130–32. *See also id.* at 126–29, 138–40. A more detailed discussion of the issue, with appropriate specific reference to Rawls' discussion can be found in George C. Christie, *The Importance of Recognizing the Underlying Assumptions of Legal and Moral Arguments: of Law and Rawls*, 28 AUSTRALIAN J. LEG. PHIL. 39, 48–52 (2003).

29. Roger Cohen, *The End of the End of the Revolution*, NEW YORK TIMES MAGAZINE, Sunday, Dec. 7, 2008, is instructive on this point. It is a somewhat lengthy commentary on life in Cuba on the 50th anniversary of "Castro's Cuba."

30. THEORY OF JUSTICE, *supra* note 19, at 74, 300. In JUSTICE AS FAIRNESS, *supra* note 24, at 162–68, he discusses the principles of justice that should be applied within the family, but confesses that it is not clear that their fulfillment "suffices to remedy the system's fault." *Id.* at 168. His suggestions, however, only relate to establishing a more just and democratic family structure, not to the "undeserved" benefit of nurturing which his suggestions might only serve to accentuate.

of society should be. After all, Rawls asks us to accept the validity of his vision of the structure of justice by taking into consideration, in our search for a reflective equilibrium, our knowledge of real people living in the real world. However we structure our thought experiments, it is we as real people, that is, as members of a species that is the product of a very long period of animal evolution, who must decide what is to be the ideal structure of justice in the societies in which we live.

Keeping this discussion in mind, we might now find it instructive to turn to the attempt that has been made to find, in Rawls' work, reasons to adopt some specific social policies which have generated an appreciable amount of litigation and that concern complex and serious human rights issues similar to those we have already discussed. One such attempt has been to show that the case for adopting affirmative action policies is based on notions of justice, not merely on notions of social policy.[31] The reason for looking for such justifications in Rawls' work is undoubtedly at least partly motivated by the fact that affirmative action policies have been attacked on the ground that, however many policy reasons can be given for adopting them, for many people there is also something disturbing about them. Support for them in Rawls' work could go a long way toward negating the effect of these criticisms and simplify the task of courts called upon to rule on their constitutionality. In exploring how Rawls' work might contribute to that debate, it has thus been asked why Rawls did not accord fair equality of opportunity the same lexical priority that he accorded to what he called "basic liberties," rather than describing it as something that should only be given priority when we reach the stage of working out the ramifications of the "difference principle."[32] The importance of the social justice considerations underlying the elimination of discrimination against minorities and the achievement of a truly egalitarian society would, it was argued, require a more prominent place for the principle of fair equality of opportunity. One reason that has been recognized as possibly justifying Rawls' failure to explore this possibility more vigorously was his perception of the difficulty of applying that principle in practice as compared to protecting the basic liberties, such as freedom of conscience and expression, from state interference.[33]

I would submit that there is an even more basic reason why Rawls, who I am prepared to accept was as much of an egalitarian as most, was unable to give fair equality of opportunity any more priority than he did. That reason is the unavoidable consequence of Rawls' express and often repeated declaration that the perspective, from which the representative persons are negotiating behind a veil of ignorance to define the basic framework of the society they wish to create, is that of rational, self-interested people and not that of people committed to a communal

---

31. *See*, e.g., Seana Valentine Shiffren, *Equal Citizenship: Race and Ethnicity: Race, Labor and Fair Equality of Opportunity Principle*, 72 FORDHAM L. REV. 1643 (2004).
32. *Ibid.*
33. *Id.* at 1660–62.

perspective on anything. Rawls' whole point was that, given the right initial conditions, even self-interested people would, if they were rational, choose his concept of how the basic structure of society should be organized. Once one talks about minorities, a person in the original position appreciates that he is unlikely to be in that position. The more likely possibility is that he would be a member of the majority that might possibly be disadvantaged by a policy of affirmative action. Knowing that he is establishing the broad framework for what Rawls calls a *modern* democratic society, that is to say, a relatively advanced society, the most on which a rational, self-interested person could definitely be expected to insist, on the basis of the maximin principle, would be a general no-discrimination requirement and perhaps some assistance to individuals who, because of injuries for which they bear no responsibility, are unable to pursue certain opportunities which they otherwise might have been capable of pursuing. Such a person would also accept that those who have themselves personally been harmed by unlawful decisions or practices should be given either monetary compensation or some type of preference to negate the effects of the discriminatory practices to which they have been subjected. That would be the essential minimum for such a rational, self-interested person. Anything more might clearly put such a self-interested person at a material disadvantage, even if these further measures were prudent social policies.

Simply put, Rawls could not do as much as many would have wished with the fair equality of opportunity principle because his initial starting assumption of a universe of rational, self-interested people put significant impediments in his way. It is not of course that equality and fairness are not important moral features that we would expect a legal order to respect. However, only people who have already adopted a communal perspective would accept that these suggested further steps flowed logically from the notion of justice rather than being measures which, though opposed by many, might nevertheless be justified, and even sometimes accepted by rational, self-interested people as a matter of practical policy, in order to accommodate complex and conflicting social, political, and ethical demands. There is more to morality than equality or even fairness and certainly more than the sort of equality and fairness that Rawls argued all rational, self-interested people would accept. In short, the perspective of a rational, self-interested person is not sufficient to form the basis of a complete theory of justice. The perspective of rational, self-interested people deliberating in the state of ignorance assumed to exist in the original position will be nowhere near adequate to resolve conflicts between freedom of expression and privacy or other important social values. These conflicts are as much political and legal in nature as they are philosophical. No philosophical shortcut exists which can enable us to avoid the laborious wrestling with the specific facts of individual cases in order to develop a legal framework that will give adequate guidance as to the appropriate outcome when human rights of equal value come in conflict. The issue is whether even case-by-case adjudication is adequate to the task.

My purpose in this extended discussion of the admittedly powerful and attractive theories of Dworkin and Rawls has thus been to demonstrate that an attempt to lay out moral principles that will not merely figure in legal argument but will actually provide the means for achieving clear answers to the types of legal disputes we have been considering is doomed to failure. The normative and factual issues involved are just too complex to be decided by armchair speculation. Whatever solutions are eventually arrived at will be reached by a combination of a long slog of case-by-case adjudication and our confronting the necessity of sometimes having to make difficult political choices.

8. THE USE OF BALANCING TESTS AND FACTOR ANALYSIS—THE INEVITABLE TENDENCY TO RESORT TO BRIGHT-LINE TESTS

The acceptance of the need for a process of case-by-case adjudication to resolve conflicts between defeasible human rights and important social objectives, as well as conflicts between two defeasible human rights, is a clear acknowledgment that the quasi-deductive model of adjudication simply is not adequate despite the effort to expand the universe of legally relevant sources to include fundamental moral principles. As we saw in the last chapter, even if these principles are universally accepted, and some clearly are not, they are still too broad in scope to provide the courts with the guidance they are seeking. It is not surprising therefore that courts should, as we have seen, talk about the need to "balance" the conflicting interests or rights at play in the circumstances of the particular case before the court. The question is whether such a process can produce clearly defined rights while, at the same time, insulating the courts from the charge that they are assuming the role of super-legislatures or possibly that of politically unaccountable administrative agencies or, worse yet, that of spokesmen for some ill-defined elite intent on imposing upon society its views on controversial social issues.

That courts have always felt obliged to engage in some type of balancing is indisputable. The image of *Justitia* holding a balance as she weighs the evidence and arguments presented by the contending parties is ingrained in the popular imagination. What is different now is the increased need for courts to do that in a world that accepts a much wider range of obligations on the part of a nation-state to its citizens. It is a role that requires courts not only to weigh the evidence presented by the contending parties but also to measure, in a particular case, the weight to be accorded to widely accepted social values and policies that inevitably come in conflict under this broadened view of the state's responsibilities. That is a much harder task but nevertheless a necessary one, if the courts are to construct, out of a number of equally valued defeasible human rights that often come in conflict, something that resembles a scheme of Hohfeldian rights.

In judicial decisions and academic discussion as to how such a process of case-by-case decision making would operate, two expressions predominate: interest balancing and factor analysis. The concepts underlying these terms are closely allied and indeed often intertwined, but in some respects, the judicial techniques to which they refer may usefully be considered as somewhat conceptually different. The most obvious possible distinction between traditional balancing and the more recent factor analysis is the implication that factor analysis is a more focused and less subjective type of balancing process. Thus, although the terms "interests" and "factors" are normally often used interchangeably, interests can more easily encompass the subjective desires of specific individuals whereas the notion of factors more readily connotes some empirically verifiable social beliefs or material conditions. But since the term "interest" is also often used by some of the authors we shall be discussing to refer to the material concerns of society, we shall, as almost all similar discussions do, often use the terms interchangeably and let the context determine whether when we use the term "interest" we are referring to the subjective preferences of individuals or to something more concrete and subject to empirical investigation. That said, when reference is made to consideration of risks and material benefits, the term "factors" seems more appropriate, unless one insists that what is involved is an individual interest in risk or in material costs and benefits rather than in these empirically dependent concepts themselves.

Balancing as a technique of judicial decision making has probably been around as long as human beings have discussed law and the legal process in a systematized way. Factor analysis, on the other hand, arose in large part out of the development, in the nineteenth century, of the modern social sciences.[1] These "new" sciences appeared to offer the promise that the social and economic structure of society could be studied with something like the same precision and objectivity as was claimed for the physical sciences. The notion was that social development was fact driven and that, if one could acquire "scientific" evidence about the nature of the social world, one could predict how a society would evolve and also understand how to influence and possibly even direct that development. As more and more knowledge of society was obtained, the choice between competing solutions would be increasingly governed by a more objective or quantifiable process rather than by a more qualitative and subjective process, such as that which we have seen in the human rights cases we considered earlier.

It is understandable that the use of factor analysis in judicial decision making came to seem attractive in the latter part of the nineteenth century. It was a period when everything seemed to be in a state of flux. The contention of traditional legal scholars, such as von Savigny[2] and later Puchta[3] in Europe and James C. Carter[4] in the United States, that the law administered by the courts was a self-contained body of doctrine that reflected and indeed was the product of the

---

1. *See* GEORGE C. CHRISTIE, THE NOTION OF AN IDEAL AUDIENCE IN LEGAL ARGUMENT 167–79 (2000), for a more extended discussion of the history of the use of factor analysis.

2. FRIEDRICH CARL VON SAVIGNY, VOM BERUF UNSERER ZEIT FÜR GESETZGEBUNG UND RECHTSWISSENSCHAFT (OF THE VOCATION OF OUR AGE FOR LEGISLATION AND JURISPRUDENCE) (1814).

3. GEORG PUCHTA, OUTLINES OF JURISPRUDENCE AS THE SCIENCE OF RIGHT (William Hastie trans., 1887, reprinted 1982) (1822).

4. JAMES C. CARTER, LAW: ITS ORIGIN, GROWTH, AND FUNCTION (1907).

natural evolution of these societies was no longer convincing. The competing Austinian view, that law was merely the expression of the will of the political sovereign, seemed equally unsatisfying because it was incomplete. Law was more than the logical arrangement of the rules and doctrines promulgated by a supreme lawmaker who had the power to effectively enforce his directives. The dissatisfaction with these traditional models of the legal process was accentuated by the fact that, to many people, decisions that ostensibly purported to be derived from tradition and/or the logical application of legal concepts seemed clearly driven by unexpressed policy preferences and ideological considerations. Rudolf von Jhering, reflecting this new intellectual climate, put "Interest instead of Will at the basis of law."[5] Accordingly, since interest suggests purpose, von Jhering concluded that "there is no legal rule which does not owe its origin to a purpose, i.e., to a practical motive."[6] Although von Jhering himself did not go much beyond the assertion that the "practical motive" of commercial law was to insure the security of transactions, many observers believed that, by examining the social and economic structure of society, the new social sciences would be capable of discovering the practical purposes of the various branches of law and hence the appropriate answers as to how to structure legal relations.

The work of von Jhering and other European scholars attracted the attention of the indefatigable Roscoe Pound who introduced this insistence upon the instrumental nature of law to the English-speaking world.[7] There it found a welcome audience, and particularly in the United States for readily understandable reasons. At the turn of the twentieth century, the American body politic was confronting the challenge of the United States' emergence as a great economic power with vast human and natural resources. Large railroads and industrial combines, such as Standard Oil, that were constituted on a scale never before seen anywhere in the world, were amassing an economic strength that seemed frightening. To many well-educated people, it seemed obvious that the economy could not be left to the clash of conflicting private interests subject to whatever piecemeal and fitful control could be exercised by the courts using traditional legal remedies. Moreover, the complexity of the modern economy could not be managed simply by legislation. Legislation was necessary but the economy needed day-to-day supervision and regulation by trained professionals. In short, in America, the time of the modern regulatory state, functioning through an array of administrative agencies staffed by experts, had arrived.

What is most relevant for any study of the role of courts in human rights litigation is the belief that the scientific study of society could also provide useful

---

5. RUDOLF VON JHERING, LAW AS A MEANS TO AN END liv (Author's Preface) (Issac Husik trans., 1924). This work, originally published in 1877, was the first volume of von Jhering's *Der Zweck im Recht (Purpose in Law)*.

6. *Id.* at liv.

7. Roscoe Pound, *Mechanical Jurisprudence*, 8 COLUM. L. REV. 605 (1908).

answers in the domain of what might be considered quintessentially private law that traditionally, in the common law world, had been the province of the courts. Factor analysis was thus seen as a methodology that was not only helpful in resolving legislative disputes about the basic structure of the economic arrangements of society or for creating an administrative apparatus to police and regulate the increasingly complex economic structure of modern society, but also as a method that would assist in the judicial resolution of disputes arising out of the day-to-day interactions of ordinary people. As is well known, a school of legal scholarship, called legal realism, evolved to exploit the promised potential of that approach. The core notion of many legal realists in the United States was the belief that a properly trained lawyer, that is one with a thorough training in the social sciences and a thorough grasp of the needs and interests of the parties involved in legal transactions, could, as an advocate and especially if he were to become a judge or even a legislator, make the law more responsive to the needs of society.[8] That way of thinking again built on earlier European roots. At the close of the nineteenth century, François Gény, who embraced von Jhering's approach, had asserted that the judge, in performing his judicial function, "finds the necessary objective support only in the *nature of the subject matter of its inquiry.*"[9] All this, of course, could be interpreted as suggesting that the "facts" spoke for themselves and that reaching the appropriate legal conclusion was just a matter of acquiring a correct and sufficiently deep knowledge of the particular situation before the court and of the broader social and economic environment. It was the equivalent of something like situational ethics applied to a whole class of legal transactions. In his later work, Llewellyn spoke of the "law of the singing reason" in which a "rule [of law] wears both a right situation-reason and a clear scope-criterion on its face," which in turn would yield "regularity, reckonability, and justice all together."[10]

The notion that, if one thoroughly analyzed a social situation and appreciated the significance of what was going on in the "real world," the right answer would just jump out at one, is not unattractive nor in conflict with some aspects of everyday experience. After all, everyone is confronted with situations in which the correct answers to practical problems, even sometimes relatively complex ones, seem intuitively obvious once a person has devoted some attention to the matter. But there are limits to how far that recognition can take one. We all know that even our considered intuitions often ultimately turn out to be wrong because the real world is almost always more complex than we originally thought. Moreover, we might ask, what exactly was the scope of Llewellyn's field of inquiry

---

8. Herman Oliphant, *A Return to Stare Decisis*, 14 A.B.A. J. 71 (1928).
9. François Gény, Méthode d'Interprétation et Sources en Droit Privé Positif 357 (Jaro Mayda trans., 2d ed. 1954) (1919).
10. Karl N. Llewellyn, The Common Law Tradition: Deciding Appeals 183 (1960).

when he tried to apply his touchstone for determining appropriate legal doctrine, that is, rules of law that could meet the demands of "singing reason"? Llewellyn recognized that the "interests," such as "security of transactions," that were bandied about by legal theorists were not very helpful.[11] For Llewellyn, interests were "groupings of behavior claimed to be significant." The materials with which one had to work were the "objective data, that specific data, claimed to represent an interest."[12] At the level of description, one was ultimately left, according to him, "at the one end with groupings of conduct (and demonstrable expectations) which may be claimed to constitute an interest; and on the other [end] the practices of courts in their effect upon the conduct and expectations of the layman in question"[13]—the latter, presumably, being among the people whose conduct and expectations had been examined in the attempt to ascertain the facts claimed to represent an interest. Assuming one could actually identify all the interests involved in a certain set of situations, what then? How does one come to the right conclusion when many interests are involved? As we know too well, intuition is often fallible.

If there were a common metric, one might hope to achieve some degree of precision in the balancing of all the relevant interests or factors. Cost expressed in monetary terms is the only conceivable common metric that can plausibly be suggested. For that approach to have any hope of succeeding, two things would have to be possible. First, that a monetary amount can also be assigned to intangible interests, which could include the values of fairness and aesthetic satisfaction; and, second, that one could identify all the relevant costs. That seems impossible. Nevertheless, one might try to preserve some notion of having an objective method of decision making by asserting that factor analysis is just about counting up all the factors pointing in one direction and then all the factors pointing in another (assuming for the sake of simplicity that one is only dealing with a situation in which it is accepted that there are just two possible solutions). But that attempt to resolve disputes involving conflicting or inconsistent interests might ultimately also be unsuccessful, even if each of the interests involved is given equal weight, when there are an equal number of factors on each side of the equation. And what if, as in real life, there are multiple plausible solutions to a practical problem involved in the dispute?

An even more serious problem is what if some of the interests on each side of the equation are specific to the individual parties and others are social interests? Roscoe Pound long ago recognized that one cannot directly weigh individual

---

11. Karl N. Llewellyn, *A Realistic Jurisprudence—The Next Step*, 30 COLUM. L. REV. 431, 445 (1930).
12. *Id*. at 446.
13. *Id*. at 448.

interests against social interests.[14] That would be like comparing apples and oranges. In order to weigh individual interests against social interests, the individual interest, say for example in one's bodily security, would have to be translated into the *social* interest in the bodily security of the individual person. Moreover, as we shall soon begin to illustrate with specific examples, those who have attempted to apply factor analysis to the resolution of concrete legal disputes have never been prepared to assign each factor equal weight nor even to assign to any one factor the same weight in every case in which it might be relevant. In short, whatever might have been its promise of applying objectively discernible features to legal decision making, factor analysis, in its application, becomes just an instance of plain old balancing as it moves beyond mere quantitative analysis and requires us to enter the world of qualitative analysis, with all the problems that such balancing entails. The belief that some sort of identifiable and empirically quantifiable policies can be found that enable us to avoid that need turns out to be wishful thinking.

The controversial cases that we discussed earlier are, for the most part, clearly instances of what, in the United States at least, has come to be called ad hoc balancing.[15] These cases are often contrasted with those in which a court may enunciate a number of factors that it has considered in the course of choosing to adopt one generally worded legal doctrine rather than another to govern a whole category of cases, a use of factor analysis that is sometimes called *definitional* balancing.[16] Llewellyn may have been talking about this latter sort of situation. Whether the distinction between ad hoc balancing and definitional balancing is as clear cut in practice as it is in theory, particularly in the value-laden area we have been discussing, is another matter. The most dramatic use of ad hoc balancing in the United States was the Supreme Court's espousal of that method for resolving disputes over the reach of the First Amendment as fear of subversion by domestic and foreign enemies led to legislation that had a substantial impact on speech-related activities. After reaching its zenith in the 1950s, the enthusiasm for resolving those disputes by some sort of ad hoc balancing waned as the Court moved towards the much more absolute view of the reach of the First Amendment that we shall discuss later in this chapter.

In a world of competing basic values, each of equal weight, the allure of ad hoc balancing is, however, irresistible. It offers what initially may seem to be an

---

14. *See* Roscoe Pound, *Individual Interests of Substance—Promised Advantages*, 59 HARV. L. REV. 1, 1–3 (1945). *See also* Roscoe Pound, *Interests of Personality*, 28 HARV. L. REV. 343 (1915).

15. *See* T. Alexander Aleinikoff, *Constitutional Law in an Age of Balancing*, 96 YALE L.J. 943, 948 (1987). This is a particularly good discussion of the issues raised by balancing in the context of constitutional law.

16. Melvin B. Nimmer, *The Right to Speak from* Times *to* Time: *First Amendment Theory Applied to Libel and Misapplied to Privacy*, 56 CAL. L. REV. 935, 942–45 (1968).

acceptable method of legal decision making in situations which are extremely fact dependent and there is no bright-line legal doctrine, derived from the cases or the applicable statutes and the cases interpreting those statutes, that can serve as the focus of the decision-making process. It is thus no wonder that the use of balancing tests has been proposed in cases like *Campbell* and *von Hannover* as a means of resolving conflicts such as those between rights of privacy and rights of freedom of expression. Since the same problem of comparing incommensurables without some method of rank ordering them has plagued the application of balancing tests in less emotionally charged areas, it may be helpful to consider what we might learn from that experience should we persist in insisting that balancing is the way ahead in the areas that we have been discussing. A few quick examples from what, in continental Europe, would be considered private law will suffice for our present purposes.

In 1938, as part of its *Restatement of Torts*, the American Law Institute summarized the common law that had developed in the United States around the notion of strict liability for the miscarriage of dangerous activities that had been enunciated in 1868 by the House of Lords in the famous case of *Rylands v. Fletcher*.[17] By strict liability is meant a regime under which those seeking to recover damages for harm caused by the miscarriage of the activity are not required to present any proof of fault on the part of those carrying on the activity. Characterizing the doctrine as applying to what it termed "ultrahazardous activities," the *Restatement* declared that strict liability would apply if the activity is one that "necessarily involves a risk of serious harm to others that cannot be eliminated by the exercise of reasonable care" and "is not a matter of common usage."[18] When the *Restatement (Second) of Torts* in 1977 returned to the same subject, it made several changes.[19] The first was largely a matter of nomenclature. Where the *Restatement* spoke of "ultrahazardous" activities, the *Restatement (Second)* spoke of "abnormally dangerous" activities. More importantly, in its statement of what determined whether an activity was "abnormally dangerous," it made the dangerousness of the activity, the possibility of eliminating the risk by the exercise of reasonable care, and the commonness of its usage merely three factors, along with three other separate factors, that the courts should consider in deciding whether an activity should be classified as "abnormally dangerous." These additional factors were not only the appropriateness of the activity for the place at which it is carried on and how great would be the damage that might be caused by the miscarriage of the activity, but also "the extent to which . . . [the activity's] value to the community is outweighed by its dangerous attributes." Moreover, in a departure from most similar types of tort issues in the United States, such as the determination of whether a product was defectively designed, the issue of whether an activity

---

17. L.R. 3 E. & I. App. 330 (1868).
18. RESTATEMENT OF TORTS § 520 (1938).
19. RESTATEMENT (SECOND) OF TORTS § 520 (1977).

was abnormally dangerous was assigned to the judge and not the jury, even though one of the justifications for using a jury is precisely to create a mechanism for ad hoc balancing that does not have any precedential effect. Furthermore, none of the six factors set forth in the *Restatement (Second)* was given priority. Indeed, the *Comments* to that *Restatement* specifically provided that the weight that should be given by the courts to any factor is "the weight . . . that it merits upon the facts in evidence," whatever that means.[20] Furthermore, as already noted, one of the six factors, "the extent to which . . . [the activity's] value to the community is outweighed by its dangerous attributes," was of an entirely different sort than the other five. The criticism[21] of these changes was sufficient to prompt the new *Restatement (Third)* to completely abandon the factor analysis approach. While retaining the *Restatement (Second)*'s use of the term "abnormally dangerous activities," the *Restatement (Third)* reverted to the approach of the original *Restatement* by focusing on the conjunction of a "foreseeable and highly significant risk of physical harm, even when reasonable care is exercised" in the event of miscarriage, and the activity's not being "a matter of common usage."[22]

A more extreme example of the fascination of the American Law Institute with factor analysis is the *Restatement (Second) of Conflicts'* criteria for choosing the appropriate law to apply in all cases which involve contacts with more than one jurisdiction. It first sets out seven factors relevant to all choice of law problems[23] and then sets out four additional factors to be considered in tort[24] cases and five additional factors to consider in contract[25] cases. This approach has met even more severe academic criticism, including the charge that it is "too unpredictable and parochial to be a plausible theory of constructive intent."[26] It is moreover contrary to the overwhelming preference outside of the United States, particularly in Europe, for more simple, bright-line tests for ascertaining the appropriate law to apply in contract and tort cases that would provide, to the affected parties as well as to the courts, a clear guidance that cannot be achieved by simply enumerating a long list of important factors that should be considered by the courts in individual cases.

One might say that the same consideration would suggest the need for bright-line tests in the areas with which we have been concerned. The fact that we are

---

20. *Id.* at Comment *l*.
21. *See* George C. Christie, *An Essay on Discretion*, 1986 Duke L.J. 747, 766–69, for a detailed presentation of those criticisms.
22. Restatement (Third) of the Law of Torts: Liability for Physical and Emotional Harm § 20 (2010).
23. Restatement (Second) of Conflicts § 6 (2) (1971).
24. *Id.* at § 145 (2).
25. *Id.* at § 188 (2).
26. Lea Brilmayer, *Interest Analysis and the Myth of Legislative Intent*, 78 Mich. L. Rev. 392, 393 (1980). *See also* Friedrich Juenger, *Conflict of Laws: A Critique of Interest Analysis*, 32 Am. J. Comp. L. 1, 12–50; John Hart Ely, *Choice of Law and the State's Interest in Protecting Its Own*, 23 Wm. & Mary L. Rev. 173, 212–13 (1981).

dealing with basic rights of supposed equal value that involve many complex and controversial issues strongly suggests, however, that this would be very difficult to achieve unless we are willing to abandon our commitment to the equal value of the rights now at issue. The question with which we are wrestling is whether we can describe a process of case-by-case adjudication and the weighing of competing values that is capable of confining the presently required exercise of judicial discretion within acceptable boundaries.

It is of course obvious that one can short-circuit the process by professing to assign equal value to the rights in question but in fact giving preference to one right over the other. There are many reasons why this will often be the case. A legal system dealing with serious matters will strive both for substantive correctness and consistency. The easiest way to do this in conflicts between two rights of supposedly equal value is to give primacy to one right over the other in some broad categories of cases. But, if these categories are sufficiently broad as in the case of many forms of "privacy" in Europe or as is the case with freedom of expression in the United States, we are likely to end up with a regime in which one of these rights is de facto the preferred right in a very broad range of situations. This is less of a problem in the United States because its constitution supports the position that freedom of expression *is* the preferred if not the predominant right. That is not to say that the present sweeping preference for expression was inevitable. Even in the United States it was not inevitable that the preference for expression over other values would achieve the heightened level of protection that it has now attained. As a matter of historical fact, in the United States much of the initial enthusiasm for the use of ad hoc balancing in constitutional adjudication involved litigation concerning the ability of the government to regulate freedom of expression.[27] The hope was that, by balancing the importance of freedom of expression with the important state interest in protecting national security and public morality, the courts might satisfactorily resolve the inevitable conflicts. In the United States, at least, that proved not to be the case. After striking down blasphemy legislation[28] and carving out a residual, somewhat narrowly defined, and now only occasionally litigated field of obscenity, the United States Supreme Court confronted the broader issues involved in punishing expression. Establishing criteria for deciding when public suppression of speech might be justified solely for reasons of national security or maintaining public order proved difficult. The notion of the dangerous tendencies of speech and its more refined variant, "clear and present danger" to public security,[29] were found to be too broad and too difficult to apply without having a chilling effect

---

27. *See* Aleinikoff, *supra* note 15, at 966–68.
28. Joseph Burstyn, Inc. v. Wilson, 343 U.S. 495 (1952).
29. *See* Dennis v. United States, 341 U.S. 494 (1951) (applying that standard to the conviction of senior leaders of the Communist Party of the United States for advocating the overthrow of the United States Government).

on speech. In the end, the Supreme Court held that the government could not "forbid or proscribe advocacy of the use of force or of law violation except where such advocacy is directed to inciting or producing imminent lawless action and is likely to incite or produce such action."[30] As we have often had occasion to note, the same privileging of expression has occurred in disputes among private parties such as in actions for defamation and, more markedly, in actions for invasion of privacy.

This ultimate resolution, whether based on a supposedly clear constitutional text or dissatisfaction with the continuing legal uncertainty, made case-by-case ad hoc balancing of interests largely unnecessary in the United States. Freedom of expression became the clearly preferred value and the foundation for generating a set of Hohfeldian rights. As such, freedom of expression could not easily be trumped by other important social values or interests. Admittedly, there would always be some cases in which it would be unclear whether the speech in question was advocating imminent unlawful behavior as well as whether the speech in question was "likely" to produce that result. The uncertainty surrounding those often largely factual questions susceptible to empirical proof is impossible to eliminate completely, although the range of uncertainty can be greatly narrowed by a process of case-by-case adjudication. Moreover, it is a type of uncertainty present in all litigation. In short, one response to how to protect some pre-eminent social value is simply to give it primacy, not necessarily absolute primacy but enough to simplify the process of case-by-case adjudication by eliminating the need for complex balancing exercises in most situations. In a sense, this is what was done in the European cases upholding laws punishing the denial of the Holocaust, in reliance in part on Article 17 of the European Convention which declares that no one has the right to use the freedom guaranteed by the Convention to advocate the destruction of any of the freedoms guaranteed by the Convention, but of course with a reversal of the priorities. If taken literally, it suggests that the Convention itself becomes more important than the freedoms it was designed to protect. It is said that, given the history of Europe in the first half of the twentieth century, this reversal of priorities is necessary. One might perhaps nevertheless ask, how does one really know that this is still necessary? If the underlying test is proportionately between the danger and the means chosen to avoid the danger, surely asking and answering that question is necessary.

The same type of questions may be asked regarding the suppression of religious expression because of the threat to "secularism" or of any other type of expression because of the threat it may pose to some other broadly accepted value. Leaving aside how one determines what social values are so important that they justify suppressing any expression that could be said to advocate the

---

30. Brandenburg v. Ohio, 395 U.S. 444, 447 (1969). *See also* Virginia v. Black, 538 U.S. 343 (2003).

rejection of such values, there remains the more fact-bound question of how likely is it that the expression in question will lead to the public rejection of these presently preferred values. Without techniques for answering these questions, we have the worst of all worlds, namely, a substantial downgrading of the value of expression without any possible offsetting benefit from an increase in the ability to decide with certainty when public advocacy is permissible and when it is not. The end result is that, despite the guarantee of freedom of expression, the government's assertion of any plausible but inchoate danger to such important unchallengeable public values immediately puts someone who challenges these values on the defensive. We shall return to these issues in Chapter 11, when we try to describe what might be an adequate process of case-by-case adjudication for deciding these disputes.

The potential impact on expression of measures designed to protect certain public values is obviously a serious political issue. Of more immediate concern in daily life, however, is the inevitable conflict between privacy and freedom of expression. Here again, the same differences in approach are evident. In the United States, the constitutionally privileged status for expression very substantially reduces the need to engage in a case-by-case balancing of conflicts between privacy and expression. The insistence in Europe of the equal value of privacy and expression would seem to make a continuing process of case-by-case ad hoc balancing almost inevitable, at least until a sufficiently rich body of precedents could be created to give some clear guidance to courts and potential litigants. What we have noted, however, is that the urge to quickly develop some bright-line doctrinally driven rules for deciding these issues has led to the privileging of one of these supposedly equal rights, namely privacy, in a broad range of situations.

In Chapter 5, we saw that, in the *von Hannover* case, the European Court of Human Rights rejected the German Constitutional Court's decision that, as a figure of contemporary society "par excellence," Princess Caroline could not complain about being photographed in public space that was not so secluded as to generate a reasonable expectation of privacy.[31] This limited privileging of expression by the German courts was rejected by the European Court on a number of grounds including the failure to allow an individual "to know exactly when and where they are in a protected sphere or, on the contrary, in a sphere in which they must expect interference from others, especially the tabloid press."[32] The Court insisted that all people, even political figures, had a legitimate expectation of privacy even in public space. Whether someone who infringed that legitimate expectation of politicians might be held legally liable would depend on the "contribution" that the challenged expression would "make to a debate in a dem-

---

31. Von Hannover v. Germany, Application No. 59320/00, Judgment of June 24, 2004, 40 Eur. H.R. Rep. 1 (2005), at ¶ 75.

32. *Id.* at ¶ 73.

ocratic society" concerning the exercise of their public functions.[33] With regard to a person like Princess Caroline who, though well known, was not a politician or public official, publication of details about her private life "cannot be deemed to contribute to a debate of general interest to society."[34] Given the vagueness of these criteria, the only clear guidance given to people wishing to exercise their right to freedom of expression is, when in doubt, do not publish; and, if you do, remember the burden, and it may be a very heavy burden, is on you to justify your expression. The attempt by the House of Lords to create a law of privacy in the United Kingdom by extending the notion of confidentiality far beyond its traditional borders, as we also saw in Chapter 5, is fraught with the same problem. The expanded notion of confidentiality is quite broad. To tell a person, whose expression has allegedly breached some general obligation to refrain from publishing matters that a reasonable person would not want disseminated widely, that he can nevertheless escape liability if he can establish that the publication is in the "public interest," is again to tell him, when in doubt, do not publish; and, if you do publish and are challenged, be prepared to carry the costly and time-consuming burden of showing that your publication was in the public interest. These again are among the difficult issues with which we shall grapple in Chapter 11 when we attempt to describe how the courts might give some clearer direction in these matters.

---

33. *Id.* at ¶ 63.
34. *Id.* at ¶ 65.

PART IV
CASE-BY-CASE ADJUDICATION

9. AN OVERVIEW OF CASE-BY-CASE ADJUDICATION, ITS POSSIBLE GOALS, AND THE INFLUENCE OF LEGAL TRADITIONS

The previous chapters of this book have highlighted the problems confronting courts attempting to decide the contentious issues that inevitably arise in the adjudication of cases involving what are accepted as basic human rights. We also considered a number of the ways that have been suggested to meet these problems in a manner that would make a universe of defeasible rights into something that would approach the Hohfeldian rights model and yet still be compatible with our traditional notions about the function of courts and the role of judges but have found them wanting. The time has now come to go further and to explore and, if possible, set forth acceptable and plausible ways that might enable courts concerned with the implementation of difficult human rights issues to meet, in an intellectually satisfying way, the challenging demands now being made on them. In other words, we must consider how, if at all, courts might meet these challenges without becoming either meek and quiescent rubber stamps to decisions made by powerful political actors or a coterie of philosopher kings who are creating a more structured system and hierarchy of rights by imposing their own views, or the views of the social elites to which they belong, on the citizens of a democratic society. This will be a difficult task which will require the discussion of many often contentious issues.

To begin with, we must decide what we would wish an adequate theory of human rights adjudication to provide. Would the only satisfying answer be one that permitted courts to achieve the correct answers to the difficult questions that they are asked to adjudicate? Or are we interested instead, and more modestly, in answers to those difficult questions that are at least consistent, that is in answers that, at the very least, enable people living in a democratic society to predict with a fair amount of certainty how these questions will likely be decided in the future and thus permit them to organize their activities accordingly? Or, finally, would we be content merely with a system of adjudication which is so structured that it at least permits most members of a society to accept the legitimacy of those decisions even if they are not prepared to accept either the substantive correctness of these decisions or even the consistency of these decisions.

For some, the last of these alternatives might at first glance appear to be a very minimal goal indeed, one that puts in doubt the worth of expending any appreciable amount of effort at all on the quest on which we have embarked. That note of despair would not, however, be completely warranted. Much can be done and is done to legitimize legal decision making, even if it does not supply either correct or consistent decisions and even if it supplies decisions which many people regard as both incorrect and inconsistent. Indeed, the use of ad hoc balancing in some ways presupposes that, in some of the areas of human rights adjudication that we have been discussing, this may be not only the most that we can expect but may also possibly be a morally and intellectually acceptable objective. Before dismissing this alternative because we might wish for more in this area of the law, we must remember that it is not only possible but often the case that decisions which are widely accepted as correct and consistent are nevertheless not considered legitimate because either the procedures utilized are not considered acceptable or the decision is considered beyond the province of courts to make, or for other reasons. Obviously, the optimal solution would be one that produces decisions that are broadly accepted as being correct, consistent, and legitimate. As the discussion in this book proceeds, all of these issues will be addressed. Although it will obviously be necessary sometimes to consider these issues separately and in isolation, they are all interrelated. How any one of these three major issues is resolved will affect how we try to resolve the other two major issues. Before we start our more detailed inquiry, therefore, let us stipulate that we are considering a world in which the persons who are making the decisions with which we are concerned, in this study the judiciary, are for better or for worse accepted as at least having the legal authority to decide the issues before them. Furthermore, we are also starting from the assumption that the cases which are to be decided involve clashes between legally recognized fundamental human rights or clashes between legally recognized fundamental human rights and basic governmental objectives that most people would accept as important and even essential governmental objectives in a democratic society. It is because these issues are so important and the resolution of the conflicts between them so difficult to resolve that reliance on case-by-case adjudication has been considered necessary and has led to the general acceptance that resort must be had to some kind of balancing process in order to decide such cases. What makes the resort to case-by-case adjudication so attractive is that it assuages our misgivings about giving courts too much leeway, by assuring us that we have at hand a process that will reduce that leeway to acceptable levels. The question is, how realistic are those hopes in the areas with which we are concerned, areas in which small factual differences, when combined with conflicting but strongly held opinions of what is the ideal legal solution, exert a strong centrifugal force.

In accepting that courts faced with the task of engaging in case-by-case adjudication to resolve a conflict between one person's right to freedom of expression and another person's right to privacy, or between an individual's right to freedom of expression and the state's ability to restrict that expression because it offends some people's religious sensibility, as in prosecutions for blasphemy, or because it offends some people's sense of sexual propriety, as in prosecutions for obscenity, what are we hoping that a process of case-by-case adjudication could achieve? And the same question arises in situations where the intervention of the state is justified on the basis of some particularly important public goal and not largely as a way of mediating, directly or indirectly, between the conflicting claims and values of private citizens.

Scholars and judges trained in the civil law tradition often express the belief that, starting with instances in which courts engage in what might be called ad hoc balancing in a particular case or in a relatively small set of such cases, the courts will be able to develop a set of general principles that can be used to settle future disputes. This was clearly evidenced in the *von Hannover*[1] case where, as we saw, the European Court of Human Rights declared that even a person as well known as Princess Caroline enjoyed a broad right to privacy that included her activities in what was clearly public space. People trained in the civil law tradition are perhaps encouraged to believe that this derivation of categorical general rules is not only possible but also desirable by the much discussed work of Ronald Dworkin, on which we commented in Chapter 7, which maintains that the essential characteristic of judicial decision making is that the discretional authority of judges is ultimately controlled by general principles that are derived from the history and moral principles of the society in question in a way that shows that society in the best moral light. They are probably also encouraged in their search for categorical legal doctrine by statements of common law trained lawyers and judges that the common law works its way pure as legal rules enunciated in one case are refined through application in similar subsequent cases into fairly precise and definite rules of law. At a theoretical level, this is an odd conclusion because these same authorities are fully aware that the basic premise of common law adjudication is that the only thing authoritative about a prior case is the actual decision on the facts in question.[2] Everything else is dictum and can be ignored by future judges if they wish. And, as has been pointed out, it is certainly possible that, in dealing with complex issues, the more decisions issued by the courts, the greater the confusion.[3]

The task of finding the "law" by extrapolating from the previously decided case is not made any easier by the feature of all common law case-by-case adjudication that the so-called facts of the previous cases can be stated at various levels of generality. The more general the level, the broader and more open ended will be the supposed "rule" derived from the previous cases.[4] That is not

---

1. Von Hannover v. Germany, Application No. 59320/00, Judgment of June 24, 2004, 40 Eur. H.R. Rep. 1 (2005), discussed at length earlier in Chapter 5.

2. *See* Julius Stone, Legal Systems and Lawyers: Reasonings 267–98, (1964); George C. Christie, *Objectivity in the Law*, 78 Yale L.J. 1311, 1313–18 (1969). *See also* Lingle v. Chevron U.S.A., Inc., 544 U.S. 528, 545–46 (2005) (O'Connor, J., writing for the Court). A more recent illustration is the Court's per curium opinion in *Thaler v. Haynes*, 130 S. Ct. 1171 (2010).

3. *See* Anthony D'Amato, *Legal Uncertainty*, 71 Cal. L. Rev. 1 (1983).

4. *See* Stone, *supra*, note 2, at 263–67.

to say that past cases are not useful in narrowing the range of possible decisions in future cases. The doctrine of precedent assumes that in fact they are. The question is, how much guidance? In some areas of the law, the narrowness of the issues and the existence of a sufficiently large number of cases may be able to provide guidance as great as would be provided by a statutory provision covering the same subject. In other areas it will not. We shall return to this issue in greater detail as the discussion proceeds and especially as we try to describe how a case-by-case process of adjudication would actually operate and explore whether such a process would be adequate to produce the guidance that we are seeking in the controversial areas with which we are concerned, where even small factual differences have significant substantive importance. Finally, lest we lose perspective, we might note that not all law that is produced by judicial decision is the product of a case-by-case process of adjudication. Sometimes it is the product of judicial fiat and not necessarily improperly. An example in the fields with which we are concerned is the decision of the United States Supreme Court in *New York Times v. Sullivan*,[5] to which we have often referred, in which for the first time in over 170 years the Court expressly applied the First Amendment to the common law of defamation and, in the course of doing so, mandated substantial changes in that law. Although there was, as is almost always the case, some relevant historical background to that decision, the Court's decision could by no means be called the culmination of an evolutionary process.

As we proceed, in this world of defeasible and conflicting rights, we are obliged to explore in as much detail as possible what we mean by the decision of a controversial case that we would consider an appropriate one, given the state of the law and our vision of what the role of courts should be in a democratic society. It is not merely a question of legal "logic." If we were to take Dworkin literally, we would be committed to the view that, in a sophisticated legal system, there are right answers to almost all legal controversies because a sophisticated legal system is able to provide answers that in most instances are the "right" answer from the perspective of the political and moral history of its society. Under such a view, the duty of the courts is to deliver those right answers. If we reject that view as utopian, as I have argued we must,[6] we might nevertheless be prepared to say that there are several correct answers from both a legal and possibly also a moral perspective to most really difficult questions and that, by reaching any one of those answers, a court has not departed from the traditional role assigned by society to courts. If even meeting that criterion also often seems unachievable, we might fall back to requiring that the decisions in all these difficult cases must at least be "reasonable," and that is not a bad description of much actual practice, but, to the extent it implies that a decision might be

---

5. 376 U.S. 254 (1964).
6. *See* the extensive discussion of Dworkin's theory in Chapter 7, *supra*.

reasonable yet nonetheless incorrect, it does present some difficulties, especially to one who is concerned with the logic of legal decision making. One way of avoiding these difficulties, which has support in moral theory, is to say that the criterion for judging the soundness of a particular legal decision is that it should not be incorrect or, in Dworkinian terms, that it should not be the wrong answer. Certainly in making many difficult judgments about controversial human actions, the most that we can often say is that a decision that the action in question was not morally wrong is not an incorrect one. Whether the action was *the* morally right thing to do, or that the judgment passed on that action was a morally correct one, is another matter. It is not only that there may be several so-called right answers, but it may also happen, as I would suggest is often true in complex and difficult cases, that there are no ascertainable clearly correct resolutions to the controversial issues in question either from a legal or a moral perspective. Nevertheless, we may still be able to agree that some possible decisions in those cases would be clearly wrong. In much of the following discussion, I shall assume, unless otherwise indicated, that sometimes this is often the most rigorous criterion of correctness that we could realistically hope for.

There of course may also finally be cases so factually complex and morally and politically difficult that we have no confidence in our being able to ascertain not only any possible correct decision to the controversy in question, but also unable to decide with any degree of confidence what might be an incorrect decision or even an unreasonable one. In situations presenting this last scenario, we must recognize that the degree of authority enjoyed by the deciding body, in our case the courts, will be a decisive factor in generating public acceptance of the decision. Much will depend on the many psychological factors which are always present in varying degrees in any institutional structure but which we can only briefly note. A society may be organized in some sort of hierarchical manner so that those with the power of decision by virtue of their status can expect a certain amount of deference to be given them by the inhabitants of their country, whatever decision they hand down. But a fairly rigid hierarchical structure is not the only basis for the successful exercise of that sort of authority, nor is it a necessary basis. Lest there be any confusion by what is meant by the term "authority," it should be clear that, in this context, the term is used to designate something beyond the formal legal authority to perform the acts in question. I am referring rather to an ability to command or decide that is accepted not merely because the person or body that has issued the command or decision has the formal legal authority to take that action and the physical power to implement it, but also because, as a matter of actual fact, that person or body is, in some broader sense, accepted as being entitled to have issued that command or decision.[7] This is the

---

7. I have discussed this set of issues at great length elsewhere. *See* GEORGE C. CHRISTIE, LAW, NORMS AND AUTHORITY (1982).

notion upon which the legitimacy of government has ultimately been usually based. No one has refuted Hume's observation that the strongest basis for successfully exercising authority over the members of a society is derived not from law but from the fact that those who are exercising that authority have possessed and exercised it for a long time.[8] There certainly is no question that the Supreme Court of the United States' decision in *Bush v. Gore*,[9] abruptly and definitively ending the legal challenge to the election results in 2000 without public violence or even public unrest, is a significant modern-day example that clearly illustrates the validity of Hume's thesis. Of course, it is not only courts that can rely on the successful long-term exercise of authority in order to successfully continue exercising that authority. It is human nature to accept the habitual way social relations are arranged as the natural way they should be arranged. As Locke said, in what has theretofore been a stable society, it takes a great deal of misgovernment to lead to sufficient dissatisfaction with the structure of government to make drastic change even remotely possible.[10] It is undoubtedly this consideration that prompted Kelsen to maintain that one reason for insisting on the separation of law and morality is to inhibit the tendency of people to accept that what is legally prescribed is indeed what is morally prescribed.[11]

We would of course naturally expect that courts would rely on more than their ancient existence and the fact that heretofore they have not so antagonized society by the manner and substance of their decisions as to alienate the society whose courts they are.[12] And indeed, the judicial machinery of a sophisticated democratic state does do much more. It insists that its judges be as impartial as possible and ideally that they be well educated and wise; that the parties have the right to counsel and the right to present evidence and argument before the courts that are adjudicating their cases; that irrelevant evidence or evidence that is more inflammatory and prejudicial than its value in contributing to the court's decision be excluded, if possible, or, at the very least, admitted under conditions that limit its potentially prejudicial effect, etc. And, finally, of course, the judicial machinery of the state relies for its legitimacy upon its ability to meet the public's conception of the proper role of courts. That conception assumes that courts base their decision on "the law," that is, something that optimally pre-exists a

---

8. DAVID HUME, A TREATISE OF HUMAN NATURE, BK. III, PT. II, § x (at 553–67) (L. A. Selby–Bigge ed., 1888) (1779).

9. 531 U.S. 98 (2000).

10. JOHN LOCKE, THE SECOND TREATISE OF GOVERNMENT § 225 (at 126–127) (T. P. Beardon ed., 1952) (1690).

11. HANS KELSEN, GENERAL THEORY OF LAW AND STATE 5–6 (A. Wedberg trans., 1949) (1945).

12. *See* KARL N. LLEWELLYN, THE COMMON LAW TRADITION: DECIDING APPEALS 219–20 (1960).

court's decision and is in theory knowable in advance by, if not the members of the public at large, then at least by their legal advisors.

But what if we are forced to recognize not only that judges to some extent are always making law as they decide the cases brought before them, but also that the pre-existing law often consists of broad, vaguely worded statements of basic social values? What happens when these broad, vaguely worded social values come in conflict in a case under judicial consideration? It would be disappointing if all one could offer the people affected by the decision is our best effort to make sure that the judges deciding the case are honest and as insulated from political influence as possible. It would also be naïve in those circumstances to believe that we possess the ability to assure the litigants that judges are the most qualified people to make these decisions. Indeed, it is hard to say who is the most qualified. Dworkin may have confidence that there is some philosopher-judge called "Hercules" who can perform that chore, but not many people have that same confidence. In point of fact, the so-called "philosophers' briefs" filed in some United States Supreme Court cases not only do not seem to have had any influence on the Court but were also rather partisan.[13]

When the issue involves social mores, why are judges or philosophers or any other group of elites better placed than any other member of the public, many of whom are as well-educated and certainly often have much more practical experience than either judges or philosophers? There is something that rings true in the late William F. Buckley's quip that he would rather "live in a society governed by the first two thousand names in the Boston telephone book than in a society governed by the two thousand faculty of Harvard University."[14] And, indeed, there has actually been a case in the United States where something like that point was actually made in a very concrete way in a judicial opinion. The case was *Repouille v. United States*,[15] decided by the United States Court of Appeals for the Second Circuit in 1947. The petitioner applied for naturalization and, under the relevant statute, was required to have been a person of "good moral character during the five years preceding his application for naturalization." The issue was whether the petitioner, who had chloroformed his thirteen-year-old, "blind, mute, deformed, idiot son who was also incontinent," met the requirement. It was accepted that Repouille who was supporting a family which included four other children, acted as he did because he was overwhelmed by his responsibilities. This prior criminal trial had excited a great deal of sympathy and, upon conviction by a jury that recommended the "utmost clemency," the sentence of five to ten years imprisonment was stayed and he was placed on probation from

---

13. Two such examples were *Roe v. Wade*, 410 U.S. 113 (1973) (abortion rights) and *Washington v. Glucksberg*, 521 U.S. 702 (1997) (assisted suicide).
14. WILLIAM F. BUCKLEY, JR., RUMBLES LEFT AND RIGHT, 134 (1963).
15. 165 F.2d 152 (2d Cir. 1947).

which he had been subsequently discharged.[16] The majority of the Court of Appeals reversed a lower court finding that petitioner had established "good moral character" but noted that the petitioner could reapply after the five-year period had expired. The majority, per Learned Hand, J., declared that, personally, they did not feel that the petitioner was not a man of "good moral character," but that they were called upon to judge the case by the standards of the ordinary man. Judge Jerome Frank in his dissent[17] pointed out the incongruity of judges with very limited contact with the public deciding what the ordinary man felt on such issues. This was a particularly apt observation regarding Learned Hand, as eminent and deservedly admired a judge that he was, who had led a particularly privileged and sheltered life.[18]

It might be germane to this discussion to recall the *Müller*[19] case, which we discussed earlier, in Chapter 4, in which judges sitting in the European Court of Human Rights were reviewing the decision of judges sitting in the Swiss courts. The case had been brought at the instigation of an irate parent and the issue was whether, under the social mores in the canton of Fribourg, the paintings in question were obscene and therefore subject to seizure and possible destruction, even though there had been no such challenge under the social mores prevalent in Basel when similar paintings were displayed there. There is indeed something to be said for the proposition that, when the question is public mores, the public at large is often in a better position to decide those sorts of issues than an elite class of judges. If there were ever situations in which a jury should be required, particularly the common law jury of twelve persons that deliberates without any judge present and is obliged to reach a unanimous verdict of guilt, these are certainly among them.

Lay participation in the judicial process has of course increasingly become a goal in many if not most democratic societies as a means of allowing citizens to participate in the performance of important government functions and as a way of buttressing the legitimacy of governmental institutions. Many civil law

---

16. In describing the prior state proceedings, Judge Hand declared: "It is reasonably clear that the jury which tried Repouille did not feel any moral repulsion at his crime. Although it was inescapably murder in the first degree, not only did they bring in a verdict that was flatly in the face of the facts and utterly absurd—for manslaughter in the second degree presupposes that the killing has not been deliberate—but they coupled even that with a recommendation which showed that in substance they wished to exculpate the offender. Moreover, it is also plain, from the sentence which he imposed, that the judge could not have seriously disagreed with their recommendation." *Id.* at 153. This was clearly an illustration of the common law's toleration of "jury nullification" that we discussed in Chapter 2.

17. *Id.* at 154.

18. *See* GERALD GUNTHER, LEARNED HAND: THE MAN AND THE JUDGE (1994).

19. Müller v. Switzerland, Application No. 107371/84, Judgment of May 24, 1998, 13 Eur. H.R. Rep. 212 (1991).

countries use lay assessors or jurors who sit with professional judges in at least some serious criminal cases and typically provide that the accused cannot be convicted without the concurrence of at least one and often more of the lay judges.[20] A few countries are even experimenting, in criminal cases, with juries that sit alone without professional judges.[21] But even this latter enlargement of lay participation in the judicial process does not approach that exercised by jurors traditionally at common law. First, as we have already noted, under the traditional common law still followed in the United States in all criminal cases and still followed in most cases by most common law countries, a jury verdict of acquittal cannot be overturned by the trial judge nor even, contrary to civil law practice, by an appellate court. Secondly, even in civil cases, as was noted in Chapter 3, the jury, like a judge trying a civil case without a jury, operates under a procedure in which the findings of fact made at the trial level cannot be overturned unless they are clearly unreasonable. Although the Supreme Court of the United States has held that a jury of as few as six persons might be adequate and that non-unanimous verdicts are permissible, many states still insist on unanimous verdicts by a jury of twelve persons, even in civil cases. Smaller juries are now also permissible in civil cases brought in the federal courts, but unanimous verdicts by twelve-person juries must be used in federal criminal cases.[22]

---

20. *See* Walter Perron, *Lay Participation in Germany*, 72 INT'L REV. PENAL L. 181 (2001); Jean Pradel, *Criminal Procedure, in* INTRODUCTION TO FRENCH LAW 143–44 (George A. Bermann and Etienne Picard eds., 2008); Kent Anderson and Emma Saint, *Japan's Quasi-Jury* (Saiban-in) *Law: An Annotated Translation of the Act Concerning Participation of Lay Assessors in Criminal Trials*, 6 ASIAN PACIFIC L. & POL. J. 233 (2005).

21. *See* Stephen C. Thaman, *Europe's New Jury Systems: The Cases of Spain and Russia*, 62 LAW & CONTEMP. PROBS. 233 (1999), *reprinted in* THE JURY SYSTEM: CONTEMPORARY SCHOLARSHIP 99 (Valerie Hans ed., 2006). The procedure is somewhat complex. General verdicts are not permitted and the jury is asked specific questions and must explain the reasons for its answers. Unanimity is not required but in Spain findings that are against the defendant must be supported by a super-majority of the jurors.

22. FED. R. CRIM. P. 23 reflects this constitutional requirement. In North Carolina, where I live, if a person being tried for a crime for which the penalty is more than 6 months imprisonment does not plead guilty, he must be tried by a twelve-person jury. There is no possibility of waiving a jury trial. *See* N.C. GEN. STAT. ANNOT. § 15A-1201. Even a petty crime tried in the state's district court without a jury, must be tried by a jury if the defendant decides to appeal his conviction for a trial de novo in superior court, the trial court of general jurisdiction. *See id.* § 1431. For a good discussion of the American jury system in operation, *see* Neil Vidmar and Valerie P. Hans, AMERICAN JURIES (2007). In England, until 2003 all "trials on indictment" were tried to a jury. By virtue of the Criminal Justice Act 2003, §§ 43, 44, complex fraud cases and cases where there is danger of jury tampering, may be tried by a judge alone. As regards cases which may be begun either by indictment or a more summary process, the defendant may choose to be tried by a jury. *See* ANDREW ASHWORTH, PRINCIPLES OF ENGLISH LAW 7 (6th ed. 2009). *See also* LORD JUSTICE

Accordingly, if the issue is what are the prevailing social mores of a society, a trial by such a jury has much to recommend it, particularly if procedures are in place to insure, as much as possible, that the jurors in point of fact do represent a cross-section of society. There does not seem to be much of an alternative to the use of some such procedure if one is really trying to bring public sentiment to bear in the resolution of cases involving public mores. Certainly, as all the societies in the developed democratic world become more ethnically, racially, and religiously diverse, it is increasingly chimerical to believe that there is some universal social consensus that enables even the most experienced and enlightened judge or even a jury that is as representative as possible to resolve all the disputes involving the contentious social issues arising in concrete social circumstances. If there is no generally accepted correct answer, a process that relies as much as possible on local participation and making the trial stage of the proceedings as procedurally fair as possible may be as much as one can realistically hope for. Certainly the common law's deference to the findings of fact by juries or local judges definitely accepts the view that local decision making, like procedural fairness, is important, and sometimes even more important than the so-called right answer, an importance that is obviously heightened when what is the right answer is itself a very contentious matter. The inflexible common law doctrine of double jeopardy that has been constitutionally adopted in the United States reflects some of the same preference for local decision making and not merely, as we have already noted, the value judgment that the interest of a criminal defendant in not being tried twice is more important than the interest of the state in achieving ultimate "justice." In an ideal world, however, one would want more than a process featuring legislative enunciation of broad and potentially conflicting nostrums that leave to courts and juries the task of sorting things out. But *faute de mieux*, we must take the world as it is and see what more the courts can do to deal with the difficult task that has been thrust upon them beyond merely perfecting the procedural safeguards and trying to incorporate greater public participation in at least some stage of the proceedings. It is to this part of our inquiry that we shall now turn.

AULD, 2001 REVIEW OF THE CRIMINAL COURTS OF ENGLAND AND WALES (http://www.criminal-courts-review.org.uk), Ch. 5 Juries, ¶¶ 119–72, a procedure that he states has been much criticized by many judges and academics. Since 1967, majority verdicts have been permitted provided 10 jurors agree when the jury consists of eleven or twelve jurors and nine if the jury has been reduced to ten. *Id.* at ¶ 75.

10. THE OPTIMAL CONDITIONS FOR CASE-BY-CASE ADJUDICATION AND ITS LIMITS

In Chapter 9 we suggested that a possible minimal goal for a process of case-by-case adjudication in the contentious cases with which we are concerned might be the establishment of a sufficient number of reference points so that one can distinguish decisions that are clearly wrong from those which it is impossible to conclude that they are incorrect even though we remain uncertain about their correctness. One might be uncomfortable with resigning oneself to accepting this seemingly perpetual diffidence but, in the areas with which we are concerned, we shall have to face up to the possibility that the more ambitious goal of eventually developing through case-by-case adjudication a sufficiently comprehensive set of reference points to enable us, in most situations, to divide results into the two categories of correct decisions and incorrect decisions may not be attainable. Although, in the short run, even achieving the more modest goal of separating the not incorrect decisions from the clearly wrong ones may prove to be a harder task than we might initially imagine, it does seem to be an achievable goal under certain conditions. It would require the European Court of Human Rights to restrict itself to the role performed by courts in the United States and also, traditionally, in the United Kingdom in reviewing the decisions of administrative bodies or the decisions of local courts on largely factual issues. Were the European Court prepared to accept such a confined view of its role, we could end this book at the conclusion of the present chapter. If we wanted a decision-making process in which courts played a more active role, we could still materially shorten the remainder of this book provided that in the areas of law coming before them, the salient issues were relatively few and dependent on a comparatively circumscribed number of factual considerations. Case-by-case adjudication is ideally suited for those sorts of situations. What we are dealing with here, however, are areas of law in which the salient features are many, highly emotive, and often rather unique. Dealing with such a complex set of issues is not made any easier by the European Court's insistence on correct decisions while accepting that often national authorities are in the best position to determine what that one correct decision is. That it should insist on the right answers to the scope of a basic human right is not only understandable but also would seem to be essential if the notion of human rights transcending national borders is to be meaningful. The problem is that delegating the authority to make that determination to local courts subject to some supervision by the European Court can lead to a world that Cicero deplored, namely one in which there is one law in Rome and another at Athens.[1] The ultimate question which we shall explore in the final two chapters is whether, under such a regime, case-by-case adjudication can provide both the reckonability of result and the legitimacy of process that we would want in the sorts of human rights controversies with which we are concerned. To set the stage for that discussion we shall, in this chapter, discuss some important formal attributes of a successful case-by-case decision-making process.

For case-by-case adjudication to do its bit to provide a workable, judicially enforceable framework for managing the basic conflicts upon which we have been focusing without resorting primarily to reliance on authority and authority's power to enforce its decisions, we must consider, in addition to procedural fairness, at the very minimum the following additional matters. First, to have any hope of giving serious guidance to future litigants and decision makers, the system must generate the necessary large number of cases involving relatively similar factual patterns over a comparatively finite period of time. Second, that guidance will be enhanced if the final decision-maker is a relatively fixed body with a relatively fixed composition. One of the features that has given so much authority to the decisions of the United States Supreme Court is that it is composed of only nine members who sit in all the Court's cases and who, because they enjoy life tenure, serve for a very long time. It is not unusual for the Court's composition to remain completely unchanged for five to ten years, and occasionally even longer. This is in sharp contrast to the forty-seven judges, serving limited fixed terms, who sit in panels no larger than seventeen and usually far fewer members, that compose the European Court of Human Rights; or even in contrast to national constitutional courts, whose judges, though normally not as numerous as those who serve on the European Court, typically also serve for relatively short, fixed terms and likewise sit in differently composed panels. It is no wonder that courts operating under such conditions of relatively continuous and perpetual change, particularly if these courts, largely composed of judges trained in a legal tradition that strives to provide right answers to legal questions, would, as we have noted in Chapter 8, want to develop bright-line tests. It is not their fault that their political masters have saddled them with a regime that insists on the equal value of rights that often come in conflict and, furthermore, makes those rights defeasible for a number of vaguely worded important social purposes, but then only when it is necessary to do so in a democratic society. To use a cliché, the judges on such courts are forced to play the cards with which they are dealt. That is why, as a means of giving legitimacy to such a system and to insulate the courts from the charge that they are merely part of a state power structure trying to enforce its views on a much less homogeneous society, we

---

1. T. MARCUS TULLIUS CICERO, REPUBLIC, Bk. III, § 22, Oxford World's Classics edition, THE REPUBLIC AND THE LAWS (N. Rudd trans., 1998). One might note that currently Holocaust denial is a crime in Berlin and Paris but not in London.

have suggested the consideration of ways of possibly including some sort of lay participation in the decisional process as a third desideratum.

Let us first discuss the last of these desiderata, the feasibility of some form of lay participation in judicial decision making. We have already discussed this possibility at several points in this book, and there is not much more that can be said about it here other than to repeat that, if a case turns on the social norms of a particular locality, it would be hard to come up with a better deciding body than a panel of citizens drawn from the local community that reflected the diverse social structure of that community. Obviously, in areas where it is felt that there is or should be a universal consensus or even merely a consensus that stretches over a large geographic area, such as the United States of America or the nations constituting the Council of Europe, that argument for lay participation in order to insure that local sentiment is considered in the decision-making process would not carry much traction.[2] Nevertheless, when the issue is whether the state may criminally prosecute someone for the alleged violation of some supposed broadly accepted social norm, the incorporation of a form of lay participation finds some support in the widely accepted value of putting a buffer between the apparatus of the state and the defendant. When issues of fact are concerned, as we have several times noted, there is even more to be said for deference to local decision makers whether the local decision maker is a judge or, as in the United States in both civil and criminal cases, either a judge or a jury. This is particularly true if, at the trial level, the proceeding involves live testimony with vigorous cross-examination and the demeanor of the witness becomes an important element in the decisional process.

The advantages of the second desideratum, a court composed of relatively few members who have long-term appointments and always sit *en banc*, also needs little additional amplification. It would certainly bring greater predictability to any process of case-by-case adjudication. The question is whether it is a realizable objective when we consider international courts, particularly those with a broad geographic reach and exercising a jurisdiction that allows suits against sovereign states, even by a state's own citizens. It is natural for a state to want to have one of its own citizens sit on such a court and even to sit as of right on any panel of judges hearing a case that has been brought against it. Indeed, up until about fifty years ago, geographical representation was considered an important consideration in the appointment of persons to sit on the Supreme Court of the

---

2. Even in this situation it has been recently suggested that establishing "constitutional juries" in a country as large as Australia might be a way of deflecting countermajoritarian criticisms of judicial reviews. *See* Eric Ghosh, *Deliberative Democracy and the Countermajoritarian Difficulty: Considering Constitutional Juries*, 30 OXFORD J. LEGAL STUD. 327 (2010).

United States.[3] There is, of course, also a structural problem that, on the international level, makes the idea of a small court with limited turnover in personnel and which always sits *en banc* seem chimerical. The constantly expanding idea of what constitutes a human right together with the inevitable conflict between competing human rights or between accepted human rights and important state interests has led to an explosion of litigation at the international level. The European Court of Human Rights had, as of December 31, 2009, 119,300 pending applications, a 23 percent increase from January 1, 2009.[4] Even with forty-seven judges, it inevitably falls further and further behind. The ratification at long last of Protocol 14 to the European Convention on Human Rights and Fundamental Freedoms that enables individual judges to dispose of what might be considered frivolous or otherwise unmeritorious cases will obviously help, but clearly neither that authority nor other new provisions allowing summary disposition of applications on the merits can be expected to solve the basic problem.[5] This crush of litigation on a truly vast variety of issues is a very serious matter that also bears on the achievement of our first desideratum, namely the ability of a process of case-by-case adjudication to generate, over a relatively short time, a sufficient number of decisions on relatively similar factual situations in order to provide the certainty and predictability that we are seeking. This is the subject to which we shall now turn as we start to discuss the core of what a successful process of case-by-case adjudication requires.

For a judicial process to provide any degree of predictability of judicial decisions, it has to be committed at the very least to achieving consistency in the decisions generated by that process. When the process operates by a method of case-by-case adjudication, that process must adopt something like the common law principle of *stare decisis* and the insistence that factually similar cases must be treated alike. Ideally, this would entail that, unless overruled, for purposes of the future direction of the law the application of a supposed norm in a given case takes precedence over the underlying norm upon which that application was based; and those who insist that "rules" are the essential basic units of the law will have to accept that the content of the supposed underlying law changes in

---

3. Some kind of religious balance was also considered essential. Although the United States is still a majority Protestant country, with Justice Stevens' retirement, the Court, for the first time in its history, currently has no Protestant members.

4. Regularly updated figures are available on the Court's website, http://www.echr.coe.int under "Reports."

5. Article 7 of Protocol 14 amended the original Article 27 of the Convention to grant authority to a single judge to declare "individual applications" (i.e., non-governmental applications) inadmissible. Article 8 of the Protocol amended the original Article 28 of the Convention by providing that a committee of three judges may declare "individual applications" admissible and, at the same time, render a judgment on the merits "if the underlying question in the case is already the subject of well-established case-law of the Court."

the process of its being applied. In a common law country, the same process operates in the course of statutory interpretation where, at any given point of time, the judicial construction of the statute becomes as much a part of the statute as its original verbal formulation and, in a manner of speaking, becomes the statute. This focus on the cases interpreting and applying a general norm or rule entails that two otherwise similar cases cannot be decided differently unless it can convincingly be maintained that there are significant factual differences between the cases, preferably more than one such difference but at the very least one such significant factual difference. If the system is sufficiently long run there may even be a sufficient jurisprudence to enable decision makers to rely on decided cases in deciding what might be considered significant or (and often more helpfully) *not* significant differences in a wide variety of situations rather than merely to rely on their own common sense evaluation of the case before them and the cases to which the instant case is being compared. Since I have described at some length a model of this type of decision making elsewhere,[6] I will not, in this book, try to give a detailed explanation of how such a system actually would operate.

For our present purposes, it would be hard not to take as a starting point Justice Kennedy's observation that "[t]he lesson of historical practice . . . is most helpful and instructive when the circumstances of a case bear substantial parallels to litigation the courts have confronted before."[7] The more such cases there have been in the past, the greater the guidance to future courts and the ability of counsel to predict the likely outcome of future cases. That seems self-evident, but the method of case-by-case adjudication of contested human rights cases would also require a view of legal reasoning that to me seems most in accord with traditional practice but that, as we have already intimated,[8] many observers, perhaps even in common law countries, would find difficult to accept. That disagreement involves the question of what is eventually to be derived, even if only over long periods of time, from the examination of the mass of similar cases. For purposes of easy access to the cases by those who research legal issues, namely judges, academics, lawyers, and law students, one would certainly want to construct propositions that would serve as classification devices to facilitate the grouping together and retrieving of the cases that constitute the raw materials of the law. For ease of application, these generalizations would furthermore normally be formed in a way that they could serve as a means of predicting how hypothetical

---

6. *See* George C. Christie, *Objectivity in the Law*, 78 YALE L.J. 1311, 1333–50 (1969). A more compressed description may be found in GEORGE C. CHRISTIE,, THE NOTION OF AN IDEAL AUDIENCE IN LEGAL ARGUMENT 146–51 (2000).

7. eBay Inc. v. MercExchange, L.L.C., 547 U.S. 388, 396 (2006).

8. See our discussion in Chapter 9, *supra* at p. 121, where we noted that Dworkin and others may be overestimating what a process of case-by-case adjudication can deliver.

future cases would be decided. These observations about the practical or operational value of generalizations about the law are largely uncontroversial.

What is controversial, as I noted in the previous chapter, is the epistemological status of these eventual generalizations. Do they have independent normative significance and power? Or are they merely the linguistic expression of our system of classification and possibly also rules of thumb for quick reference in dealing with legal issues but with no superseding normative significance as is suggested by the fact that, as the law evolves, the content of these generalizations, the so-called rules of law, has to be adjusted to reflect the accumulated case law? In making this statement, I in no way mean to deny that in some areas of the law there are so many previously decided cases and, accordingly, so many rules of thumb that capture so much of the richness of the decided cases, that for all practical purposes they attain normative force, something like the definition in a prestigious dictionary of a standard term used in ordinary discourse. But, particularly in times of social change, legal propositions, like all linguistic expression, consciously or perhaps more often unconsciously, change in nuance and reach. This is particularly likely to occur when, as in the areas with which we are concerned, the conscientious decision of a case requires the consideration of a large number of factual issues of serious normative significance. Even in less controversial areas, as we noted in Chapter 9, there is some truth to the observation that sometimes a series of cases on the same subject can actually create more confusion than clarity in "the law."[9] Accepting this possibility, which can never be completely eliminated when conflicting basic values are constantly at stake, the normative element of a process of case-by-case adjudication is best captured in the requirement of consistency among the cases. As explained and stressed several times already, this means that unless the instant case presents a significant factual difference from the previously decided cases, it must be decided like the previous case. What is a significant difference is one that the person stressing that difference, whether he is an advocate or a judge or an academic observer, believes has already been determined by past cases to be significant or which he believes legally trained observers would accept as significant, or that he believes the ideal audience which he envisions, and perhaps refers to as the personification of "justice," would accept as significant. As pointed out earlier in this book, these beliefs necessarily depend on some sort of prediction of the reaction of the audience presupposed by the person expressing those beliefs. So long as one is talking about case-by-case adjudication as an ongoing process that has yet to reach its end-point, there is no other alternative.

What is accepted as significant will naturally also change over time. That is inevitable and is an important way in which the law can achieve social change. At one time, the difference between male and female was considered significant for

---

9. *See* Anthony D'Amato, *Legal Uncertainty*, 71 CAL. L. REV. 1 (1983).

all sorts of important functions, such as voting or serving on juries or practicing law or even controlling one's own property. That has changed, and thankfully so, over time. Nevertheless, in the operation of a system such as the one being described, if one gives some priority to predictability of result, one must also accept Justice Brandeis' observation that "in most matters it is more important that the applicable rule of law be settled than that it be settled right."[10] To quote Justice Breyer, "[t]o overturn a decision . . . simply because we might believe that decision is no longer 'right' would inevitably reflect a willingness to reconsider others. And that willingness could itself threaten to substitute disruption, confusion, and uncertainty for necessary legal stability."[11] Justice Breyer described this legal stability in a later case as being the base "upon which the rule of law depends" and as something which must endure "whether judicial methods of interpretation change or stay the same."[12] In recent times, certainly the refusal of Justices O'Connor and Kennedy in the *Casey*[13] case to overrule *Roe v. Wade*,[14] a decision of which they both disapproved, was based on such a view.

That is not to say that precedent must be followed regardless. Sometimes it may be felt necessary to overrule a body of cases and start all over again. The House of Lords did this in the not too distant past, as noted earlier in Chapter 7, in the economic loss cases where it implicitly but very obviously rejected Dworkin's expansive view of the "principle" underlying tort liability.[15] More recently, in the *Citizens United*[16] case, the Supreme Court of the United States, despite over a century of legislative practice and several of its own decisions in the last decades of the twentieth century, held that statutory restrictions on campaign expenditures by for-profit corporations were unconstitutional. What is accepted in all such instances is that the departure from precedent must be justified. The same may be said for any major departure, even by a "higher" court, from what has been widely accepted as settled law based on decisions of a court of lesser hierarchical status. An illustration is the Privy Council's rejection, in the first *Wagon Mound*[17] case, of the theory of causation enunciated in the *Polemis*[18] case on the ground that that judicial landmark was based on a shaky

---

10. Burnet v. Coronado Oil & Gas Co., 285 U.S. 393, 406 (1932) (Brandeis, J., dissenting).
11. John R. Sand & Gravel Co. v. U.S., 552 U.S. 130, 139 (2008).
12. CBOCS West, Inc. v. Humphries, 128 S. Ct. 1951, 1961 (2008).
13. *See* Planned Parenthood of SE Pa. v. Casey, 505 U.S. 833, 866–69 (1992).
14. 410 U.S. 113 (1973).
15. *See* pp. 92–93, *supra*.
16. Citizens United v. Federal Election Commission, 130 S. Ct. 876 (2010) [hereafter *Citizens United*].
17. Overseas Tankship (U.K.) Ltd. v. Morts Dock and Engineering Co., Ltd. (The Wagon Mound), [1961] A.C. 388 (P.C.).
18. *In re* an Arbitration between Polemis and Furness, Withy & Co., [1921] K.B. 560 (C.A.).

precedential basis, that its doctrine was unworkable as evidenced by its often being honored in the breach rather than the observance, and finally that it led to arbitrary and unjust results. Ideally, the occasions requiring such an extreme volte-face in the law should be rather few. The world changes and the law must therefore also change, but a law whose content constantly changes is no law, but merely the set of individual directives through which power is exercised. As has been pointed out so often that it needs no citation of authority, law and society will always be somewhat out of synchronization even in relatively placid times, let alone the turbulent and dynamic period in which we now live.

The *Citizens United* case is worth examining in some detail not merely because it departed from past practices. Its greater significance for our purposes lies in the fact that it involved core aspects of freedom of expression and raises the possibility that some types of controversy over the reach of the guarantee of the right of freedom of expression may not be capable of judicial resolution by any practically achievable process of case-by-case adjudication. Citizens United was a nonprofit corporation and as such, unlike a for-profit corporation, could make election expenditures. Citizens United, by means of video on demand, wished to distribute, within the statutorily proscribed 30-day period before a primary, a 90-minute film called *Hillary: The Movie*, which was highly critical of Mrs. Clinton, who was at the time seeking to be the Democratic candidate for president of the Unites States in the 2008 election. Because, however, some of the funding for the production and distribution of the movie came from for-profit corporations, Citizens United sought and was denied a ruling that its conduct was constitutionally protected. Eventually the case reached the Supreme Court.

The *Citizens United* case involved the interrelation of a number of provisions of what, to say the least, was a very complex statutory regime. The most important provisions in dispute involved those prohibiting contributions or expenditures by any for-profit corporation or labor union in connection with any federal election or in the primaries, caucuses, or conventions in which candidates for those elections were selected.[19] These prohibitions included the making by for-profit corporations and labor unions of what were called "electioneering communications," defined as "any broadcast, cable or satellite communication which refers to a clearly identifiable candidate" made within 60 days of a general election or within 30 days of a primary, caucus, or other selection process.[20] Broadcast media were exempted from such restrictions even though they were owned by

---

19. 2 U.S.C. § 441b (2006). In a prior case, the Court had held that this prohibition was unconstitutional insofar as it was not limited to the "functional equivalent of express advocacy . . . [of a] vote for or against a specific candidate." Federal Election Commission v. Wisconsin Right to Life, Inc., 551 U.S. 449, 469–70 (2007). In *Citizens United* the Court held that *Hillary: The Movie* was such "express advocacy." *Citizens United* at 889–90. Citizens United had argued that the movie was a documentary.

20. 2 U.S.C. § 434 (f) (3) (A) (i).

for-profit corporations so long as they were not owned or controlled by "a political party, a political committee, or candidate."[21] Communications by nonprofit corporations such as Citizens United were likewise not treated as prohibited "electioneering communications" if their funds came from "individuals" who were citizens or nationals of the United States or persons admitted for permanent residency in the United States.[22] Persons whose communications were considered permissible "electioneering communications" were, however, subject to various disclosure and disclaimer requirements. Accordingly, if the Court struck down the prohibitions on contributions or expenditures by for-profit corporations, Citizens United would be required to disclose the name of the for-profit corporations from which it had received funding. That part of the underlying statute was also attacked by Citizens United.[23] In a five-to-four decision on the most controversial issue in the case, the Court held that a for-profit corporation enjoyed the same freedom of speech regarding independent election expenditures as a nonprofit corporation and indeed any other entity, natural or not, that had legal personality. The Court upheld the disclosure and disclaimer requirements, however, with only Justice Thomas in dissent.

The opinion of the Court was written by Justice Kennedy. The dissent written by Justice Stevens was joined by the three other dissenters. The dissent argued that precedent required the contrary result. The majority responded that the earlier cases were incorrectly decided and furthermore led to increased uncertainty in the law. To this argument the dissent argued that, although its members would have still dissented, at the very least the majority should have decided the case on narrower grounds and, in a controversial area such as this, the narrowest possible grounds.[24] One such ground would have been that the statute was not primarily aimed at feature-length films, but rather at spot advertisements on television and therefore the Court's decision should have been confined to the particular facts before the Court. This is a legitimate point because the essence of case-by-case adjudication is that courts should, when possible, decide on narrower rather than on broader grounds in order not to hinder the future gradual evolution of the law and thereby increase the pressure for abrupt changes in the law as social conditions change. The majority did not dispute this basic postulate of case-by-case adjudication and accepted the need to justify departures from it, as the House of Lords had done when it rejected the causal theory espoused in the *Polemis* case.

---

21. *Id.* at § 434 (f) (3) (B) (i).
22. *Id.* at § 441b (c) (2).
23. The FEC claimed the authority under the statute to exempt nonprofit corporations, such as Citizens United, from providing the disclosures normally required but, after an attempt to exercise that authority was successfully challenged in Shays v. FEC, 337 F. Supp. 2d 28, 124–29 (D.D.C. 2004), the FEC abandoned the effort.
24. *Citizens United* at 936–38.

The majority argued that the Court's prior decisions ratifying the policy of restricting independent election expenditures by for-profit corporations had not only been wrongly decided but were also of relatively recent origin. The majority noted that the argument that the statute was aimed at combating corruption or the appearance of corruption in the election process was not pressed by the government. They also noted that 26 states, something more than half of the states, did not restrict independent expenditures by for-profit corporations and there was no claim by the government that elections in those states were more corrupt than in states where they were forbidden.[25] Indeed, the dissenters' claim that business corporations and even foreign business corporations would have a major influence in elections seems exaggerated. Four members of the majority and all four of the dissenters agreed on the constitutionality of the statute's requirement 1) of some disclosure of the sources funding electioneering expenditures, and 2) that all electioneering communications by political committees through any type of public advertisement and, in the case of a communication paid by other entities, any such communication advocating the election or defeat of a clearly identified candidate, must disclose not only the entity that paid for the communication but also a statement that the communication is not authorized "by any candidate or candidate's committee."[26] Given the skittishness of American corporations with public stockholders and a broad customer base to putting anything in their advertisements that might offend an even arguably appreciable segment of the public, the claim that the Court's decision opened the way for business corporations to materially influence federal elections seems misplaced. If corporate election expenditures are the concern, the problem arises primarily with regard to privately held corporations and is the same as that presented by the election expenditures of wealthy individuals and non-profit corporations supposedly funded by the dues or contributions of their members, including corporate members. The obvious remedy to the dangers presented by all these types of political expenditures is to strengthen disclosure requirements so that the public is made aware, in a timely manner, of who is financing large election expenditures. It is somewhat hyperbolic to claim that the Court's decision might indirectly open the way for foreign corporations to influence federal elections. To posit that the American subsidiaries of Deutsche Bank or UBS or BMW would wish to be seen as trying to do so is scarcely credible.[27] This is one of many reasons why the Court could be said to have been

---

25. *Id.* at 908–09.
26. 2 U.S.C. §§ 437 (f) (2), 441d (a) (3). Furthermore, all such communications made by radio or television must contain an oral statement and with regard to television communications also a written statement that they are or are not authorized by a candidate. *Id.* at § 441d (d) (1) and (2).
27. While the Court struck down the distinction between corporate speech and individual speech, it in no way indicated that the prohibition against any contributions, directly or indirectly by *any* foreign national in connection with *any* federal, state, or local election

justified in ignoring the corporate governance issue despite the fact that it was also one of the arguments stressed by the dissent.[28] If that argument were to be taken seriously, individual stockholders should be able to challenge and even block a corporation's use of treasury funds for charitable contributions to organizations that provide abortion counseling and services.

In this book I am not concerned with whether restrictions on independent election expenditures by for-profit corporations are or are not good public policy. What I am concerned with is how, if at all, the difficult questions raised by any such regulatory regime can be adequately managed by a process of case-by-case adjudication. Perhaps the most salient and difficult issue in this entire litigation was the crazy-quilt nature of the statutory regulation. It is the obvious complexity and in some ways inconsistent character of the legislative scheme in question that gives the greatest practical support to the majority's resort to a bright-line approach that clearly privileged freedom of expression over all other considerations.[29] For example, the disclosure requirements did not apply to the broadcast media. Furthermore, despite the fact that all the major broadcast media are owned by for-profit corporations, the prohibitions on election expenditures by for-profit corporations applied neither to them nor to the print media defined as including newspaper, magazines, or other periodical publications not owned or controlled by a political party, political committee, or candidate.[30] Like the broadcast media, all these entities, even if owned by for-profit corporations, could endorse candidates. Why the media should be so privileged raises many intriguing issues. Surely no one ever accused Fox News, owned by the Murdoch interests, of an exaggerated sense of impartiality; and of course there is the even more fundamental question of what entities were included in the term media and why

---

was constitutionally suspect. As regards whether contribution by American subsidiaries of foreign corporations could now engage in making election expenditures in connection with federal elections one would presume that the Federal Election Commission would follow the approach it has taken to such expenditures by American subsidiaries of foreign corporations in state and local elections when allowed under state law, namely to permit them if no foreign national exercises decision-making authority over the contribution and if the funds are not provided or reimbursed by the foreign parent. *See* JAN BITOLD BARAN, THE ELECTION LAW PRIMER FOR CORPORATIONS 75 (5th ed. 2008), citing FEC Advisory Opinion 1989-29 and other earlier advisory opinions. It should be noted that, in the dissent, Justice Stevens opined that "the majority's reasoning would appear to afford the same protection to multinational corporations controlled by foreigners as to individual Americans." *Citizens United* at 947–48.

28. *Id.* at 977–79.

29. In an op-ed piece in the *Wall Street Journal*, eight former Commissioners of the Federal Election Commission referred to an *amicus curiae* brief they had submitted in the *Citizens United* case in which they noted that "the FEC now has regulations for 33 types of contributions and speech and 71 different types of speakers." Joan Aikens et al., *Chuck Schumer vs. Free Speech*, WALL ST. J., May 19, 2010, at A19.

30. 2 U.S.C. § 431 (9) (B).

the media should now enjoy special privileges that are not enjoyed by others. Would a widely and regularly distributed newsletter published by a group supported, in whole or in part, by for-profit corporations qualify as a periodical? The somewhat inflammatory and certainly extreme newsletter published by the John Birch Society that was at issue in the *Gertz*[31] case comes to mind as an example of what such a publication might look like. If the media are to enjoy special privileges, should courts then use the notion of "responsible journalism" developed by some common law jurisdictions to ameliorate the rigors of the traditional law of defamation to decide which types of mass communications media are sufficiently "responsible" to qualify for the "media" exemption? The notion of "responsible journalism" was developed in an area in which the expression in question was accepted as being false. Whether it can also be used to determine what truthful communication can survive a privacy challenge will be discussed in the next chapter.[32] For the moment, it suffices to ask who has ever thought that, in a democratic society, the state could establish criteria for determining what is "responsible" electioneering rhetoric by an avenue of mass communication or anyone else, much less enforce those criteria. There is an even more troublesome feature of the legislative scheme at issue, namely that corporately owned publishers of books were not granted the exemption afforded to media. The government in oral argument accepted that, if it had tried to apply the prohibition to books, the publisher would have a "good as applied challenge."[33] Finally, one might note that the rapidly changing technology of mass communication makes many of these attempts to control any kind of expression of questionable value. Is a blog controlled by or supported by a for-profit corporation entitled to be treated as part of the media?

The basic question with which we are concerned here is how one can make any of these distinctions in the United States when, as just indicated, the Court, on the few situations in which it had to decide the issue, has held that the media have no superior expressive rights than any other persons or entities.[34] The dissenters tried to address this issue in several indirect ways. The prohibitions only applied for a limited time and there were other avenues for some roughly equivalent communication because the election laws permitted the formation of political action committees. These are separately established entities funded by "voluntary" contributions from the shareholders and employees of a corporation—in practice, largely relatively senior executives—or from the members of a labor union. These so-called PACs cannot only make independent election expenditures but can also, subject to contribution limits, even contribute directly

---

31. Gertz v. Robert Welch, Inc., 418 U.S. 323 (1974).
32. *See* p. 153, *infra*.
33. *Citizens United* at 904.
34. *See*, e.g., Dun and Bradstreet, Inc. v. Greenmoss Builders, Inc., 472 U.S. 749 (1985); Branzburg v. Hayes, 408 U.S. 665 (1972).

to the campaigns of individual candidates. This is certainly a somewhat, but not completely, comparable avenue of expression but, to the extent it is comparable, it does suggest that the danger of permitting for-profit corporations and labor unions to make independent election expenditures is overrated. For our present purposes, what is most troubling is the admission of Justice Stevens who wrote the principal dissent that, while freedom of expression was an important value, it was not the only value at stake and that therefore some accommodation had to be made, even if there was some restriction on expression.[35] This hint that the Court might be prepared to accept some inroads on the current near-total primacy of expression over other basic social values in the United States suggests that, like its European counterparts, the Court might conceivably be prepared to engage in the type of analysis that we shall discuss in the next chapter when we return to discussing how to resolve the conflicts between the supposedly equally important rights of expression and privacy, as well as conflicts between expression and important state interests. What I shall do in the remainder of this chapter is present the argument that, even if it were possible over time to design a method of case-by-case adjudication to resolve those conflicts, the attempt to use those same methods to solve the current controversies about election expenses is much more difficult and, arguably, impossible.[36] In trying to make this argument, I in no way want to be thought of as not taking seriously the fact that many responsible observers, foreign as well as American, have decried the expenditures of vast amounts of money in American election campaigns. These critical reactions are understandable and not without substantial merit. The question is what can be done about the situation in the light of the current state of the law and, even more importantly, the basic political structure of the United States.

Given the express language of the First Amendment to the United States Constitution that "Congress shall make no law abridging the freedom of speech or the press," one might have thought that almost any attempt to restrict either election contributions or expenditures would be bound to fail.[37] We have seen, however, that this has not proved to be the case. As noted in the series of cases described in the *Citizens United* case, the Court had struck down most expenditure limitations as restrictions of speech but had upheld limitations on campaign

---

35. *Citizens United* at 945–48.
36. In Gideon v. Wainwright, 372 U.S. 335 (1963), the Court overruled its prior decision in which it had held that the obligation to provide indigents with counsel in felony cases depended on "special circumstances." The Court instead adopted a blanket requirement for providing counsel to indigents in all felony cases because, as noted by Harlan, J., in his concurring opinion, *id.* at 348–52, that standard was administratively complex and produced inconsistent results. *See also* Jerold H. Israel, Gideon v. Wainwright: *The Art of Overruling*, 1963 SUP. CT. REV. 211, 222.
37. For a recent defense of a fairly absolute interpretation of the First Amendment, *see* DAVID L. LANGE & H. JEFFERSON POWELL, NO LAW (2009).

contributions. In our discussion of the *Citizens United* case, we saw that, if there were to be any expenditure limitations, the enormous number of seemingly minor but legally significant factual differences that would arise in the application of such a regime would tax the ability of any court trying to exercise the tight control mandated by the constitutional protection of expression, at least if it were to behave like a court rather than some administrative agency whose decisions are only reviewable by Congress and then not on all issues. It should be noted that, despite the expedited process of review provided in the legislation,[38] the *Citizens United* case, begun in December 2007, was not decided until over two years later, in 2010. Some of the delay was the result of the Court's insistence on re-argument but, even without re-argument, the case would probably not have been decided before June 2009, long after the general election of November 2008, let alone the primary elections in the first few months of 2008 with which the expression in question was concerned. Only an administrative agency totally committed to election issues could deal with such a case-load. Moreover, many of those cases will involve serious constitutional questions that cannot be definitively resolved by an administrative body or, at least, most certainly should not.

To examine the types of issues that might arise in trying to resolve those types of potential constitutional issues, it may be helpful to examine how a few of these seemingly administrative issues have been handled by the Court in a case decided in 2006[39] that involved both expenditure and contribution limitations imposed by the state of Vermont. As might have been expected, the Court struck down the expenditure limitations but this time it also struck down the contribution limitations on the ground that the limits set by the Vermont legislature were too low. These limits were $400 for contributions to candidates for statewide offices and lesser amounts for contributions to candidates for election to Vermont's bicameral legislature. Similar limits on contributions to individual candidates by political parties were also struck down. The dissenters pointed out that given Vermont's small population—estimated in 2005 by the Census Bureau as roughly 623,000—the limits were not that low and, furthermore, were higher on a per capita basis than those imposed by a number of other states.[40] Somewhat curious was the comment in Justice Stevens' dissent that "[j]ust as a driver need not use a Hummer to reach her destination, so a candidate need not flood the airways with ceaseless sound-bites of trivial information in order to provide voters with reasons to support her."[41] Although the American philosopher John Rawls has expressed similar thoughts, and remarks about the low value of material printed in tabloids have been expressed in judgments of the European Court

---

38. 2 U.S.C. § 437h (2006).

39. Randall v. Sorrel, 548 U.S. 230 (2006).

40. *Id.* at 284–85 (Souter, J., joined by Stevens and Ginsburg, J.J., the two other dissenters).

41. *Id.* at 277.

of Human Rights, it is very surprising to find them in the opinions of justices of the United States Supreme Court. Moving on, however, the main point is obvious: When a court, such as the United States Supreme Court, is considering whether a $400 contribution limitation for state wide elections is too low as a matter of constitutional law but a $500 limitation is perhaps not, surely we have reached the point where courts are acting more like administrative bodies charged with implementing the policy decisions of the body politic than they are like courts in the traditional sense.

The need to construct a regime that is largely administrative because it involves a potentially large number of specific issues that must be decided within a limited period of time, and yet require access to courts because so many of these issues involve serious constitutional questions, makes the task of constructing a satisfactory regime of election-financing in the United States practically impossible. The impossibility arises, in part, from the large size of the election districts in the United States. That such large election districts would probably favor the well-off and well-connected members of society was recognized even before the Constitution was ratified and entered into force. In the ratification debates in the separate states, two recurrent issues were raised concerning the proposed House of Representatives: The first, which is no longer of any concern, was that the representatives would have two-year terms, whereas the then almost universal practice in the states was for annual elections of state legislators and of governors as well.[42] The second issue was the size of the electoral districts. In sharp contrast to the ratio of legislators to inhabitants in the states, the United States Constitution provided for a ratio of one to thirty thousand.[43] Representation in the Senate was not an issue at that time because, until

---

42. All of the thirteen original states, other than South Carolina provided for annual elections at the time the Constitution of the United States was being drafted. *See* GORDON S.WOOD, THE CREATION OF THE AMERICAN REPUBLIC 166 (1969). The common mantra was "Where Annual Election ends, Tyranny begins." *See ibid.*

43. This was the result of a "last-minute" amendment of the proposed Constitution shortly before its adoption by the Constitutional Convention on September 17, 1787. The first apportionment was actually made, however, on the basis of one to 40,000 inhabitants as provided in the draft presented to the convention. Under that apportionment, the membership of the original House of Representatives was 65 once all the states ratified the Constitution. U.S. CONST. Art. 1, § 2, ¶3. Virginia which, as the most populous state was allocated ten members, had a legislature whose lower house in 1773 had a membership of 122. Massachusetts, which was one of several states which were allocated eight members, is recorded as having had a legislature whose lower house had 117 members in 1765. *See* Jackson T. Main *Government by the People, the Americanization and the Democratization of the Legislature.* WM. AND MARY Q., 3d Series, 23 at 391, 396–97 (1966). Melancton Smith, a delegate to the "Convention of the State of New York on the Adoption of the Federal Constitution," was one of many people opposing the ratification of the proposed United States Constitution who stressed the anti-democratic and aristocratic concentration of legislative power in the hands of a few people. *See* THE ANTI-FEDERALIST

the ratification of the Seventeenth Amendment in 1913, senators were chosen by the legislatures of the several states. At present, the number of representatives is 435. With a population estimated as being about 305,000,000 in 2009, that makes an average of one representative for each 690,000 inhabitants. If the ratio of representatives to inhabitants were determined on the basis used in France or the United Kingdom, the United States House of Representatives would have over 3,000 members. In such a body, the individual members would have very little power. Even the promise of government office is of limited use in keeping the members of Congress "on side" because the Constitution prohibits any member of the Congress from serving at the same time in any civil office of the United States nor, should the member resign, may he be appointed to any office created during that member's present term.[44] Any power exercised by the body would have to be by some central committee or by some form of strict party discipline. The latter as a practical matter is not possible. In the United States the national parties are weak and the state parties are in many instances even weaker. In the states that select candidates by primary elections, all an individual typically needs to do to be a candidate is to register himself as a member of the party in whose primary he wishes to enter, fulfill the age and residence requirements applicable to the position sought, and pay the requisite registration fee.[45] From then on it is a free-for-all. There is no central party elite, either on a federal or state level, that can effectively control the process.

In the Senate, all the factors that favor the well-off or the famous or incumbents are present, in most cases to a considerably greater extent. The extreme example is California with an estimated population of 36 million in 2009. At the other extreme, the population of Wyoming in 2009 was estimated at approximately 510,000. Both states are entitled to two senators chosen on a statewide basis. It would be very difficult for anyone in a state with a large area and large population to be elected a senator unless he were very rich or very famous. The public funding of candidates at any but the general elections would be practically impossible. Given the open structure of American politics which with its powerful national legislature and, despite its size, considerable sensitivity to local sentiment, the present somewhat anarchic election procedure on which it is based

---

342–46 (Herbert J. Storing ed. 1985). *See also id.* at 73–79 (letter vii of The Federal Farmer).

44. *Id.* at U.S. CONST. Art. I, § 6, ¶2. Should he resign, the same provision forbids appointing a member of Congress to any office the "Emoluments" of which were increased during his term. It has been feasible to avoid that problem by passing legislation freezing the pay for the office at the level that existed before any increase was approved during the member's term of office.

45. In North Carolina, the filing fee for all state or county offices and for U.S. Senate or House of Representatives is 1% of the annual salary of the position in question. N.C. GEN. STAT. ANNOT. § 163–107 (2009).

has its merits. Moreover, as President Obama has shown, with the advent of the Internet, it is not impossible for someone who can create at least some public notoriety for himself to raise the vast sum needed to run for major offices in the United States from the public at large without the need to rely so heavily on the rich and powerful. President Obama, it should also be recalled, refused to accept the available federal funding for the general election of 2008 because to do so would have limited his expenditures to the amount of the government grant. If such efforts to obtain mass public financial support become more widespread and effective, we might be able to ameliorate the current problem and rely instead on instant disclosure of sums greater than some de minimis amount and, at least within some reasonable period before an election, the names of those financing independent election expenditures, a requirement that eight of the justices who decided the *Citizens United* case found to be clearly constitutional.

Being realistic, even if it were logically possible to make a clear distinction between the judicial and administrative roles, it would be difficult to enforce such a distinction in practice however much one believed that courts have no business getting involved in anything resembling the day-to-day administration of public affairs. There are always extreme circumstances that may require some departures from accepted customary practice. In the United States, there certainly have been situations in which the courts have assumed regular administration functions generally performed by other branches of government. The most important and, undoubtedly, best known is the use of federal courts to implement the United States Supreme Court's decision in *Brown v. Board of Education*[46] that maintaining segregated public schools was unconstitutional. The federal district courts spent decades dealing with issues such as compulsory busing and student assignment within a school district. Some of this judicial supervision still continues. Other examples of courts having assumed administrative functions include litigation concerning prison conditions and in litigation involving legislative apportionment, when state legislatures were unable to act or, when they did act, came up with plans for legislative apportionment that did not meet constitutional criteria established by the Supreme Court. In such circumstances, courts, often the federal courts, became obliged to prescribe the appropriate prison conditions or to delineate the election districts. In both of these situations, as in the school desegregation cases, the primary role of the lower courts was not so much the interpretation and making of law but employing the prestige of courts and often the powers of the federal government to enforce compliance with law laid down by the United States Supreme Court or the highest court in the states in question. The expectation moreover was that once compliance was obtained, the role of the courts in continual administration would be reduced if not even completely eliminated. There is no such reachable

---

46. Brown v. Board of Education of Topeka, 347 U.S. 483 (1954).

goal in the election cases if the Court is not prepared to abdicate its role as the guardian of the First Amendment by accepting any plausible reasonable argument in favor of limiting campaign financing. Unless, or more hopefully until, the technological developments noted earlier largely moot the importance of the issues involved, or, less likely, Congress can come up with a less complex and more justifiable scheme for regulating contributions and expenditures in federal elections, the Court might have no alternative but to abide by the bright-line test articulated in *Citizens United*. Fortunately, at least in the United States, for the moment, dealing with quasi-administrative tasks has not been the major concern that the recognition of welfare rights would entail.[47]

---

47. At the state level, the recognition by some state supreme courts that some minimal level of state support for public education was required by the state constitution obliged the lower state courts to implement decisions ordering the state either to take measures to equalize the amount of money available to each of the school districts in the state or even to increase the funds available for primary and secondary education. The latter is a particularly difficult problem since, on the state as well as the federal level, only the legislature can authorize expenditures. These cases can become extremely controversial and can lead to solutions that do not fully satisfy anyone. *See* Mary J. Amos, Comment: Derolph v. State: *Who Really Won Ohio's State Funding Battle?* 30 Cap. U.L. Rev. 153 (2002). *See also* Larry J. Obhof, *Rethinking Judicial Activism and Restraint in School Finance Litigation*, 27 Harv.J.L. & Pub. Pol'y 569 (2004). One difference between the United States and some European countries is that the United States Supreme Court has not recognized any constitutionally based welfare rights. *See* Dandridge v. Williams, 397 U.S. 471 (1970). Even the dissenters in that case only took issues with the majority on the issue of whether the courts were precluded from ruling on how funds provided for needy families with dependent children were allocated, not on the quantum of funds provided for the program. The plan upheld by the majority allocated funds per family, per child until six children. The dissenters thought the available funds should be allocated solely per child. At the other end of the spectrum is the jurisprudence of the Federal Constitutional Court of which its decision in the *Hartz IV* case, BVerfG, 1BvL from 9.2.2010 is an important illustration. In that case, the Court ruled that the standard benefits provided under the new provisions of the Social Code did not meet the subsistence minimum in line with human dignity required by Art.1.1. of the Basic Law.

11. CASE-BY-CASE ADJUDICATION OF CONTENTIOUS HUMAN RIGHTS CONTROVERSIES

In the preceding chapter, we noted that the process of developing a consistent legal framework in any area of the law by a case-by-case process of adjudication is greatly facilitated if the legal system can generate a large number of cases with a high degree of similar facts over a relatively short period of time. This endeavor will be materially advanced if two other factors are present. The first is an accepted clear and relatively concrete objective for the area of the law in question. The second is the nature of the factual issues that the courts are required to resolve. The more concrete and narrowly focused these issues are, the greater the likelihood that a case-by-case process of adjudication will be able to achieve satisfactory results. Take a case involving commercial matters. Contractual and other forms of commercial legal arrangements have as a goal the facilitating of commercial activity, including of course limiting transaction costs and doing so in a socially acceptable manner. Indeed, if there is any area where consistency and predictability of results are perhaps even the predominant values, this is it. The goals of this area of the law are widely accepted as the appropriate ones and the factual issues involved are relatively narrow, at least in comparison with those raised by the types of human rights litigation upon which we have been focusing. The comparative clarity and consistency of application of law in the commercial area is more than adequate testimony to the tremendous assistance that a process of case-by-case adjudication provides when it operates in an area of the law where the social goals are widely accepted, narrowly defined, and dependent on a comparatively narrow range of relatively concrete factual issues.

Something of the same can be said in the major areas of traditional tort law. The social goal is redress for physical injury to person or property and, nowadays, for emotional harm suffered by a human being from a reasonable fear of serious bodily injury to himself or a loved one. The factual question of what is physical injury is not always clear but it is certainly a fairly concrete issue compared to the potential damage to a state's interest in preserving a secular order or the damage to a person's interest in privacy if activities conducted in public are revealed to a wider audience. Furthermore, the question of fault that is encapsulated in the terms "tort" and "delict" normally turns on matters as to which people largely agree on the appropriate legal criteria, such as an intent to injure or a reckless or blamable failure to foresee possible physical injury to others. In this area, moreover, there will be no shortage of cases arising over a very short period of time for the courts to fine-tune the applicable law in these areas. The insurance industry obviously presupposes, with good reason, that this is in fact the case.

To a greater or lesser degree, all the features just mentioned are obviously not present in the areas of the law which have served as the principal focus of this book. The goal of maintaining and furthering a democratic society is very amorphous and quite abstract. It is not of course that anyone would doubt that this is the bedrock of contemporary society. The problem is that rational and sensible people have different notions of the ideal audience to which they are addressing their words and actions when, as judges, they try to justify their decisions that some particular measure that restricts some accepted right is or is not "necessary" in a democratic society. As applied in the cases we have been discussing, what is necessary in a democratic society has obviously been dependent on the resolution of many contested value questions that cannot in any concrete sense be reduced to anything that would satisfy our notion of what it means for something to be a factual question. In short, the enormous range of disagreement about so many value-laden issues in a potentially infinite range of factual situations presents real difficulties. This is particularly true of many disputes about privacy issues or about what are the threats to social order posed by various types of speech or social practice. Because so many issues of values are involved, we find ourselves in a world that is achieving greater economic harmony but, from a social perspective, is becoming more heterogeneous. The achievement of a world of relatively clear human rights in such an environment by a process of case-by-case ad hoc balancing will not be easy.

Among the difficult types of cases that must be handled by courts through a process of case-by-case adjudication, let us start with those in which freedom of expression, or freedom of religion that is manifested in ways that are not simply speech, is curtailed to advance some particular social good. The most easily justifiable of such restrictions is the suppression of expressive activities whose aim is the instigation of immediate violence against individuals or property or the immediate violent overthrow of the state. No society can exist for long without suppressing such expressive activity and surely no one other than a revolutionary, or an anarchist who totally rejects the legitimacy of any state-like apparatus, would object to such prohibitions. The difficult issues in these cases are in a sense largely both linguistic and factual. On the linguistic level, what is meant by "advocacy" or by "violence" or the phrase "immediate or imminent violence," and when does a challenged expression actually advocate such violence against an individual or the apparatus of government? On the more factual level, even if the expression in question might plausibly be said to advocate violence, how likely is it that the expression in question could possibly lead to such violent consequences so as to be taken seriously? These are all issues that lend themselves to a process of case-by-case adjudication. As to these sorts of issues, it would also be the process which most people would admit is the one most capable of achieving the reasonable objectivity and predictability to which judicial decision making ideally aspires.

The issue is whether this degree of objectivity and predictability can be achieved when the reason for restricting speech is the more subjective determination that it attacks a supposedly fundamental value such as secularism or that it proposes, albeit in a non-violent manner, some fundamental social change such as the repeal of all or some of the provisions of the European Convention on Human Rights or of similar provisions of the United States Constitution. Likewise, if the state is prepared to permit people to wear clothes with offensive or vulgar statements imprinted on them or to go around scantily clad or possibly even naked, why should it forbid religiously motivated people from wearing certain types of clothing that conceal more of the body than some people believe is appropriate? The only conceivable justification based on a concern for public safety that might plausibly be given for outlawing the wearing of the burqa in public, as in legislation now pending in Belgium and recently enacted in France,[1] is to protect against suicide bombers. If that were the reason, then the wearing of all bulky clothing in public should be banned. Moreover, the usual concrete reason given for banning the burqa is that it hides a woman's face, not that it covers her body in a bulky envelope. To say that one is protecting "secularism" is not all that satisfactory. What exactly is secularism, and what is realistically likely to be an "imminent" danger to it? A case-by-case process of adjudication would have to labor hard to produce a convincing and precise enough jurisprudence to allow the courts to escape the criticism that they have eviscerated the heart of what are accepted as fundamental human rights by serving as a rubber stamp for the decisions of political actors who attempt to restrain the exercise of such freedoms. And more fundamentally, why should the freedom of expression not include the freedom to advocate a theocracy? Are the courts to decide which changes of government structure are permissible and which are not? If one accepts that peaceful criticism of government is permitted, why should peaceful advocacy of change of governmental structure through the use of existing, legally available methods be proscribed, such as amendment of national constitutions in the legally prescribed manner? A similar criticism can be made of the criminalization of public expression that most of us would assert flies in the face of historical fact, such as the denial of the Holocaust. Perhaps at one time such a denial could arguably be linked to an imminent attempt to overthrow post-World War II democratically established governments, but surely no one can make that claim today. If the justification of such laws against the denial of the Holocaust are based on the offense they inflict to the feelings of large portions of the citizenry, it would surely be difficult to refuse to prosecute expression that is deemed blasphemous or otherwise offensive by a significant portion of society but not by a traditional majority. The attempt to suppress such speech brings back memories of the time when people were punished in England for denying the existence of the Trinity or the

---

1. The bill passed the lower house of the Belgian Parliament on April 29, 2010, and is expected to be passed by the upper house later in 2010. *See* Kayvan Frazaneh, *Foreign Policy: Europe's Burqa Wars*, NPR.org, May 12, 2010, http://www.npr.org/templates/story/story.php?storyId=126772691. The French law is Loi 2010-161 du 14 septembre 2010.

necessity of an episcopal religious regime on the ground that eliminating bishops would ultimately undermine the established monarchical order.

In the absence of an objectively discernable incitement to violence, one may well question whether judges are in any position to say what speech can be proscribed. There is, moreover, a certain arbitrariness to all these probations. As we have already noted, many religions popular in the Western world deny certain facts about the world, and its history and origin, that the large majority of educated people think are undeniably and even demonstrably true. No one would dream of putting in jail someone who denied the validity of the evidence pointing to the evolutionary development of life, even if widespread adoption of that view actually might have deleterious material consequences on education and many scientific endeavors. If the courts are not prepared to accept such measures, were they to be attempted, why should they accept such restrictions regarding denial of the Holocaust or other historic events absent some convincing evidence of a real threat of social violence? In the United States, some people think that the CIA instigated the assassination of President John Kennedy and some people even think that the CIA was responsible for engineering the disasters of "9/11," but there is no danger that the republic will not survive despite those assertions. Absent some real concrete present threat to public order, to have courts blithely accept political decisions as to what beliefs can be expressed in public is to cheapen the authority of courts. Surely a proportionality test would require a more detailed examination of means and ends and the feasibility of using less drastic means for achieving the desired end. To have courts themselves decide case by case what is or is not a belief that can be publicly expressed without a judicial finding of imminent threat to public order borders on the intolerable in a free society.

The types of difficult cases that, given the present state of society, are likely to occur most often are of course those in which courts are forced to decide which of two competing fundamental human rights, of supposedly equal value, should prevail in disputes between private parties. These are the cases that test most dramatically our notions of the appropriate role of courts in human rights adjudication. We have thus been focusing the major part of that discussion on the conflict between the right of freedom of expression and the right to respect for one's private life. These largely involve conflicts between individuals rather than conflicts that are primarily between the state and some of its citizens. As we have seen, the natural and indeed inevitable tendency is for courts to divide each of these categories, particularly speech, into several sub-categories, some of which will end up giving primacy to expression over an asserted right to privacy while other sub-categories lead to expression being trumped by the assertion of a privacy claim. A number of considerations have been asserted as relevant to the resolution of these conflicts between freedom of expression and privacy. One way of approaching the matter has focused on the nature of the publication in which the offending expression has appeared. Is the publication a tabloid, or is it what the House of Lords has described as a "serious" publication?[2] How does one distinguish between these two categories? And why should any such distinction matter? A tabloid certainly deals with matters in which the public is interested but not always with matters that the deciding court believes are in a real or legitimate sense of public interest. Many people, however, would not take such a harsh view of what tabloids do. The scandal involving sometime United States Senator/Vice Presidential candidate on the 2004 Democratic ticket, and aspirant for the 2008 Democratic presidential nomination, John Edwards, was uncovered by a tabloid.[3] Like most Americans, I would think that the disclosures showed character defects that indicated he was clearly unqualified to hold any of these offices.

What for some people is particularly obnoxious about tabloids is that they provide a market for, and thus encourage, paparazzi. Newspapers that are classified as serious publications, on the other hand, are accepted to be serving an important public purpose by providing the public with information that it is in the public interest that they should know. But, as the House of Lords accepted in the *Campbell* case, some of the information provided by the *Daily Mirror* clearly fell into that latter category even if some of their lordships felt that other information was not something the public was entitled to know. As we saw when we discussed the case in Chapter 5, what made the difference for some of the majority was the publication of a photograph taken outside the premises in which Naomi Campbell was attending meetings of Narcotics Anonymous, even though none of the Law Lords challenged Lord Hoffman's assertion that the *Daily Mirror* could have used a file photograph of Ms. Campbell without suffering any adverse legal consequences. If the nature of the medium has some independent bearing on the issue of whether freedom of expression can overcome privacy concerns, we would want some greater specificity as to what is a serious publication and what is a tabloid or, in other words, what is not a serious publication. Many if not most publications would likely have some of the characteristics of the accepted paradigms of a "serious publication," say the European edition of the *Wall Street Journal*, which was involved in the *Jameel*[4] case, or the similar *Financial Times*, but also would have some of the characteristics of what is considered a tabloid,

---

2. *See* Jameel v. Wall Street Journal Europe SPRL, [2007] 1 A.C. 359 (2006), at ¶ 150, where Lady Hale declared that the defendant was "as the journalist quoted by my noble and learned friend [Lord Hoffman] said 'gravely serious' (indeed some might find it seriously dull). We need more such serious journalism in this country and our defamation law should encourage rather than discourage it."

3. *See* Stephanie Clifford, *From Rumor to a Hint of Respect*, N.Y. TIMES, March 8, 2010, at B1 (discussing the *National Enquirer*). *The Wall Street Journal* has itself also published the tawdry details revealed in divorce proceedings between, among others, the Governor of Nevada and his wife. Dionne Searcey, *Dirty Laundry Aired: The Fight Over Revealing Divorce Details*, WALL ST. J., May 28, 2009, at A10.

4. Cited in note 2, *supra*.

taking as a paradigm the *Daily Mirror* in the United Kingdom or the *National Enquirer* in the United States. Assuming it were even appropriate for the courts to define and apply this distinction, or for judges to express this contempt for tabloids in their opinions, it would take quite a few decisions to define the categories sufficiently to avoid the chilling effect on expression of legal uncertainty.

One possible source of assistance would be to focus not so much on how one should characterize the publication in which the challenged material appeared but to focus instead on the manner in which the material was obtained and possibly how it came into the possession of the publication in question. The precedents to which one might turn are those in which the common law courts outside the United States have developed the notion of "responsible journalism" to soften the rigors of the common law of defamation in order to make some accommodation for the concerns which prompted the United States Supreme Court to make even more drastic changes in that law by requiring public officials and public figures to prove intentional publication of false material that the defendant either knew was false or as to which he was recklessly indifferent to its truth or falsity;[5] and, if the plaintiff was neither a public figure nor a public official, he was nevertheless still required to prove at least some fault on the part of defendant.[6] In both instances, the burden of persuasion on the issue of truth or falsity was transferred to the plaintiff. Unwilling to take such radical steps, these other common law courts extended the common law qualified privilege attached to the publication of material that, even if false, is germane to some common interest of the publisher and recipient to encompass in varying degrees a broader "public interest," that is, an interest shared by the public at large. By making the "public interest" a common interest, these courts introduced into the law of defamation the notion that is now being used in Europe to decide when the public disclosure of private facts might be justified, as we shall discuss at length again shortly. The developments in the common law world are not completely uniform. In the United Kingdom[7] and Canada,[8] the courts have thus far been unprepared to hold that, in the area of defamation, political speech has, as a general category, greater public interest value than other categories of expression. In Australia[9] and to a greater extent New Zealand,[10] political speech has

---

5. *See* New York Times Co. v. Sullivan, 376 U.S. 254 (1964).

6. *See* Gertz v. Robert Welch, Inc., 418 U.S. 323 (1974).

7. *See* Reynolds v. Times Newspapers Ltd., [2001] 2 A.C. 127 (1999), which has been extensively amplified by the *Jameel* case, *supra* note 2.

8. *See* Grant v. Torstar Corp., [2009] 3 S.C.R. 640; Quan v. Cusson, [2009] 3 S.C.R. 712.

9. *See* Lange v. Australian Broadcasting Corp., 189 C.L.R. 520 (1997).

10. *See* Lange v. Atkinson, [2000] 3 N.Z.L.R. 385 (C.A.). At least where political speech is involved, the defendant can escape liability if he has an honest belief in the truth of his statement.

been accorded more solicitous treatment. What seems to have been generally agreed, however, is that the defamatory material in question, in addition to concerning a matter of public interest, should also have been the product of "responsible journalism" or "responsible communication." As used in the defamation context, the notion of "responsible journalism" refers primarily to the care the defendant has taken to ascertain the truth, that is to say, it introduced some element of fault into the mix. The application of that concept, however, would also seem to have some influence on the issue of whether the publication in question should be deemed to have been in the public interest. Of course where invasions of privacy actions are concerned, there is no question of falsity, but the notion of "responsible journalism" can be used to denote not only fault in ascertaining its truth but fault in the sense of the unethical if not even illegal manner in which the information in question was obtained. Whether the defendant acquired the information it divulged in what the courts believe was a responsible fashion clearly seems to be of some relevance to whether the defendant's publication was in the public interest. Certainly the condescending treatment accorded to "tabloids" is undoubtedly influenced by the view that they not only pander to the baser interests of the masses but that they are also presumed to use questionable methods of securing that information.

Even if one accepts that all so-called media, including those that do not scrupulously observe the canons of responsible journalism, fulfill some particularly important function owing to their wider distribution and ability to serve some watchdog purpose, and that therefore it is in the public interest that they should enjoy some greater privileges than the public at large—a development I would strenuously oppose—some problems remain. If one accepts that books and pamphlets have important social value, as surely we must, we would be faced with the problem that *some* books or pamphlets and *some* types of authors could be considered more serious than others; and this might tilt the balance in their favor when the question is whether their publication of supposedly private facts is in the public interest. How a case-by-case process of adjudication would sort out which authors should be accorded some kind of preferential treatment without resorting to stereotypes escapes me. Moreover, giving the "press," including the broadcast media, some privileged status would also introduce the same difficulties we noted in our extended discussion of the *Citizens United* case in the previous chapter. Who qualifies as a member of the media is not as self-defining as it might appear.

The likely need to refine both the stature of the publication and the status of the author only begins to describe the tasks faced in deciding what publication of supposedly private facts is in the public interest. The more difficult and more serious issues concern the content of expression challenged as being an invasion of someone's privacy. In this regard we should not forget that the status of the person whose privacy is alleged to have been invaded is also part of the content of the expression, even if we might normally think of content as referring to some particular factual assertion, or more generally some particular category of speech, say "political" or "artistic" or perhaps even "idle" or "scurrilous" speech. The European Court of Human Rights certainly recognized this in the *von Hannover* case[11] where it drew a sharp distinction between public officials and all other persons, even those who, like Princess Caroline, would clearly be characterized as public rather than private figures under American law. At the same time, the European Court declared that even public officials enjoyed some protections from the curious if the matters disclosed did not concern their official duties. How easy a task it would be to decide what revelations might be relevant to a public official's performance of his official duties is another matter. Assuming that some relatively clear and easily applied criteria could be established to distinguish matters germane to an official's official duties and those that are not, anyone who disclosed little-known private facts about a public official or about someone as well-known as Princess Caroline relating to activities carried on in public space would have to demonstrate that the disclosure was in the public interest. Certainly publication in what that Court would consider a tabloid would, to say the least, not help the case for disclosure to the general public.

The Court in *von Hannover* proceeded on the assumption that the criterion of activities carried on in public space by public figures gives, among other things, less certain protection to public personalities than the criteria of public interest or contribution to a debate of general interest. Conversely, in making it more difficult for plaintiffs to succeed in defamation actions, the United States Supreme Court chose instead to give the greatest protection to speech about public officials or public figures rather than relying on the criterion of whether the speech in question concerned a matter of public interest. The reason given for that choice was skepticism that courts were the appropriate decision makers as to what was speech of genuine public interest.[12] And indeed, public notoriety does seem to be somewhat more of an empirical question than the issue of what is really in the public interest. Nonetheless, as we have noted, the House of Lords, in giving greater, but more limited, protection to defamatory speech also chose to base that protection on the judicial determination of what is truly a matter of public interest and reserving to the courts the authority to make that determination. In the *Campbell* case, it carried over that insistence on the public interest in publication to the field of privacy. But dealing with statements that are true is different from dealing with statements that are false. False speech is tolerated because of the desire not to stifle speech. It is not *prima facie* entitled to protection for its own sake. Speech that is true, however, is not something that is

---

11. Von Hannover v. Germany, Application No. 59320/00, Judgment of June 24, 2004, 40 Eur. H.R. Rep. 1 (2005).

12. *See* Gertz v. Robert Welch, Inc., 418 U.S. 323, 346 (1974), where the Court, per Justice Powell, declared that "[w]e doubt the wisdom of committing this task [of determining what is in the public or general interest] to the conscience of judges."

tolerated by the state *merely* as an instrumental good. Barring exceptional circumstances, one would think that truthful expression is always, to some extent, a good in itself as an aspect of exercising one's personal freedom.

It is surely not unreasonable to suggest that, when true statements are involved, one would want sharper lines between permitted and unpermitted speech. The easiest bright line to apply therefore would be to distinguish between statements concerning activities that are carried out in public space or that can be observed by someone standing in public space and those which are not carried on either in public space or in areas visible from public space. In effect, this is undoubtedly the practical reality. All that cases like *von Hannover* and *Campbell* do is prohibit a person from publishing a photograph, for which he is perhaps paid, in a mass circulation print medium. In the digital age in which we live, there is, as a practical matter, little that can be done to stop someone from circulating photographs, taken from a place accessible to the public, on any one of the available websites, many of which are situated in places beyond the reach of courts wishing to prevent that publication. Moreover, there is always private distribution within a circle of friends. What most people would call private information, if circulated among a sufficient number of close associates, soon becomes a matter of common knowledge and enters the public domain. The end result may be that all that is accomplished is making it harder for paparazzi to make a living but otherwise not giving much protection to someone in whom a sufficiently large number of the public are interested regardless of whether that interest is considered worth catering to or not.

There is indeed a certain contradiction in the notion that a person can be in the public space and yet still enjoy some of the benefits of being in a "private" space. If it may be made an offense for someone to wear a burqa in public, or to walk around nude in public, the notion of private activities in public space becomes somewhat strained. If such legislation were enacted and actually survived judicial challenge, could a celebrity or even an ordinary person who is not a public official who wore a burqa in public complain if her photograph were published in the press? After all, she would have committed a crime. I raise the issue because it would be possible, and in some countries it is actually the case, that, although someone may not be able to prevent himself from being photographed in public space, such a person is given something like a copyright in the photograph that would presumably allow him to prevent the person who took the picture from selling it to a "tabloid" or otherwise distributing the photograph. But surely that would not be possible if the event at which the photograph was taken was a newsworthy one, for otherwise there could be no photographs published in newspapers reporting such events. This is clearly the case in Germany where, for example, pictures of a person's involvement in "contemporary history" may be published without consent, as may pictures in which the person seeking redress only appeared as an accessory to a depiction of a landscape or other physical location or which relate to a meeting or similar public gathering attended by the complainant.[13] Finally in both Germany and France, it is a crime to photograph without consent an individual in what might be called private space, such as in Germany "an apartment or a specially protected area" or, as in France, "a private place."[14] One would hope that the Grand Chamber of the European Court of Human Rights, which is now in the process of adjudicating a second *von Hannover* case,[15] will be able to provide some further and more helpful guidance on these difficult issues.

In what is popularly described as an "anti-paparazzi" law, California makes physical trespass with intent to capture a visual, audio, or other physical impression of someone engaged "in a personal or familial activity" actionable where the physical invasion occurs in a manner that is "offensive to a reasonable person," and also subjects the offender to a "civil fine."[16] A somewhat more questionable provision provides the same regime for what is called "constructive trespass" when the person capturing the images just described is only able to do so by the use of enhanced visual or audio devices.[17] I express no opinion on whether this latter prohibition passes constitutional muster. Regardless of the legal niceties, as a practical matter, the person who took such photographs could surely look at them from time to time and probably even show them to a small circle of friends.

The great divide between the United States and most other countries obviously relates to photographs not taken in anything that might be called private space. In the United States, one can get legal redress for the use of photographs or other types of representation taken or made in public space or otherwise lawfully obtained only if they are used without consent for what might be called advertising or trade purposes, that is, they are used primarily to obtain some economic benefit. That also seems to be the law in New Zealand.[18] In California, where this matter is covered by statute, there is an explicit exception for uses of images in connection with "news, public affairs, or sports broadcasts or accounts."[19] There is, furthermore, case law exempting description and images

---

13. *See* KUG § 23.
14. *See* StGB § 201 (a); C. PÉN. § 226-1. The French provision expressly declares that consent is presumed when the person taking the photograph is within the sight of the person being photographed and that person knows that he is being photographed. The more general French law on privacy is derived from Article 9 of the French Civil Code enacted in its present form in 1970 and earlier judge-made law. There is a good discussion of the French law of privacy in Helen Trouille, *Private Life and Public Image: Privacy Legislation in France*, 49 INT'L & COMP. L.Q. 199 (2000).
15. Von Hannover v. Germany, Application No. 40660/08.
16. CAL. CIV. § 1708.8 (a) (West 2009).
17. *Id.* at § 1708.8 (b).
18. *See* Hosking v. Runting, [2005] 1 N.Z.L.R. 1 (2004) (C.A.).
19. *See* CAL. CIV. § 3344 (d).

used as part of "artistic expression."[20] In New York, the first state to deal with these issues by statute, the courts have construed statutory prohibitions of the use, without consent, of a person's name, likeness, voice, etc. for economic purposes[21] not to reach reports or discussions of newsworthy matters nor matters of public interest, with both exceptions being defined very broadly;[22] nor do they reach use as part of artistic expression, such as paintings or other works of art, of which only a limited number are sold.[23] The prohibitions also do not cover caricatures. In short, under this approach, the more a challenged use of a person's image, likeness, voice, or even description without consent resembles advertising for a product or service, the greater the likelihood of the challenge succeeding and of course the converse is also true. The gist of an action that succeeds would be the loss of the plaintiff's ability to exploit to the fullest the economic advantages of those attributes. Leaving aside the broader questions with which we have been concerned, there is no question that this narrower, largely economic approach can take advantage not only of a much more general agreement as to what is or is not permissible, but also of the availability of a relatively objective measure of the damages to which a successful plaintiff is entitled. The further we stray from this economic core, the more subjective becomes the decision of whether the use in question should be actionable and what should be the appropriate monetary remedy. This will be especially true if semi-objective criteria such as public space or what the public is interested in are rejected in favor of criteria that rely primarily on judges' beliefs as to what privacy people are "entitled" to enjoy.

Images of course are often, if not usually, employed with textual description but that only complicates the decisional process. As we have several times noted, at least one of the three Law Lords who ruled in favor of Naomi Campbell clearly indicated that, but for the picture of Campbell outside the Narcotics Anonymous meeting place, he would have ruled with the two dissenters, in which case Campbell would have lost her action.[24] That is to say, publication accompanied by a photograph taken in a public place that was in no way embarrassing, but

---

20. *See* Winter v. DC Comics, 30 Cal. 4th 881 (2003).
21. *See* N.Y. Civ. Rights Law §§ 50–51 (McKinney 2009).
22. *See,* e.g., Howell v. New York Post Co., 81 N.Y.2d 115 (1993).
23. *See* Simeonov v. Tiegs, 602 N.Y.S.2d 1014 (N.Y.C. Civ. Ct., 1993). In *Altbach v. Kulon,* 754 N.Y.S.2d 709 (App. Div. 2003), the Appellate Division held that not only a painting caricaturing a judge but also the use of a picture of the judge on a flyer advertising the exhibition of the painting at an art gallery were not covered by the statute. A similar case in Europe is *Vereinigung Bildender Künstler v. Austria*, Application No. 68354/01, Judgment of January 25, 2007, which involved a somewhat salacious caricature of a number of well-known figures including the applicant, a prominent politician, in which the European Court in a four-to-three decision held that the prosecution of the organization that displayed the paintings violated Article 10 of the Convention.
24. Campbell v. MGN Ltd., [2004] 2 A.C. 457, at ¶ 121 (per Lord Hope).

might have indicated to a very astute observer where the Narcotics Anonymous meeting was held, constituted a breach of the expanded notion of what it is for information to be confidential; but publication without the photograph would not amount to such a breach of confidence. That seems a rather odd distinction if the essence of the tort is breach of confidence.[25] One appreciates that a major reason that the British courts have resorted to the expansion of the law of confidentiality is to accommodate British law to the determinations of the Parliamentary Assembly of the Council of Europe and of the European Court of Human Rights that the rights of privacy and of freedom of expression are of equal value. They have tried to make that accommodation in a manner that is more focused and less broad ranging and thus capable of giving more guidance than the approach taken by the European Court. The question remains, however, whether it gives sufficient guidance or just discourages speech since, at least in litigation involving private parties, it is almost always the plaintiff complaining about the invasion of his privacy and the defendant who has chosen to speak.

There have been relations between people that have been recognized as confidential for a very long time. In mature legal systems, the relationship between a lawyer and his client is a paradigm of a confidential relationship and the publication by a lawyer of information obtained from his client through that relationship is strictly forbidden with very few exceptions. There are similar protections extended to the priest/penitent relationship and to the doctor/patient relationship. There is a substantial amount of case law defining those relationships and what is the content of the relevant duty of confidentiality. It is worth noting that one of the cases from which the House of Lords in the *Spycatcher*[26] case derived the extended version of confidentiality was the acrimonious litigation surrounding the divorce of the Duke and Duchess of Argyll, in which one of the parties disclosed to a newspaper, possibly for a monetary payment, details about the other spouse's sex life.[27] Regardless of whether this extension of the duty of confidentiality was wise, recent cases like the *Campbell* case have certainly gone a long way past that.

The difficult cases with which we are concerned involve the extension of a duty of confidentiality to a person who does not fit into any of the traditional relationships nor is engaged in anything that could be classified as commercial speech or trying to make use of another's name or image for advertising or trade purposes but knows of information about an individual that he should realize the individual in question would not want to be generally known. There are, however, so many things a reasonable person would realize that a person would not want to be generally known about himself that, if applied literally, such a doctrine would impose a very heavy burden on expressions. As we noted earlier,

---

25. At least Lord Hoffman thought so. *Id.* at ¶¶ 76–77.
26. Attorney General v. Guardian Newspapers (No. 2), [1990] 1 A.C. 109, 144 (1988).
27. Margaret, Duchess of Argyll v. Duke of Argyll, [1967] Ch. 302 (1965).

in order to sort out what expression would be possible, we would need to have a series of cases illustrating what sort of information could be proscribed and who exactly might be said to have a duty of non-disclosure. In the United States, as we have seen, the law seems to be that if one confides to a person, without some express promise of confidentiality, one accepts the risk that the recipient might disclose that information to others. Thus, when a person who had been the subject of an article about "body surfing" complained about the publication of information obtained about some of his idiosyncrasies in the reporter's conversations with his friends and with his ex-wife, he was denied recovery.[28] Obviously, in Europe, the law appears to be different. Seemingly the disclosure by a person of embarrassing facts about himself to a stranger while drinking at a bar would also come under this obligation of confidentiality. If there is to be a duty of confidentiality in such situations, the courts would also have to decide how widespread knowledge of the information can be and still held to be confidential with regard to a general audience. Surely it would be relevant to know to whom else the plaintiff might have disclosed that information while drinking at a bar or at a private dinner.

Our discussion thus far only begins to show the complexity of the task of sorting out when a right to freedom of expression will prevail over an equally important right to the privacy of one's personal life and when it will not. Let us assume that we live in a world in which a public figure, even a public official, has a right to privacy relating to his private life, such as has been declared in the *von Hannover* case, or relating to matters about himself which a court is prepared to accept that a reasonable person would not wish to have communicated to others by persons who have no legal relation to him other than that they are privy to information that the aggrieved person would not wish to be widely circulated. This seems to be the teaching of the *Campbell* case. This primacy of privacy over freedom of expression may be overcome by a showing that the information in question is not merely something in which a substantial number of the public is interested but is also something which it is in the genuine public interest that the public should know. To answer that crucial question, as we have seen, certain categories of preferred speech have been enunciated. They include political speech, scientific or educational speech, and artistic or literary speech. These categories are themselves quite broad and by no means self-explanatory. Of these categories, most people would probably rate political speech as the most important in the sense of deserving the most legal protection. But what is included in the term political speech is by no means self-evident. It could be as narrow as speech related to an election, or somewhat broadened to include information germane to pending legislation or current public policy disputes. But could it not also include publication of information about a politician's private life, say his

---

28. Virgil v. Time, Inc., 527 F.2d 1122 (9th Cir. 1975), *cert. denied*, 425 U.S. 998 (1976).

affairs with women who are neither his employees nor otherwise involved in public life, or his preference for very rare wines or his belonging to snobbish clubs with very socially and ethnically restricted memberships? The disclosure of such information would undoubtedly show a politician in what he might reasonably believe to be an unfavorable light, even if only to suggest that, despite his professed belief in the value of family life, he has a troubled marriage or that he is a faux egalitarian.

If such speech is subject to legal sanction, it would reflect a very narrow view of what is legitimate political speech and a very elitist view of what information a voter is permitted to consider in judging his elected representatives or in casting his ballot. And, should the matter be published and a suit for injunction against further publication or an action for damages were brought, would it be possible to restrict press reports of those proceedings? Even if one accepted that speech about candidates for office could escape legal sanction for publication of the sort of information described above, would information about senior, non-elected government officials receive the same forbearing treatment? And what about celebrities who are not themselves candidates but endorse candidates for public office? Would information about people involved in issues of public policy, such as environmental issues or the safety of genetically modified crops or even of drug policy or the merits of teaching creationism in the public schools, also receive preferential treatment? It is significant that, in the *Campbell* case, it was the plaintiff's public denial of taking drugs that made her to some extent fair game and not her having spoken out, as a well-known celebrity, on a frequently discussed issue of some public importance. If she had never said anything about her own possible use or non-use of drugs, it would seem that disclosure of her actual use of drugs might well have been actionable even though she had entered the public debate on the subject. And finally, what about powerful business figures, whether they are corporate raiders or senior executives of major banks or industrial enterprises or who perhaps are only executives of banks or enterprises that, though not significant on an international or national level, exert major influence in the locality covered by the offending publication? All this would have to be worked out in some detail before a prudent person of moderate means could even dare to mention these matters in a public forum for fear of facing the crippling litigation costs that has increasingly been exploited by the rich and powerful to silence critics of their actions.[29]

Similar difficult problems will arise in fleshing out the other ostensibly privileged types of expression. Let us begin with a concrete example taken from the United States as to what might constitute "scientific" or "educational" speech

---

29. It is worth recalling that, as we pointed out in Chapter 5, at p. 58, *supra*, while Campbell only recovered a total of £3,500 in compensation and aggravated damages, she was awarded almost £1,100,000 in costs by the House of Lords in a decision now in the process of being challenged in the European Court of Human Rights.

that was mentioned as a sub-category of speech that might sometimes trump privacy concerns on grounds of public interest. The example is *Commonwealth v. Wiseman*,[30] decided by the Supreme Judicial Court of Massachusetts. Wiseman had obtained official permission to make an educational, documentary film at the Massachusetts Correctional Institute at Bridgewater. The permission was subject to certain conditions designed to protect the privacy of the inmates and patients. Wiseman in due course produced a film about the criminally insane entitled *Titicut Follies*. The film is not without sympathy for the staff, who were struggling with excruciatingly difficult problems in an obsolete institution with inadequate resources, or concern for the depressing plight of the inmates, but it shows inmates in pathetic and embarrassingly indecent situations. The film contains scenes of forced nose feeding, skin searches of naked patients, and pathetic attempts by prisoners to hide their genitals. Unknown to the Massachusetts authorities, the film was shown at two film festivals, in one of which it won first prize as the best documentary film of the year. Wiseman contracted for the commercial distribution of the film, and it was first shown in New York where it was advertised as making "'Marat Sade' look like 'Holiday on Ice.'" The Attorney General of Massachusetts, concluding that the film went beyond the scope of the consent granted by Massachusetts authorities and that the film was an unauthorized invasion of the inmates' privacy, brought suit to enjoin future exhibitions. In appealing the trial court's decision in the Attorney General's favor, Wiseman argued that the distribution of the film was in the public interest as a means of bringing the plight of the inmates to the public's attention. The Supreme Judicial Court of Massachusetts agreed with the trial court, however, that Wiseman had not adequately complied with the conditions of the permission to make the film, one of which was to photograph only inmates legally competent to sign releases. This seems clearly correct. Treating Wiseman as primarily a collector of information who had breached the conditions under which he was allowed to make the film, one can see little difficulty with the legal system's providing remedies to protect the interests of the inmates. Furthermore, regardless of the conditions that were or were not imposed, I would strongly argue that the court should have held that no one may grant permission to photograph mentally incompetent inmates within a state institution unless the photographs are necessary for treatment of the patients or would aid in the efficient administration of the institution, such as for identification purposes.

What is curious about the case is that the Massachusetts Supreme Judicial Court modified the trial court's decree, that the film must be destroyed, to permit exhibition to specialized audiences, such as "legislators, judges, lawyers, sociologists, social workers, doctors, psychiatrists, students in these or related

---

30. Commonwealth v. Wiseman, 356 Mass. 251, 249 N.E.2d 610 (1969), *cert. denied*, 398 U.S. 960 (1970), *decree modified in minor respects*, 360 Mass. 857, 275 N.E.2d 148 (1971).

fields, and organizations dealing with the social problems of custodial care and mental infirmity," provided that "a brief explanation that changes and improvements have taken place in the institution" be included in the film. Relying on this modification of the original decree, the film was shown from time to time at a number of law schools and other educational institutions.[31] The court's decision implies that some people's right to know is better than others.[32] Given that, in the United States, there are over 150,000 students enrolled at any one time in law schools with combined faculties of at least 5,000 and considerable support staff, plus many hundreds of thousands, perhaps even millions, of other persons in the other enumerated preferred audiences, the class of privileged viewers is sufficiently large as to make one wonder what privacy means in such a context. Although the regime of balancing favored in Europe has generally favored privacy over freedom of expression, an interest-balancing test turning on what courts consider "the public interest" can also have some unfavorable consequences for privacy. In the *Wiseman* case, a public interest test could have lead to eroding the protection of what many would consider the very core of privacy and, in doing so, might perhaps have encouraged a cynical person to conclude that, in a world of conflicting, defeasible human rights, the cost of protecting the basic rights of the individual under a regime so dependent on the concept of public interest is to make him a public resource. It would certainly take a large number of authoritative cases and a firm commitment to *stare decisis* to provide a sufficiently detailed legal background to give one assurance that whether he is to be treated as such a public resource is not left solely to the discretion of courts composed of judges who themselves are frequently replaced by other judges.

It would not be difficult to take each of the other categories of speech that are to be given some degree of preference in the difficult task of balancing privacy interests against freedom of expression and point out the myriad and, in many important ways, *sui generis* situations in which the courts will be forced to engage in that task in the hope that, at some point perhaps, the parameters of when the public interest defeats privacy concerns, and when it does not, will become sufficiently clear so that we can actually have a world of meaningful rights. Rather than unduly extend the present discussion, I will close this chapter with some

---

31. I myself saw the film when it was shown under this exemption at Duke Law School.

32. An earlier federal district court decision, *Cullen v. Grove Press, Inc.*, 276 F. Supp. 727 (S.D.N.Y. 1967), denied relief to guards at Bridgewater who sought to enjoin the film's showing in New York. The restrictions on the distribution of *Titicut Follies* have now been lifted by the Massachusetts courts. William H. Honan, *Judge Ends Ban on Film of Asylum*, N.Y. TIMES, August 3, 1991, § 1 at 12. The passage of time was a decisive factor. What if all the inmates portrayed in the film had not died? Should that have been the decisive factor? For the actual order lifting the restrictions, *see Commonwealth v. Wiseman Civ. Action No. 87538* (Mass. Superior Ct., Suffolk Cty., July 29, 1991). Wiseman, however, was not permitted to reveal the names of the inmates who appeared in the film.

comments on the conflict between privacy and literary or artistic expression such as the graphic and performing arts. It is certainly well-known that characters in many important works of fiction are based on real people, many of them otherwise obscure but still living, with whom the author has interacted during his life. If it is possible for some of the public to identify the characters portrayed albeit with changes of name and other characteristics, the law in common law countries, and I should imagine in the civil law as well, allows the person in question to bring an action when the portrayal ascribes false and defamatory attributes to his literary impersonation.

But what if the literary portrayal presents an accurate and true description of the identifiable person on whom it is modeled? D.H. Lawrence, to take one example, is said to have often modeled his characters, not always in a flattering way, on people he knew.[33] The same has been said about Thomas Wolfe.[34] Can the aggrieved model bring an action? Should the answer depend on whether the work is considered of "literary value," that is, as "literature"? And who is to make that decision? If one is diffident about the ability of courts to make that decision, to whom should he turn? Are there really "experts" on these matters? There was a time when many literary experts would undoubtedly have condemned Henry Miller's work as not being literature; and James Joyce's *Ulysses* and *Finnegan's Wake* were not greeted with universal acclaim by experts. And why should that matter? From the perspective of the person who feels that his privacy has been invaded, it is not unreasonable to suppose that it is the size of the audience to which his foibles have been exposed that matters most rather than the literary quality of the publication in which that exposure appears. Graphic art can similarly be based to a greater or lesser extent on real-life people, even on people whom the artist has casually seen on the public street or in cafés, as in the work of Toulouse-Lautrec, or the sketches of lawyers and judges by Daumier. That is to say nothing about the vast and constant output of cartoons. Is viability of an action to depend on the perceived quality of the art? That judges as well as experts have strong opinions on that subject is indisputable.[35] Again, all these matters

---

33. Lawrence acknowledged as much in correspondence to Catherine Carswell when he described modeling the character Halliday from *Women in Love* on the composer Philip Heseltine. HARRY T. MOORE, THE INTELLIGENT HEART 219 (1954). Heseltine later threatened to sue Lawrence for libel over the portrayal. *Id.* at 284.

34. *See* FLOYD C. WATKINS, THOMAS WOLFE'S CHARACTERS: PORTRAIT FROM LIFE (1957).

35. Judge Loucaides' dissent in the *Vereinigung Bildender Künstler* case, involving a salacious and satirical painting that included a representation of the applicant, a prominent politician, that was discussed *supra* note 23, is a clear recent example. He declared:

It is my firm belief that the images depicted in this product of what is, to say the least, a strange imagination, convey no message; the "painting" is just a senseless, disgusting combination of lewd images whose only effect is to debase, insult and ridicule each and every person portrayed. Personally, I was unable to find any criticism or satire in this "painting." Why were Mother Teresa and Cardinal Hermann Groer ridiculed?

must be sorted out. It will not be easy and, from the perspective of the litigants, it will not be a low-cost endeavor with the need to pay for literary and/or art critics as expert witnesses in addition to the normal legal costs of litigation. Unless these issues are sorted out rather quickly, the only result is the inhibition of expressive activities. In place of socialist art, one might have a sanitized and perhaps even politically correct art or literature.

Why were the personalities depicted naked with erect and ejaculating penises? To find that situation comparable with satire or artistic expression is beyond my comprehension. And when we speak about art I do not think that we can include each and every act of artistic expression regardless of its nature and effect. In the same way that we exclude insults from freedom of speech, so we must exclude from the legitimate expression of artists insulting pictures that undermine the reputation or dignity of others, especially if they are devoid of any meaningful message and contain nothing more than senseless, repugnant and disgusting images, as in the present case.

Vereinigung Bildender Künstler v. Austria, Application No. 68354/01, Judgment of January 25, 2007 (Loucaides, J., dissenting).

PART V

CONCLUSION

12. WHAT IF WE MUST CHOOSE?

It is very possible that, despite our best efforts, a process of case-by-case adjudication cannot produce the specificity and clarity that we are seeking. There are a number of reasons why this might be the likely outcome. First of all, there is a limit to the certainty that any continuing process of case-by-case adjudication can deliver even in the best of circumstances. The amount of uncertainty that we are prepared to tolerate in the areas with which we are concerned requires us to consider not merely the expectations of judges and scholars but also what reasonable people would consider tolerable. To the extent that an adjudicatory regime puts comparatively greater stress on process-related features, the greater might be the degree of inconsistency in results it must be prepared to tolerate. In the areas with which we are concerned, areas which involve very important and often conflicting values, it is hard to feel comfortable embracing a regime which emphasizes process and giving litigants their day in court but leads to a significant degree of inconsistency between what substantial numbers of rational observers would consider similar cases. In this area, a case law which often produces only decisions that we can merely describe as neither clearly wrong nor clearly correct is not an adequate legal regime. That is to say, when basic human rights are concerned, a regime which affords a wide margin of appreciation to local decision-makers' notions about the content of such rights demeans the whole notion of what it means for individuals to be endowed with basic human rights that transcend national boundaries. That is why we have seen that in both Europe and the United States there has, as a practical matter, been a significant drift towards bright-line tests. In short, whether we are prepared to openly acknowledge it or not, we are in fact choosing between values. It is important therefore to recognize the implications of the choices we have already made and to decide how we shall make the choices with which we shall be confronted in the future.

This need to choose is most clearly presented in a regime in which the principal competing values are represented as being of equal value. Whether, but for the circumstances surrounding the death of Princess Diana, Europe would have so easily decided that rights of privacy and rights of freedom of expression are of equal value is an interesting but now moot point.[1] At this point in time, the question before us is how to deal with conflicts between those two equal values. To

---

1. The language of Resolution 1165 of the Parliamentary Assembly of the Council of Europe (1998) leaves no doubt that it was largely prompted by Princess Diana's tragic death in August of 1997.

state simply that "on balance" one or another of those values should prevail on a given set of facts is to state a conclusion not to describe a process. To even begin to have any hope of coming up with an adequate solution, one would need to come up with some common metric that could be used to "balance" the "values" (or "interests") involved. This is of course what Dworkin sought to do, as we saw in Chapter 7, when he asserted that the basic legal conflicts in society were reducible to a moral dimension, and therefore resolvable by working out the correct moral solution to the underlying conflicts involved. Even if it were possible to reduce the conflicts with which he was concerned to a single moral dimension, I questioned whether the ultimate moral principle put forth by Dworkin, namely society's moral obligation to show equal moral concern for all of its members, was adequate to the task. The problem in the areas with which we are concerned is that there is no adequate and truly common metric against which to measure the conflicting values.

The concept of privacy has both a moral and political dimension. When the issue is the intrusion of the state into what are considered the private lives and activities of people, the political dimension of privacy may become of equal if not even greater importance than its moral dimension. There certainly are political as well as moral reasons why we do not want the state to invade people's homes, read their mail, or listen to their phone conversations without demonstrating some very important reason for doing so. When the invasion of privacy concerns constraints on the activities of private people who are trying to exercise their acknowledged right to freedom of expression in order to convey to others information that they have lawfully obtained, it is the moral dimension of privacy that is being primarily relied upon. Since the concept of freedom of expression in the context of an organized social structure is largely a political notion, what the plaintiff in such a privacy action against another private individual is asking of the state is that it should use its power to curtail the political freedom of another to uphold a moral entitlement of the plaintiff. This in turn creates a conflict between the largely moral entitlement of the plaintiff and the largely political entitlement of the defendant.

A few illustrations will make clear what I mean by these assertions. In late October 2004, almost six months after its decision in the *Campbell* case, the House of Lords refused a request that, in the reporting of a criminal trial, the press should be restrained from printing the name of an eight-year-old boy as well as the names and pictures of his mother and his deceased brother for whose murder the mother was on trial in the proceedings in question.[2] While the case was pending, the newspapers involved agreed not to publish the surviving brother's name. There was testimony from experts as to the possible psychic harm to the younger brother should his schoolmates become privy to his associating with

---

2. In re S, [2005] A.C. 593 (2004).

those involved in the criminal prosecution; and his mother had joined in this request that the press be enjoined from publishing the material in question. Looked at from a moral perspective, it would be a hardhearted person indeed who would refuse this request from the child's guardian. But of course the morality of the disclosure was not the issue. The only issue was whether in a free country the press, if it wished, could publish the names and the pictures and that is a matter to be governed ultimately by political values. I would submit that the primacy of this political value was more than tacitly recognized in the speech of Lord Bingham in which he responded to a criticism that the Court of Appeal had made of how the trial judge had approached the case. Although the Court of Appeal had, in a two-to-one decision, affirmed the trial judge's refusal to enjoin the newspaper, all three of its judges criticized the fact that the trial judge had proceeded from a perspective in which the freedom of the press to publicize was the preferred value rather than from the perspective recognized by the European Convention on Human Rights, namely that the rights of freedom of expression and privacy were of equal value. In his speech agreeing with the unanimous decision of the House of Lords affirming the judgment in favor of the newspaper, Lord Bingham declared:

> In agreement with Hale LJ the majority of the Court of Appeal took the view that Hedley J had not analyzed the case correctly in accordance with the provisions of the ECHR. Given the weight traditionally given to the importance of open reporting of criminal proceedings, it was in my view appropriate for him, in carrying out the balance required by the ECHR, to begin by acknowledging the force of the argument under article 10 before considering whether the right of the child under article 8 was sufficient to outweigh it. He went too far in saying that he would have come to the same conclusion even if he had been persuaded that this was a case where the child's welfare was indeed the paramount consideration under section 1(1) of the Children's Act 1989. But that was not the shape of the case before him.[3]

It is unclear how the European Court of Human Rights would have handled this case if a proceeding challenging that decision had been brought before it. Several recent cases indicate that the European Court might have held that a decision either way would have passed muster having regard to the margin of appreciation enjoyed by national authorities in these matters, a solution that, from the perspective of someone who believes in truly universal human rights is less than optimal. For example, two recent judgments of the European Court of Human Rights seem to follow the British lead.[4] Both involved press reports in Finland of an altercation that occurred at the home of a "National Conciliator,"

---

3. *Id.* at ¶ 37.
4. Tuomela v. Finland, Application No. 25711/04, Judgment of April 6, 2010; Flinkkilä v. Finland, Application No. 25576/04, Judgment of April 6, 2010.

that is, a person who was part of a corps of public officials who mediated labor disputes. The person in question, who had been drinking heavily, brought a woman with whom he had been having an affair to his home late one night. His wife and an adult son were at home. There was an altercation, the police were called, and he and his lover were arrested and eventually convicted on criminal charges. His conviction for resisting arrest and criminal damage carried a "four-month conditional prison sentence." Her conviction for assault carried only a fine. She eventually instigated criminal proceedings, joined with a claim for damages, against the reporters and editors of three nationwide magazines that published her name, workplace, picture, or some combination of those items. The defendants in both cases were convicted and fined and the woman recovered damages. The European Court of Human Rights held that these judgments in the Finnish courts violated the applicants' rights to freedom of expression.

Like the House of Lords, the European Court spoke of the watchdog function of the press. I would suggest that this is not the best way to look at what is involved in these cases. Whatever the watchdog function the magazines were fulfilling in naming the public official involved in the Finnish cases, it does seem rather ambitious to claim that the magazines were also fulfilling some watchdog function in providing the name, picture, or other information about his lover. It is certainly hard to believe that anyone would have argued that they were under any quasi-fiduciary obligation to the public to provide that information. Indeed, if morality is the criterion, there is much to be said for not publishing this information even if that argument is not as strong as the argument for not publishing the name of the young boy involved in the British case. I would submit that the most sensible basis on which to justify these decisions is that the state should not punish someone for reporting about public events and publicly available material even if the purpose of publication was primarily the monetary one of increasing their circulation.

Other recent decisions of the European Court make it clear, however, that the Court is not about to adopt that categorical approach. Both cases involved Norway. One concerned two newspapers which, in publishing reports about the convictions of a woman for a particularly brutal triple murder, included in their reports photographs of the woman, who had just been convicted of these crimes and sentenced to 21 years in prison, as she was leaving the courthouse.[5] A criminal prosecution was brought against the editors-in-chief of the two newspapers. The defendants were acquitted in the trial but, on appeal, the Supreme Court of Norway found the defendants guilty and fined them. They then brought the case to the European Court which unanimously held that their rights of freedom of expression under Article 10 of the Convention had not been violated because the actions of the Norwegian authorities were within what was called their "wide

---

5. Egeland v. Norway, Application No. 34438/04, Judgment of April 16, 2009.

margin of appreciation."⁶ The European Court relied on a Norwegian statute forbidding the taking of photographs of accused or convicted persons on their way to or from court. The application of the statute in the circumstances in the case was justified as being necessary both to protect the privacy interests of criminal defendants guaranteed by Article 8 and to avoid putting additional pressure on them so as to ensure their rights to a fair trial guaranteed by Article 6. In the other case, decided a week previously, the same section of the Court (the First Section) had found against Norway in a case in which the applicant, previously convicted of murder, had been refused a remedy in the Norwegian courts against reports on a TV broadcast and in a "subscription newspaper" of his interrogation in connection with police attempts to solve the rape and murder of two young girls.⁷ The TV report included some pictures of the applicant. The Court unanimously held that Norway had violated his rights under Article 8, even though the matter in question had attracted very wide public attention. This somewhat inconsistent case law will, as a practical matter, inevitably privilege privacy over expression because defendants wishing to exercise their freedom of expression will think twice before publishing anything that could be the subject of a plausible privacy claim and even possible criminal prosecution. On the more general level, these cases show that, in this particular area, the hope of getting anything seriously resembling clear-cut Hohfeldian rights to freedom of expression out of a process of case-by-case adjudication is unlikely and possibly largely illusory.

This is not to say that there may not be some situations in which the moral dimensions of a problem are given presumptive preference over other types of rights or even absolute preference over any political or policy consideration. An obvious example is the International Convention on Torture which practically every country in the world has signed and ratified and which admits of no permissible use of torture. Whether, if one of the extreme scenarios that all of us can easily conjure up in which the lives of millions of people are at stake should ever arise, we can expect the obligations imposed by that treaty and similar national legislation and multinational conventions to be observed is a question that one would hope we shall never be obliged to confront. Something like that possibility is nevertheless raised by the German Federal Constitutional Court's decision in early 2006 striking down the Aviation Security Act of 2005 which, *inter alia*, authorized the German armed forces to shoot down a passenger plane "where it must be assumed under the circumstances that the aircraft is intended to be used against human lives, and where this is the only means to avert the imminent danger."⁸ In its decision, the Court first decided that, under the Basic Law

---

6. *Id.* at ¶ 55.
7. A. v. Norway, Application No. 28070/06, Judgment of April 9, 2009.
8. Judgment of February 15, 2006, 1 BVR 357/05. I am relying on the English language translation provided on the Constitutional Court's website at http://www.bundesverfassungsgericht.de/en/decisions/. The decision has received a more positive reaction in

(or Constitution) of the German Federal Republic, the authority to take the measures required, even if they were legally permissible, was lodged in the Länder and not in the Federal Government. That would have been enough to end the case. Since the provision was a reaction to the events of September 11, 2001, with the passage of time it was unlikely, given the considerable criticism that its enactment provoked, that any attempts would have been made to resurrect the provision by finding legal means to avoid that difficulty. The Court reached out, however, to rule that the right to life under Article 2.2 of the Basic Law, in conjunction with the guarantee of human dignity under Article 1.1 of the Basic Law, forbade such action to the extent that it affects innocent people on board the aircraft. In doing so, it stressed that one could never be absolutely sure that the plane was going to be flown into a building and that, moreover, given the limited extent of German airspace, the time needed to organize a response to the threat would make it impossible to exercise the authority granted by the act. The Court did not discuss the possibility that the intention of those in control of the aircraft might have become known well before it crossed into German airspace and thus have allowed time for sufficient resources to be mobilized to be able to destroy the aircraft if there were no other alternative. One wonders again what would happen in practice if that situation actually arose. After all, the occupants of the office building are also innocent and they may be far more numerous. Would the authorities actually sit still or would they act and claim that their action if not "justified" was nevertheless "excused"?

Fortunately, we are not required to answer the question of whether in some particular circumstances even a legal right incorporating some pre-eminent moral value may ever be infringed. For our purpose, all it would be necessary for us to assert is that, when extremely important but defeasible fundamental rights of supposedly equal value are at stake, if we are not prepared to accept a degree of inconsistency which might be acceptable in other less emotionally charged areas, we may be forced to accept that our so-called balancing is really driven by a host of largely subjective beliefs and attitudes and that judges are no more free of those attributes than other rational human beings. We would then be forced to choose. I have furthermore argued that freedom of expression, including religious expression, should prevail over state interests unless that expression incites immediate violence against others or urges the overthrow of the political order and there is realistic likelihood that it can have either of those effects. When

---

Germany than in other parts of Europe. *Compare* Oliver Lepsius, *Human Dignity and the Downing of Aircraft: The German Federal Constitutional Court Strikes Down a Prominent Anti-Terrorism Provision in the New Air-Transport Security Act*, 7 GERMAN L.J. 761 (2006) *with* Miguel Beltrain de Felipe and Jose Maria Rodriguez de Santiago, *Shooting Down Hijacked Aeroplanes? Sorry We're Humanists*, 14 EUR. PUB. L. 565 (2008).

privacy conflicts with freedom of expression, I have maintained that, in disputes among private parties, freedom of expression should presumptively prevail in most circumstances, that is, that any balancing should have a strong bias towards freedom of expression. The foremost reason for that preference is that a democratic society cannot exist without freedom of expression. Only the most pressing moral considerations or reasons of state security should change that bias in favor of freedom of expression. That is not to say there should not be social sanctions which might inhibit our legally protected freedom of expression. Such social or, if you wish, moral sanctions based on group morality have always existed. I am only saying that, in a free country, the state should stay out of the way as much as possible.

In preferring speech over privacy, I am also relying on the fact that the emotional harm people suffer from what they consider an invasion of their privacy is ultimately based on what they perceive as the amount of emotional tranquility to which they feel that they are entitled. This is in turn based to a great extent on how much emotional tranquility a person is led to expect. An army recruit cannot expect to enjoy the emotional tranquility of a professor of mathematics. Moreover, the emotional tranquility anyone can expect, whether he might be an army recruit or a mathematics professor, differs over both time and place. The belief that emotional tranquility is a good may be universal, but there is no such agreement as to the actual quantum of that good to which an individual is entitled.

My position is basically that the public space is truly public. It belongs to everyone and no one should be able to monopolize it by asserting that true statements made by a person who has lawfully acquired information about what has transpired in public space should be subject to legal regulation except in truly exigent circumstances. I would assert that the same should be true of any information a person acquires while engaged in lawful activities unless he has some pre-existing legal relationship with the person to whom that information pertains. The alternative is to permit the rich and powerful to silence others, even without legal justification, by threatening expensive litigation. This is not an idle fear. In the *Campbell* case, as we have several times noted, the *Daily Mirror* was ordered to pay almost £1,100,000 in costs even though the plaintiff herself only recovered £3,500.

One situation I have scarcely touched on but which is germane to this discussion is the intentional use of expression, including vituperation or sarcasm, to cause someone emotional distress. In a not very intellectually satisfying way, the various *Restatements of the Law of Torts* produced by the American Law Institute have tried to deal with the general subject of intentionally causing emotional distress while responding, often seemingly grudgingly, to the constitutional difficulties raised by the fact that much of the intentional infliction of emotional distress people inflict on others is through the use of expressive activities. The present version of the tort of intentional infliction of emotional harm in the

Restatement (Third),[9] largely repeating the language of the *Restatement (Second)*,[10] makes actionable the intentional or reckless infliction of severe emotional harm by extreme and outrageous conduct. In the *Falwell*[11] case, however, the United States Supreme Court held that, barring a statement known to be false or a statement about whose truth the speaker was recklessly indifferent, a public figure could not recover for any emotional distress inflicted by expressive conduct.

There is a case[12] now pending before the United States Supreme Court which may test the fairly general assumption, which I share, that neither may an adult private figure secure any such recovery for statements which are true or are statements, such as opinions or invective, that are neither true nor false. The case involves a demonstration close to a church in which a funeral for an American Marine killed in Iraq was being held and in which placards declaring that "God hates the USA," "Thank God for dead soldiers," and similar diatribes were displayed as part of the demonstrators' assertion that God hates America because of its tolerance of homosexuality. The father of the dead Marine, who first became aware of the demonstration from television news reports, had recovered substantial damages in the trial court, but this award was vacated by the court of appeals. It will be interesting to see what the Supreme Court does with this case. Given that the Court has already ruled that loud and vociferous anti-abortion demonstrations outside of abortion clinics cannot be prohibited so long as there is no reasonable threat of violence or physical impediment to women seeking to enter such facilities,[13] it is hard to see how the Court could reverse the decision of the court of appeals unless it were prepared to carve out a special exemption for demonstrations at funerals. Admittedly, there is some common law precedent for such a distinction. Relatives of a deceased person have been able to recover for emotional distress they have suffered as a result of the negligent desecration of the body of the deceased; and, more directly relevant to the point with which we are concerned, relatives of mentally incompetent, institutionalized patients have been able to recover for negligence when they were mistakenly informed that their loved one had died. I would nevertheless be disappointed if the Court were to allow recovery for the admittedly grossly tasteless and insensitive

---

9. *See* RESTATEMENT (THIRD) OF TORTS: PHYSICAL AND EMOTIONAL HARM. Although portions of this *Restatement* have been published, this part of that project has not yet been officially published in final form. The material with which we are concerned will almost certainly be what is presented as § 46 in A CONCISE RESTATEMENT OF TORTS 27 (Ellen M. Bublick ed., 2010).

10. *See* RESTATEMENT (SECOND) OF TORTS § 46 (a) (1964). The *Restatement (Third)* substitutes "emotional disturbance" for the *Restatement (Second)*'s "emotional distress."

11. Hustler Magazine v. Falwell, 485 U.S. 46 (1988).

12. Snyder v. Phelps, *cert. granted*, 130 S.Ct. 1737 (2010). The court of appeals' decision is reported in 580 F.3d 206 (4th Cir. 2009).

13. *See* Schenk v. Pro-Choice Network of Western New York, 519 U.S. 357 (1997); Madsen v. Women's Health Center, Inc., 512 U.S. 753 (1994).

demonstration involved in the case now before it.[14] In the event that it did allow recovery, all one can say is that state-enforced political correctness "lite" is better than state-sanctioned, full-strength political correctness. A special exception for funerals would be preferable to embarking on a mission to define and regulate so-called hate speech. From the perspective of the present study, that would be even more regrettable.

It is hard not to have qualms about giving judges, with their own strongly held views as to what an ideal society should look like, the power to decide what is artistic expression worthy of legal protection[15] or what lawfully obtained information can be divulged to others or what expressive activities are potential threats to the social order. To have in addition to live in a world in which judges can decide what tasteless and grossly offensive speech directed at fully competent adults can be legally sanctioned would only compound that discomfort. Here again is a situation in which society should, if at all possible, rely on social sanctions to reign in what might generally be accepted to be extreme language. The state itself ought not be the final moral arbiter. Even more importantly, being made a judge does not qualify a person to be a philosopher king.

---

14. One can accept that a child or someone known to the actor to be suffering from diminished mental capacity or from illness might have a different and more plausible case.

15. *See* Chapter 11, *supra*, at note 35.

BIBLIOGRAPHY

Aikens, Joan et al., *Chuck Schumer vs. Free Speech*, Wall St. J., May 19, 2010, at A19.

Aleinikoff, T. Alexander, *Constitutional Law in an Age of Balancing*, 96 Yale L.J. 943 (1987).

Alter, Karen J., *Delegating to International Courts: Self-Binding vs. Other-Binding Delegation*, 71 Law & Contemp. Probs. 37 (2008).

Amos, Mary J., *Comment:* Derolph v. State: *Who Really Won Ohio's State Funding Battle?* 30 Cap. U. L. Rev. 153 (2002).

Amos, Merris, *Problems with the Human Rights Act 1998 and How to Remedy Them: Is a Bill of Rights the Answer?* 72 Mod. L. Rev. 883 (2009).

Anderson, Kent and Emma Saint, *Japan's Quasi-Jury* (Saiban-in) *Law: An Annotated Translation of the Act Concerning Participation of Lay Assessors in Criminal Trials*, 6 Asian Pacific L. & Pol. J. 233 (2005).

Arai-Takahashi, Yutaka, THE MARGIN OF APPRECIATION DOCTRINE AND THE PRINCIPLE OF PROPORTIONALITY IN THE JURISPRUDENCE OF THE ECHR (2002).

Ashworth, Andrew, PRINCIPLES OF ENGLISH LAW (6th ed. 2009).

THE ANTI-FEDERALIST (Herbert J. Storing ed., 1985).

AULD, LORD JUSTICE, 2001 REVIEW OF THE CRIMINAL COURTS OF ENGLAND AND WALES, available at http://www.criminal-courts-review.org.uk.

Austin, John, LECTURES ON JURISPRUDENCE (R. Campbell ed., 5th rev. ed. 1885).

Baran, Jan Bitold, THE ELECTION LAW PRIMER FOR CORPORATIONS (5th ed. 2008).

Barnett, Hilaire, CONSTITUTIONAL & ADMINISTRATIVE LAW (2009).

Beck, Gunnar, *The Mythology of Human Rights*, 21 Ratio Juris 312 (2008).

Bell, Bernard W., *Legislatively Revising* Kelo v. City of New London: *Eminent Domain, Federalism, and Congressional Powers* (2005), available at http://ssrn.com/abstract=800174.

Beltrain de Felipe, Miguel and Jose Maria Rodriguez de Santiago, *Shooting Down Hijacked Aeroplanes? Sorry, We're Humanists*, 14 Eur. Pub. L. 565 (2008).

Bentham, Jeremy, OF LAWS IN GENERAL (H.L.A. Hart ed., 1970).

Brilmayer, Lea, *Interest Analysis and the Myth of Legislative Intent*, 78 Mich. L. Rev. 392 (1980).

Buchanan, Allen E., HUMAN RIGHTS, LEGITIMACY, AND THE USE OF FORCE (2010).

Buckley, William F. Jr., RUMBLES LEFT AND RIGHT (1963).

Burri, Suzanne, *The Position of the European Court of Justice with Respect to the Enforcement of Human Rights*, in CHANGING PERCEPTIONS OF SOVEREIGNTY AND HUMAN RIGHTS: ESSAYS IN HONOUR OF CEES FLINTERMAN 311 (Ineke Boerefijn and Jenny E. Goldschmidt eds., 2008).

Buxton, Sir Richard, *Sitting en Banc in the New Supreme Court*, 125 L.Q. Rev. 288 (2009).

Cananea, Giacinto della, *Beyond the State: The Europeanization and Globalization of Procedural Administrative Law*, 9 Eur. Pub. Law 563 (2003).

Carter, James C., LAW: ITS ORIGIN, GROWTH, AND FUNCTION (1907).

Chrisafis, Angelique, *French MP's Back Law to Bar Media from Promoting Anorexia*, Guardian, Apr. 16, 2008, *available at* http://www.guardian.co.uk/world/2008/apr/16/france.law (last visited Nov. 21, 2009).

George C. Christie, LAW, NORMS AND AUTHORITY (1982).
   THE NOTION OF AN IDEAL AUDIENCE IN LEGAL ARGUMENT (2000).
   Dworkin's Empire, 1987 Duke L.J. 157.
   An Essay on Discretion, 1986 Duke L.J. 747.
   The Importance of Recognizing the Underlying Assumptions of Legal and Moral Arguments: of Law and Rawls, 28 Australian J. Leg. Phil. 39 (2003).
   Judicial Review of Findings of Fact, 87 Nw. U. L. Rev. 14 (1992).
   The Model of Principles, 1968 Duke L.J. 649.
   Objectivity in the Law, 78 Yale L.J. 1311 (1969).
Cicero, Marcus Tullius, THE REPUBLIC AND THE LAWS (N. Rudd trans., Oxford World's Classics ed. 1998).
Clifford, Stephanie, *From Rumor to a Hint of Respect*, N.Y. Times, Mar. 8, 2010, at B1.
Cohen, Roger, *The End of the End of the Revolution*, N.Y. Times Magazine, Sunday, Dec. 7, 2008.
Colby, Thomas B. and Peter J. Smith, *Living Originalism*, 59 Duke L.J. 239 (2009).
A CONCISE RESTATEMENT OF TORTS (Ellen M. Bublick ed., 2010).
Corbin, Arthur, *Legal Analysis and Terminology*, 29 Yale L.J. 163 (1919).
Croft, Jane and Jim Pickard, *Gagging Order Eased*, FT.com, Oct. 13, 2009.
D'Amato, Anthony, *Legal Uncertainty*, 71 Cal. L. Rev. 1 (1983).
Damaška, Miryan, THE FACES OF JUSTICE AND STATE AUTHORITY (1986).
Defeis, Elizabeth F., *Human Rights and the European Court of Justice: An Appraisal*, 31 Fordham Int'l L.J. 1104 (2008).
Dembour, Marie Bénédicte, WHO BELIEVES IN HUMAN RIGHTS? (2006).
van Drooghenbroeck, Sérieux, LA PROPORTIONNALITÉ DANS LE DROIT DE LA CONVENTION EUROPÉENNE DES DROITS DE L'HOMME (2001).
Dunne, Finley Peter, MR. DOOLEY'S OPINIONS (1901).
Dworkin, Ronald, JUSTICE IN ROBES (2006).
   LAW'S EMPIRE (1986).
   A MATTER OF PRINCIPLE (1985).
   TAKING RIGHTS SERIOUSLY (1977).
   Judicial Discretion, 60 J. Phil. 638 (1963).
   The Model of Rules, 35 U. Chi. L. Rev. 14 (1967).
   Rights as Trumps, in THEORIES OF RIGHTS 153–68 (Jeremy Waldron ed., 1985).
Ely, John Hart, *Choice of Law and the State's Interest in Protecting Its Own*, 23 Wm. & Mary L. Rev. 173 (1981).
Fitzsimons, Peter, *Insider Trading in New Zealand*, in SECURITIES REGULATION IN AUSTRALIA AND NEW ZEALAND 595 (G. Walker and B. Fisse eds., 1998).
Fletcher, George P., *Comparative Law as a Subversive Discipline*, 46 Am. J. Comp. L. 683 (1998).
Frazaneh, Kayvan, *Foreign Policy: Europe's Burqa Wars*, NPR.org, May 12, 2010, available at http://www.npr.org/templates/story/story.php?storyId=126772691.
Fuller, Lon L., THE LAW IN QUEST OF ITSELF (1940).
Gardbaum, Stephen, *The "Horizontal Effect" of Constitutional Rights*, 102 Mich. L. Rev. 387 (2003).
Gény, François, MÉTHODE D'INTERPRÉTATION ET SOURCES EN DROIT PRIVÉ POSITIF (Jaro Mayda trans., 2d ed. 1954) (1919).
Ghosh, Eric, *Deliberative Democracy and the Countermajoritarian Difficulty: Considering Constitutional Juries*, 30 Oxford J. Legal Stud. 327 (2010).

Greenawalt, Kent, *Discretion and Judicial Decision*, 75 Colum. L. Rev. 359 (1975).
  Policy, Rights and Judicial Decisions, 11 Ga. L. Rev. 991 (1977).
Greer, Steven, THE EUROPEAN CONVENTION ON HUMAN RIGHTS: ACHIEVEMENTS, PROBLEMS AND PROSPECTS (2006).
Guess, Raymond, THE IDEA OF A CRITICAL THEORY: HABERMAS AND THE FRANKFURT SCHOOL (1981).
Gunther, Gerald, LEARNED HAND: THE MAN AND THE JUDGE (1994).
Hart, H.L.A., THE CONCEPT OF LAW (1961).
  Scandinavian Realism, [1959] Camb. L.J. 233.
Habermas, Jürgen, BETWEEN FACTS AND NORMS (W. Rehg trans., 1996).
Hobbes, Thomas, LEVIATHAN (Everyman's Library, 1914) (1651).
Hohfeld, Wesley N., FUNDAMENTAL LEGAL CONCEPTIONS (1919).
Honan, William H., *Judge Ends Ban on Film of Asylum*, N.Y. Times, Aug. 3, 1991, § 1 at 12.
Hruschka, Joachim, *The Permissive Law of Practical Reason in Kant's Metaphysics of Morals*, 23 Law & Philosophy 45 (2004).
Hume, David, A TREATISE OF HUMAN NATURE, BK. III (L.A. Selby–Bigge ed., 1888) (1779).
Hutcheson, Joseph C., *The Judgment Intuitive: The Function of the "Hunch" in Judicial Decision*, 14 Cornell L.Q. 274 (1929).
Israel, Jerold H., *Gideon v. Wainwright: The Art of Overruling*, 1963 Sup. Ct. Rev. 211.
von Jhering, Rudolf, LAW AS A MEANS TO AN END (Issac. Husik trans. 1924).
Juenger, Friedrich, *Conflict of Laws: A Critique of Interest Analysis*, 32 Am. J. Comp. L. 1 (1984).
Kelsen, Hans, GENERAL THEORY OF LAW AND STATE (A. Wedberg trans., 1949) (1945).
Knight, C. J. S., *Bi-Polar Sovereignty Restated*, 68 Cambridge L.J. 361 (2009).
Lange, David L. and H. Jefferson Powell, No LAW (2009).
Leftsas, George, A THEORY OF INTERPRETATION OF THE EUROPEAN CONVENTION ON HUMAN RIGHTS (2007).
Lepsius, Oliver, *Human Dignity and the Downing of Aircraft: The German Federal Constitutional Court Strikes Down a Prominent Anti-terrorism Provision in the New Air-Transport Security Act*, 7 German L.J. 761 (2006).
Lewis, Tom, *What Not to Wear: Religious Rights, the European Court, and the Margin of Appreciation*, 56 Int'l & Comp. L. Q. 395 (2007).
Lindseth, Peter L., *Democratic Legitimacy and the Administrative Character of Supranationalism*, 99 Colum. L.Rev. 628 (1999).
Llewellyn, Karl N., THE COMMON LAW TRADITION: DECIDING APPEALS (1960).
  A Realistic Jurisprudence—The Next Step, 30 Colum. L. Rev. 431 (1930).
Locke, John, ESSAYS ON THE LAW OF NATURE (ESSAY I) (W. von Leyden trans., 1954).
  THE SECOND TREATISE OF GOVERNMENT (T.P. Beardon ed., 1952) (1690).
Macaulay, Thomas Babington, CRITICAL & HISTORICAL ESSAYS (Rev. ed. 1850).
Main, Jackson T., *Government by the People, the Americanization and the Democratization of the Legislature*, Wm. and Mary Q., 3d Series, 23 at 391 (1966).
Mason, Sir Anthony, *Envoi to the House of Lords—A View From Afar*, 125 L.Q. Rev. 584 (2009).
McClintock, Henry L., EQUITY (2d ed. 1948).
Mead, George Herbert, MIND, SELF, AND SOCIETY (1934).
Miettinen, Samuel, CRIMINAL LAW AND POLICY IN THE EUROPEAN UNION (2010).
Moore, Harry T., THE INTELLIGENT HEART (1954).

Moyn, Samuel, THE LAST UTOPIA (2010).
Murphy, Liam and Thomas Nagel, THE MYTH OF OWNERSHIP (2002).
Nimmer, Melvin B., *The Right to Speak from Times to Time: First Amendment Theory Applied to Libel and Misapplied to Privacy*, 56 Cal. L. Rev. 935 (1968).
Nozick, Robert, ANARCHY, STATE AND UTOPIA (1974).
Obhof, Larry J., *Rethinking Judicial Activism and Restraint in School Finance Litigation*, 27 Harv. J.L. & Pub. Pol'y 569 (2004).
Oliphant, Herman, *A Return to Stare Decisis*, 14 A.B.A. J. 71 (1928).
Osiatyski, Wiktor, HUMAN RIGHTS AND THEIR LIMITS (2009).
Perelman, Ch. and L. Olbrechts-Tyteca, THE NEW RHETORIC: A TREATISE ON ARGUMENTATION (J. Wilkinson & P. Weaver trans., 1969).
Perron, Walter, *Lay Participation in Germany*, 72 Int'l Rev. Penal L. 181 (2001).
Pierce, Richard J. Jr., ADMINISTRATIVE LAW TREATISE (4th ed. 2002).
Pound, Roscoe, *Individual Interests of Substance—Promised Advantages*, 59 Harv. L. Rev. 1 (1945).
  Interests of Personality, 28 Harv. L. Rev. 343 (1915).
  Mechanical Jurisprudence, 8 Colum. L. Rev. 605 (1908).
Pradel, Jean, *Criminal Procedure, in* INTRODUCTION TO FRENCH LAW (George A. Bermann and Etienne Picard eds., 2008).
Puchta, Georg, OUTLINES OF JURISPRUDENCE AS THE SCIENCE OF RIGHT (William Hastie trans., 1887) (reprinted 1982) (1822).
von Pufendorf, Samuel, DE JURE NATURAE ET GENTIUM, BK II (1672).
Rawls, John, JUSTICE AS FAIRNESS: A RESTATEMENT (2001).
  POLITICAL LIBERALISM (1993).
  A THEORY OF JUSTICE (1971).
  A THEORY OF JUSTICE (rev. ed. 1999).
  Justice as Fairness: Political not Metaphysical, 14 Phil. & Pub. Aff. 223 (1985).
Rider, Barry A. K., *Insider Trading: An English Comment in New Zealand, in* ESSAYS ON INSIDER TRADING AND SECURITIES LITIGATION 60 (C. Richett and R. Grantham eds., 1997).
Ross, Alf, ON LAW AND JUSTICE (1958).
von Savigny, Friedrich Carl, VOM BERUF UNSERER ZEIT FÜR GESETZGEBUNG UND RECHTSWISSENSCHAFT (Of the Vocation of Our Age for Legislation and Jurisprudence) (1814).
Searcey, Dionne, *Dirty Laundry Aired: The Fight Over Revealing Divorce Details*, Wall St. J., May 28, 2009, at A10.
Shiffren, Seana Valentine, *Equal Citizenship: Race and Ethnicity: Race, Labor and Fair Equality of Opportunity Principle*, 72 Fordham L. Rev. 1643 (2004).
Simpson, A.W. Brian, HUMAN RIGHTS AND THE END OF EMPIRE: BRITAIN AND THE GENESIS OF THE EUROPEAN CONVENTION (2004).
Smith, Adam, THE THEORY OF MORAL SENTIMENTS (1759) (Liberty Fund Facsimile ed. 1982).
Stanly, Paul, THE LAW OF CONFIDENTIALITY: A RESTATEMENT (2008).
Stone, Julius, LEGAL SYSTEMS AND LAWYERS: REASONINGS (1964).
Summers, Robert S., INSTRUMENTALISM AND AMERICAN LEGAL THEORY (1982).
Sweet, Alec Stone, GOVERNING WITH JUDGES (2000).
Swiss Convict Turk of Denying Armenian Genocide, Reuters, Mar. 9, 2009, available at http://www.reuters.com/article/latestCrisis/idUSL09197269.

Thaman, Stephen C., *Europe's New Jury Systems: The Cases of Spain and Russia*, 62 Law & Contemp. Probs. 233 (1999), *reprinted in* THE JURY SYSTEM: CONTEMPORARY SCHOLARSHIP 99 (Valerie Hans ed., 2006).

Third Time Unlucky; Criminal Justice, The Economist, Sept. 16, 2006, at 66.

Trouille, Helen, *Private Life and Public Image: Privacy Legislation in France*, 49 Int'l & Comp. L.Q. 199 (2000).

Tushnet, Mark and Katya Lezin, *What Really Happened in* Brown v. Board of Education, 91 Colum. L. Rev. 1867 (1991).

UNITED STATES ATTORNEYS' MANUAL

Vidmar, Neil and Valerie P. Hans, AMERICAN JURIES (2007).

Watkins, Floyd C., THOMAS WOLFE'S CHARACTERS: PORTRAIT FROM LIFE (1957).

Williams, Andrew, *Respecting Fundamental Rights in the New Union: A Review*, *in* THE FUNDAMENTALS OF EU LAW REVISITED (Catherine Barnard ed., 2007).

Williams, Bernard, ETHICS AND THE LIMITS OF PHILOSOPHY (1985).

Wood, Gordon S., THE CREATION OF THE AMERICAN REPUBLIC (1969).

Zucca, Lorenzo, CONSTITUTIONAL DILEMMAS (2007).

TABLE OF CASES

A. v. Norway, Application No. 28070/06, Judgment of
   April 9, 2009 .... 171*n*7
A. v. United Kingdom, Original Application No. 2599/94,
   judgment of Sept. 23, 1998, 27 Eur. H.R. Rep. 611 (1999) 29, 30, 51
Aksoy v. Turkey, Application No. 21987/73, Judgment of
   18 December 1996, 23 Eur. H.R. Rep. 553 (1997) 40*n*10
Alcock v. Chief Constable of the South Yorks. Police, [1992]
   A.C. 310, (1991) 94*n*16
Altbach v. Kulon, 754 N.Y.S.2d 709 (App. Div. 2003) 157*n*23
Anns v. Merton London Borough Council, [1978] 1 A.C. 410 (1977) 93, 93*n*11
Attorney General v. Guardian Newspapers Ltd (No. 2) [also referred
   to as the *Spycatcher* case], [1990] 1 A.C. 109 (1988) 55*n*8, 158

Bartnicki v. Vopper, 532 U.S. 514 (2001) 68
Benmax v. Austin Motor Co., [1955] A.C. 370 .... 24*n*12
Bily v. Arthur Young & Co., 3 Cal. 4th 370 (1992) 92*n*8
Bose Corp. v. Consumers Union of the United States, Inc.,
   466 U.S. 485 (1984) 23*n*8, 23*n*9
Brandenburg v. Ohio, 395 U.S. 444 (1969) 114*n*30
Branzburg v. Hayes, 408 U.S. 665 (1972) 140*n*34
Briscoe v. Readers Digest Ass'n, 4 Cal. 3d 529 (1971) 65*n*42
Brown v. Board of Education of Topeka,
   347 U.S. 483 (1954) 79*n*3, 145, 145*n*46
Burnet v. Coronado Oil & Gas Co., 285 U.S. 393 (1932) 135*n*10
Bush v. Gore, 531 U.S. 98 (2000) 124, 124*n*9
Bushell's Case, 6 State Trials 999, 124 Eng. Rep. 1006 (C.P. 1670)......... 31*n*30

Campbell v. MGN Ltd, [2004] 2 A.C. 457 .... 8, 53–58, 59, 61, 62–63, 65,
                66–67, 68, 70, 72, 80, 111, 151, 154, 155, 157–60, 168, 173
Campbell v. MGN Ltd (No. 2), [2005] 1 W. L. R. 3394 (H.L. 2004)......... 58*n*17
CBOCS West, Inc. v. Humphries, 128 S. Ct. 1951 (2008) 135*n*12
Chevron U.S.A., Inc. v. National Resources Defense Council, Inc.,
   467 U.S. 837 (1984) 28*n*22
Citizens United v. Federal Election Commission,
   130 S. Ct. 876 (2010)............................. 135–42, 145, 146, 153

184 TABLE OF CASES

Cohen v. Cowles Media Co., 501 U.S. 663 (1991)......................66n47
Commonwealth v. Wiseman, 356 Mass. 251 N.E.2d 610 (1969)..........161–62
Commonwealth v. Wiseman Civ. Action No. 87538,
    Mass. Superior Ct., Suffolk Cty., July 29, 1991....................162n32
Cullen v. Grove Press, Inc., 276 F. Supp. 727 (S.D.N.Y. 1967)............162n32

Dandridge v. Williams, 397 U.S. 471 (1970).........................146n47
Dempsey v. Addison Crane Co., 247 F. Supp. 584 (D.D.C. 1965)..........27n20
Dennis v. United States, 341 U.S. 494 (1951).......................113n29
Deutsche Telekom v. Schröder, Case C-50/96, [2000] ECR I-743............ xivn2
Dirks v. SEC, 463 U.S. 646 (1983)..................................67n49
Dogru v. France, Application No. 27058/05, Judgment of
    4 December 2008..46nn25–26
Dun and Bradstreet, Inc. v. Greenmoss Builders, Inc.,
    472 U.S. 749 (1985)...140n34

eBay Inc. v. MercExchange, L.L.C., 547 U.S. 388 (2006).................133n7
Editions Plon v. France, Application No. 58148/00, Judgment
    of May 18, 2004..59n24
Egeland v. Norway, Application No. 34438/04, Judgment of
    April 16, 2009...170n5
Ehrenfeld v. Mahfouz, 518 F.3d 102 (2d Cir. 2008).....................70n55

Falwell Case, see *Hustler Magazine v. Falwell*
Federal Election Commission v. Wisconsin Right to Life, Inc.,
    551 U.S. 449 (2007)...136n19
Flinkkilä v. Finland, Application No. 25576/04, Judgment
    of April 6, 2010..169n4
First Cypress Case, see *Greece v. United Kingdom*

Garaudy v. France, Application No. 65831/01, Judgment
    of 24 June 2003..41n13
Gates v. Discovery Communications, Inc., 34 Cal. 4th 679 (2004)..........65n42
Gertz v. Robert Welch, Inc., 418 U.S. 323 (1974), 140, 152n6.............154n12
Gideon v. Wainwright, 372 U.S. 335 (1963).........................141n36
Grant v. Torstar Corp., [2009] 3 S.C.R. 640 ....152n8
Greece v. United Kingdom, Application 175/56, Report of
    26 September 1958, [also referred to as the
    First Cypress Case]....................................39–40, 39n6
Greece v. United Kingdom, Application 299/57, Report of
    8 July 1959, [also referred to as the *Second Cypress Case*]......39n6, 40, 40n7

Gündüz v. Turkey, Application No. 35071/97, Judgment of
   4 December 2003 44

Handyside v. United Kingdom, Application No. 5493/72,
   Judgment of 7 December 1976, 1 Eur. H.R. Rep. 737
   (1979–80) 50n41, 72–73n59
Hood v. Naeter Brothers Publishing Co., 562 S.W.2d 770
   (Mo. App. 1978) 64n41
Hosking v. Runting, [2005] 1 N.Z.L.R. 1 (2004) (C.A.) 69n53, 156n18
Howell v. New York Post Co., 81 N.Y.2d 115 (1993) 157n22
Hustler Magazine v. Falwell, 485 U.S. 46 (1988), [also referred
   to as the *Falwell* case] 174

In re G, [2009] 1 A.C. 173 (2008) 22n3, 29n23
In re an Arbitration between Polemis and Furness,
   Withy & Co., [1921] K.B. 560 (C.A.) 135n18
In re S, [2005] A.C. 593 (2004) 168n2
*Internationale Handelsgesellschaft v. Einfuhr und Vorratsselle für
   Getreide und Futtermitel*, Case 11/70, [1970] ECR 1125 . . . . xivn1
Ireland v. United Kingdom, Series A, No. 25, Application
   No. 5310/71, Judgment of 28 January 1978, 2 Eur. H.R. Rep.
   25 (1979–80) 40nn8–9

Jameel v. Wall Street Journal Europe SPRL,
   [2007] 1 A.C. 359 (2006) 151, 151n2, 151n4, 152n7
John R. Sand & Gravel Co. v. U.S., 552 U.S. 130 (2008) 135n11
Joseph Burstyn, Inc. v. Wilson, 343 U.S. 495 (1952) 113n28

Kelo v. City of New London, 545 U.S. 469 (2005) 18
Kervanci v. France, Application No. 31645/04, Judgment of
   4 December 2008 . . . . 46n25

Laird v. Tatum, 408 U.S. 1 (1972) 72n58
Lange v. Atkinson, [2000] 3 N.Z.L.R. 385 (C.A.) 152n10
Lange v. Australian Broadcasting Corp., 189 C.L.R. 520 (1997) 152n9
Lautsi v. Italie, Application No. 30814/06, Judgment of
   3 November 2009 . . . . 42n17
Lawless v. Ireland, Application No. 332/57, Judgment of
   1 July 1961, 1 Eur. H.R. Rep. 15 (1979–80) 40n8
Leyla Sahin v. Turkey, Application No. 44774/98, Judgment
   of 10 November 2005, 44 Eur. H.R. Rep. 5 (2007) 44–48, 44nn18–19,
                                                                44n21, 45n22, 51, 80

186 TABLE OF CASES

Lingle v. Chevron U.S.A., Inc., 544 U.S. 528 (2005) 121n2
Lord Browne of Madingley v. Associated Newspapers Ltd, [2008]
    Q.B. 103 (2007)..65n45

Madsen v. Women's Health Center, Inc., 512 U.S. 753 (1994) 174n13
Margaret, Duchess of Argyll v. Duke of Argyll, [1967]
    Ch. 302 (1965).....................................55n8, 158, 158n27
McKennit v. Ash, [2008] Q.B. 73 (C.A. 2006)...........................65n44
McLeod v. Comm'r of Police of the Metropolis, [1994]
    4 All E. R. 553 (C.A.)...25n15
McLeod v. The United Kingdom, Application No. 24755/94, Judgment
    of 23 September 1998, 27 Eur. H. R. Rep. 493 (1999) 24–29, 30
McLoughlin v. O'Brian, [1983] A.C. 410 (1982).........................93–94
Murphy v. Brentwood District Council, [1991] 1 A.C. 398 (1990) 93n10
Murray v. Express Newspapers LLC, [2008] 3 W.L.R. 1360 (C.A.) 69n53
Müller v. Switzerland, Application No. 10737/84, Judgment of
    24 May 1988, 13 Eur. H.R. Rep. 212 (1991) 48–50, 51, 126

New York Times Co. v. Sullivan, 376 U.S. 254 (1964) 23nn8–9, 122, 152n5
New York Times v. United States, 403 U.S. 713 (1971),
    [also referred to as the *Pentagon Papers* case] 63n36, 68

Otto-Preminger-Institut v. Austria, Application No. 13470/87, Judgment
    of 20 September 1994, 19 Eur. H.R. Rep. 34 (1995).................49–50
*Overseas Tankship (U.K.) Ltd. v. Morts Dock and Engineering Co.,
    Ltd. (The Wagon Mound)*, [1961] A.C. 388 (P.C.) 135–36, 135n17

Parents Involved in Community Schools v. Seattle School District No. 1,
    551 U.S. 701 (2007) 7, 7n16
Pentagon Papers Case, see New York Times v. United States
Planned Parenthood of S.E. Pa. v. Casey,
    505 U.S. 833 (1992) 60n32, 135, 135n13
Prosecutor v. Duško Tadi , Case No. It-94-1-T, Ruling of
    August 10, 1995, on Prosecutor's Motion for Protective
    Measures for Victims and Witnesses 64n40

Quan v. Cusson, [2009] 3 S.C.R. 712 ....152n8

*R (on the application of X) v. Head Teacher and Governors
    of Y School*, [2008] 1 All E.R. 249 (Q. B. 2007).....................47n30

R (Shabina Begum) v. Governors of Denbigh High School,
 [2007] A.C. 100 (2006) 22n3, 46n27
Randall v. Sorrel, 548 U.S. 230 (2006) 142nn39–41
RB (Algeria) v. Secretary of State for the Home Dep't, [2009]
 4 W.L.R. 1045 (H.L.) 71n56
Refah Partisi v. Turkey, Application No. 41340/98 et al.,
 Judgment of 13 February 2003 (Grand Chamber),
 37 Eur. H.R. Rep. 1 (2003) 45n23
*Regina v. Bow Street Metropolitan Stipendiary Magistrate,
 ex parte Pinochet Ugarte (No. 3)*, [2000] A.C. 147 (1999) 7n15
Repouille v. United States, 165 F.2d 152 (2d Cir. 1947)..................125–26
Reynolds v. Times Newspapers Ltd., [2001] 2 A.C. 127 (1999) 152n7
Riggs v. Palmer, 115 N.Y. 506 (1889) 90n4
Roe v. Wade, 410 U.S. 113 (1973) 125n13, 135
Rosenblum v. Adler, 93 N.J. 324 (1983) 92n7
Rylands v. Fletcher, L.R. 3 E. & I. App. 330 (1868) 111

SARL Louis Feraud Int'l v. Viewfinder Inc.,
 406 F. Supp. 2d 274 (S.D.N.Y. 2005) 70n55
Schenk v. Pro-Choice Network of Western New York,
 519 U.S. 357 (1997) 174n13
SEC v. Falbo, 14 F. Supp. 2d 508 (S.D.N.Y. 1998).......................67n48
SEC v. Switzer, 590 F. Supp. 756 (W.D. Okla. 1984) 67n48
Second Cypress Case, see Greece v. United Kingdom
Secretary of State v. AF (No. 3), [2009] 3 All E.R. 643 (H.L.) 7n15
Shays v. FEC, 337 F. Supp. 2d 28 (D.D.C. 2004) 137n23
Simeonov v. Tiegs, 602 N.Y.S.2d 1014 (N.Y.C. Civ. Ct., 1993) 157n23
Snyder v. Phelps, 130 S. Ct. 1737 (2010) 174n12
Socash v. Addison Crane Co., 346 F.2d 420 (D.C. Cir. 1965)..............27n20
Spycatcher Case, see Attorney General v. Guardian Newspapers Ltd (No. 2)

Thaler v. Haynes, 130 S. Ct. 1171 (2010) 121n2
The Florida Star v. B. J. F., 491 U.S. 524 (1989) 63–65
Tuomela v. Finland, Application No. 25711/04, Judgment of
 April 6, 2010 ....169n4

Vereinigung Bildender Künstler v. Austria, Application
 No. 68354/01, Judgment of January 25, 2007............157n23, 163–64n35
Virgil v. Time, Inc., 527 F.2d 1122 (9th Cir. 1975)................66n46, 159n28
Virginia v. Black, 538 U.S. 343 (2003) 114n30

188 TABLE OF CASES

von Hannover v. Germany, Application No. 59320/00, Judgment
   of June 24, 2004, 40 Eur. H. R. Rep. 1 (2005) 53*n*4, 58–61, 63, 66,
   68, 70, 72, 73, 80, 111, 115–116, 115*nn*31–32,
   116*nn*33–34, 121, 154–55, 159
von Hannover v. Germany, Application No. 40660/08 156
   (case awaiting decision)

Washington v. Glucksberg, 521 U.S. 702 (1997) 125*n*13
W.E.B. DuBois Clubs of America v. Clark, 389 U.S. 309 (1967) 72*n*58
Winter v. DC Comics, 30 Cal. 4th 881 (2003). 157*n*20
Witzsch v. Germany, Application No. 41448/98, Judgment
   of 20 April 1999 . . . . 41*n*13
Witzsch v. Germany, Application No. 7485/03, Judgment
   of 13 December 2005 . . . . 41*n*13, 42*n*14

Yahoo! Inc. v. La Ligue Contre Le Racisme,
   433 F. 3d 1199 (9th Cir. 2006) 70*n*55

INDEX

Abstract right, 15, 19. *See also* Rights
Ad hoc balancing, 54, 120, 121. *See also* Balancing
   distinguished from definitional balancing, 110
   use in constitutional adjudication, 110–11, 113–15
Adjudication
   case-by-case. *See* Case-by-case adjudication
   principle-driven theory of, 78
   quasi-deductive model of, 84, 105
Administrative Procedure Act, 28*n*22
Affirmative action policies, 102
African Charters on Human and People's Rights (1981), 19*n*11
Aikens, John et al., 139*n*29
Alenikoff, T. Alexander, 110*n*15, 113*n*27
Alter, Karen J., 3*n*1
American Bill of Rights of 1791, 17
Amos, Mary J, 146
Amos, Merris, 28*n*22
Anderson, Kent, 127*n*20
American Convention on Human Rights (1969), 19*n*11
Anti-paparazzi law, 156
Appellate courts, 7, 27, 28, 79*n*3, 80, 82, 84, 86, 127. *See also* Court(s)
   limitations on the authority of, 23–24
Appropriations Act of 2006, 18
"Arbitrary or capricious" test, 28*n*22
Arai-Takahashi, Yutaka, 41*n*11
Ashworth, Andrew, 127*n*22
Auld, Lord Justice, 127-28*n*22
Austin, John, 6
Authority of courts, 123–24
   over the members of a society, exercising, 124
Aviation Security Act of 2005, 171

Balancing, 105–16
   ad hoc, 54, 110–11, 113–15, 120, 121
   definitional. *See* Factor analysis
   degree of precision in, 109
   individual interests versus social interests, 109–10
   moral rights against political rights, 168–73
   the protection of private life against freedom of expression, 53–61
   role in judicial decision making, 106, 108
Baran, Jan Bitold, 138-39*n*27
Barnett, Hilaire, 22*n*2, 28*n*22
Barreto, Judge Ireneu Cabral, 61
Basic Law (or Constitution) of the German Federal Republic, 171–72
Basic liberties, 99, 102
Bell, Bernard, 18*n*9
Bentham, Jeremy, 9
Brandeis, Justice Louis D., 135
Breach of confidence, 54–56, 68, 158
Breach of contract, 18–19
Breyer, Justice Stephen, 135
Brilmeier, Lea, 112*n*26
Buckley, William F., 125
Burri, Suzanne, xiv*n*3
Buxton, Sir Richard, 7*n*15

Canadian Charter of Rights and Freedoms, 19*n*12
Canadian Criminal Law, 31
Carswell, Lord, 8, 56-57
Carter, James C., 106
Case-by-case adjudication, 50, 67
   ad hoc balancing, use of, 54, 110–11, 113–15, 120, 121
   of contentious human rights controversies, 147–64
   of contested human rights cases, 133
   legal development by, 79–80
   limitations of, 130

Case-by-case adjudication (*contd.*)
  minimal goal for, in contentious cases, 110–11, 113–15, 119–28
  optimal conditions for, 129–46
Children Act 2004, 30*n*29
Chilling effect, 113–14
Chrisafis, Angelique, 42*n*17
Christie, George C., 22*n*6, 77*n*1, 89*n*1, 90*n*4, 91*n*6, 101*n*28, 106*n*1, 112*n*21, 121*n*2, 123*n*7, 133*n*6
Cicero, Marcus Tullius, 5, 129–30
Civil law, 21–24
  right to privacy, 121
Civil law courts. *See also* Court(s)
  and common law court, structural differences between, 21–22
  finding of a specific fact, 23–24
  limitations on the authority of, 23
  trial by a judge, 22–23
Claim rights, 13–14. *See also* Rights
Clayton Act of 1914, 81
Clifford, Stephanie, 151*n*3
Colby, Thomas B., 86
Commercial law, practical motive of, 107
Common law
  jurisdiction, 26
  privilege, 25
  prohibition against double jeopardy, 31–32
  reasonableness in, 27–28, 29
  right to privacy, 121
  stare decisis, 132
  statutes, 79
  tolerance of jury nullification, 30–31
Common law courts. *See also* Court(s)
  and civil law courts, structural differences between, 21–22
  finding of a specific fact, 24
  trial by a judge, 22–23
  trial by jury, 22–23
Confidentiality, 65, 116
  duty of, 55, 55*n*8, 66
Conflicting human rights, 83*n*13, 122 and *passim*
Convergence theory of truth, 6
Corbin, Arthur, 14

Corporate speech versus individual speech, 138–39*n*27
Court(s). *See also* House of Lords; Supreme Court of the United Kingdom; United States Supreme Court
  civil law. *See* Civil law courts
  common law. *See* Common law courts
  dealing with human rights litigation, 18
  decision over contentious questions, 7–8
  to protect human rights, 4
  role of, in controversial case, 122–23
Court decisions in controversial cases. *See also* Court(s)
  degree of confidence, 123
  logic of legal decision making, 122–23
  sharply divided decisions, 8
Court of Appeal, 8, 24, 25, 31*n*34, 47, 54, 69*n*53, 93, 126, 168, 174
Criminal Justice Act of 2003, 31*n*34, 33*n*37
Croft, Jane, 69*n*54

Damaška, Mirjan, 21
D'Amato, Anthony, 121*n*3, 134*n*9
Declaration of the Rights of Man, 17
Defeasible rights, 29, 37–50, 122, 105. *See also* Rights
Defeis, Elizabeth F., xiv*n*3
De Felipe, Miguel Beltrain, 171–72*n*8
Definitional balancing. *See* Factor analysis
Della Cananea, Giacinto, 32-33*n*36
Dembour, Marie Bénédicte, 39-40*n*6, 40*n*8
Democratic society, 20, 43, 44, 50, 59, 95, 119, 120, 122, 132, 140, 148, 173
  modern, 96, 100, 103
  role of government in, 21
  secularism and, 45
De Santiago, Jose Maria Rodriguez, 171-72*n*8
Diana, Princess, 167*n*1
Difference principle, 98, 99, 102
Distributive justice, 99. *See also* Justice
Diversity jurisdiction, 84. *See also* Jurisdiction
Douglas, Justice William O., 72
Dunne, Finley Peter, 82*n*9

Dworkin, Ronald, 37*n*2, 77, 78, 80, 81, 86, 89–95, 121-22, 135, 168

Eady, Mr. Justice, 73*n*61
Edwards, John, 151
Electioneering communications, 136–37, 138
Election expenditures, prohibitions on, 139–40
Ely, John Hart, 112*n*26
Emotional harm, 147, 173–74
Emotional tranquility, 173
English Bill of Rights of 1689, 17
Entitlement, 13
Equality
    fair equality of opportunity, 96–97, 98, 103
    and veil of ignorance, 98–99
European Commission of Human Rights, 26, 27, 40, 49
European Convention for the Protection of Human Rights and Fundamental Freedoms. *See* European Convention on Human Rights
European Convention on Human Rights, 17–18, 19, 22, 26, 28, 78, 132, 149
    allowing retrial of a previously acquitted defendant after the prosecution, 31
    discrimination, 46
    prohibition of abuse of rights, 42
    prohibition of punishment without law, 39
    prohibition of slavery, 39
    protection against "inhuman treatment or punishment," 30, 38, 39, 52
    protection of right to life, 39
    right to an education, 45
    right to freedom of speech or expression, 38, 41, 43, 49, 52–53, 54, 114, 169–71
    right to privacy, 41, 45, 52–53, 169–71
    right to respect for one's private life, 43, 44, 46–50, 54
    state to derogate freedom of expression, permitting, 39
European Court of Human Rights, 3, 41–44, 46, 48, 51–52, 54, 58–63, 121, 129, 132, 169–71. *See also* Court(s)
    appeals of questions of fact, 24–27
    judicial review, standard of, 28
    margin of appreciation, 28–29
    proportionality requirement, 28
    view of protection of freedom of expression, 39

Factor analysis, 96–97, 102, 103, 105–16
    distinguished from ad hoc balancing, 110
    lexically prior to difference principle, 98, 99
    role in judicial decision making, 105, 106–8, 112
Federal Election Law, 135–41
Federal Rules of Civil Procedure, 22–23
Federal Rules of Criminal Procedure, 127*n*22
Findings of fact, appellate review of, 21–28
First Amendment to the United States Constitution
    express language of, 141
    freedom of expression, 38
Fitzsimons, Peter, 67*n*48
Fletcher, George, 27–28
Frank, Jerome, 126
Frazaneh, Kay von, 149*n*1
Freedom of speech or expression, 23, 167–72
    about public officials or figures, protection of, 153–54
    balancing the protection of private life against, 53–61
    constitutional right of, 14–15
    corporate speech versus individual speech, 138–39*n*27
    dangerous tendencies of, 113–14
    European Convention on Human Rights, 38, 41, 43, 52–53
    First Amendment of the United States Constitution, 38
    infringement of, 44
    intentional use to inflict emotional harm, 173–74
    legal sanction for publication of information, 160
    moral dimension of, 172–73
    political dimension of, 168

Freedom of speech or expression (*cont.*)
  protection of, 43
    and rights of privacy, conflict between equal values of, 167–71
    scientific or educational, 160–61
    suppression of, 148–50
Freeland, Sir John, 26
French Penal Code, 68*n*52

Gardbaum, Stephen, 9*n*20
German Code of Criminal Procedure, 31*nn*31-32
Gény, François, 108
German Federal Constitutional Court, 171
German law
  allowing retrial of a previously acquitted defendant after the prosecution, 31
  allowing subsequent prosecution in a new proceeding, 31
Ghosh, Eric, 131*n*2
Goodhart, Arthur L., 24*n*11
Gray, John Chipman, 15
Greenawalt, 94*n*17
Griffiths, Lord, 55*n*8
Guaranteed-minimum-welfare capitalist regime, 99, 100–101
Guess, Raymond, 6*n*14
Gunther, Gerald, 126*n*18

Habermas, Jürgen, 6, 85
Hale, Lady, 22*n*3, 56-57, 151*n*2
Hand, Judge Learned, 126
Hans, Valerie P., 127*n*22
Hart, H.L.A., 77, 78, 80, 82–83
Hate speech, 174-75
Hobbes, Thomas, 15
Hoffman, Lord, 22, 56-57, 58*n*17, 151
Hohfeld, Wesley Newcomb, 13–15, 18–20, 37, 38, 46, 47
Homosexuals, rights of, 16.
  See also Rights
Honan, William H., 162*n*32
Hope, Lord, 56-57
House of Lords, 3, 25, 47, 53–58, 168–69.
  See also Court(s)
  appellate jurisdiction of, 3*n*1
  decision-making processes of, 7–8, 8*n*18
  finding of a specific fact, 24

law of privacy, creating, 116
reasonable foreseeability doctrine in economic loss cases, adopting, 92–93
Hruschka, Joachim, 16
Human dignity, 71, 81, 85, 89, 172
  inviolability of, 37*n*2
Human rights, 8. *See also* Rights; Universal human rights
  basic, 17, 167
  historical development of, 16–20
Human Rights Act of 1998, 78*n*2
Hume, David, 124
Hutcheson, Joseph C., 85

Ideal audience, 85–87, 134, 148
  prediction of the reaction of, 85–86, 85*n*19
Ideal society, structure of, 96
Ideal speech situation, 6*n*14
Individual speech versus corporate speech, 138–39*n*27
International Covenant on Civil and Political Rights (1960), 19*n*11
International Convention on Torture, 171
International Criminal Court for the former Yugoslavia (ICTY), 64

Joyce, James, 163
Juenger, Friedrich, 112*n*26
Judges
  discretional authority of, 78, 89–90, 91, 121
  philosopher-judge, 125
  role of, 84–85, 108, and *passim*
Judicature Act of 1873, 23
Judicial Committee of the Privy Council, 8*n*18
Judicial construction of statute, 133
Judicial decision making
  assumptions of, 77
  epistemology of, 77–87
  factor analysis, use of, 106
  interest balancing, use of, 106
  lay participation in, 126–27, 131
  policy-based consequential reasoning, 78, 80–82, 91

predictive process, 82–84, 83n13, 132
quasi-deductive methods of, 84
role of judge in, 84–85, 108
steadying factors, 82
Judicial discretion, 78, 113
Judicial machinery of the state, 124
Judicial review, standard of, 28
Jurisdiction
  appellate, 3n1
  diversity, 84
Jury
  nullification, 125–26, 126n16
  trial by, 22–23
  verdict, 29–30
Justice, 63, 95–96, 128
  distributive, 99
  personification of, 134
  social, 53, 59, 73
Justice as fairness, 96–104

Keith, Lord, 55n8
Kelsen, Hans, 14n3, 124
Kennedy, Justice Anthony McLeod, 60n32, 133, 135, 137
Knight, C.J.S., 20n13

Lange, David L., 72n57, 141n37
Law. *See also individual entries*
  based on experience, 5
  content or meaning of, 79
  impact on social change, 134–36
  and morals, 124
  questions of fact and, 23
  of the singing reason, 108
Lawrence, D.H., 163
Lawyer/client relationship, 158
Lay participation, in judicial decision making, 126–27, 131. *See also* Judicial decision making
Legal argumentation, principle-based theory of, 89–95
Legal development, by case-by-case adjudication, 79–80
Legal positivism, 15
Legal realism, 108
Legal rights, 15. *See also* Rights
  logical structures of, 19
Leftsas, George, 46n24
Lepsius, Oliver, 171-72n8

Lewis, Tom, 46n24
Llewellyn, Karl N., 79n3, 108–10, 124n12
Locke, John, 5, 124
Loucaides, Judge Loukis, 163-64n35

Margin of appreciation, 28–29, 40–41, 41n11, 46, 49, 50, 57, 73, 167, 169, 170–71
Macaulay, Thomas Babington, 73n60
Main, Jackson T., 143n43
Maximin principle, 96–100, 103
Maxwell, Robert, 98
McClintock, Henry L., 22-23n6
Mead, George Herbert, 5, 85
Media
  print, 139–40
  as watchdog, 153
Miller, Henry, 163
Moore, Harry T., 163n33
Moyn, Samuel, 4n3
Murphy, Liam, 15n6

Nagel, Thomas, 15n6
Narcotics Anonymous, 67n50
Natural law, discovering the content of, 5–6
ne bis in idem provisions, 71
Nicholls, Lord, 54-57
Negligence, 23n10, 92, 93, 174
New Zealand Bill of Rights Act, 1990, 19n12
North Carolina General Statutes, 127n22, 144n45
Nozick, Robert, 97

Obama, President Barak, 145
O'Connor, Justice Sandra Day, 60n2, 121n2, 135
Oliphant, Herman, 108n8

Perelman, Chaïm & Olbrechts-Tyteca, L., 4–5, 85
Perron, Walter, 127n20
Phillips, Lord, 71n56
Philosopher-judge, 125. *See also* Judges
Philosophers' briefs, filing of, 125
Physical injury to person or property, 147, 174–75
  strict liability for, 92, 93–94

Pickard, Jim, 69n54
Policy and principle, distinction between, 94
Pound, Roscoe, 107n7, 110n14
Powell, H. Jefferson, 72n57, 84, 141n37
Powell, Justice Lewis F., 154n12
Pragmatism, 78
Precedent, 80, 122, 132–36
Predictivism, 82–84
Preliminary injunction pending trial
   against publication of information,
   63–66, 68
Principle-driven theory of adjudication,
   78, 89-95. *See also* Adjudication
Privacy, right to, 113, 167–72
   cases, public interest defense in, 53–58
   civil law, 121
   common law, 121
   European Convention on Human
      Rights, 52–53
   individual, 68
   legitimate expectation of, 61
   moral dimension of, 168, 173
   political dimension of, 168
   reasonable expectation of, 61
   and rights of freedom of expression,
      conflict between equal values of,
      167–71
Private activities, in public space, 155–60
   use of photographs, redressing, 156–60
Privileges
   common law, 25
   defined, 14
   practical implications of, 14
Privy Council, 8n18
Property rights, 15–16. *See also* Rights
Proportionality, 28, 41n11, 45–46, 150
Protection against torture or inhuman or
   degrading treatment or punishment
   European Convention on Human
      Rights, 38, 39
Publication of information
   preliminary injunction pending trial
      against, 63–66, 68
Public interest, 56, 57, 61, 62, 66, 72, 116,
   151–54, 157, 159, 161, 162
   defense, in privacy cases, 53–58
Pure economic loss
   reasonable foreseeability test for, 92
   recovery of, 92–93
Puchta, Georg106

Quasi-deductive model, of adjudication,
   84, 105. *See also* Adjudication

Rational discourse, 5
   Rawls, John86, 89, 90, 96–103
Reasonable foreseeability
   test, 92
Reasonableness, 27–28, 29
Referral to the court, 77
Religious expression, 172
   suppression of, 114–15
Resolution 1165 of the European
   Parliamentary Assembly, 53, 167n1
Responsible journalism, 140, 152, 153
Restatement (Second) of Conflicts, 112
Restatements of the Law of Torts, 55,
   111-12,173–75
   emotional harm, 173–74
   physical harm, 174–75
   strict liability for miscarriage of
      dangerous activities, 111–12
Rider, Barry A.K., 67n49
Rights, 13–20. *See also* Human rights;
   Universal human rights
   abstract, 15, 19
   categories of, 18–19
   claim, 13–14
   defeasible, 29, 37–50
   of equal value, conflict of, 51–73 and
      passim
   function in human rights litigation, 13,
      16–20
   function in legal discourse, 13–16
   of homosexuals, 16
   legal, 15
   property, 15–16
   of supposedly equal value, conflicts
      between, 113
   as trumps, 37n2
   to counsel, 124
   to an education, 45
   to do something. *See* Privileges
   to freedom of speech or expression. *See*
      Freedom of speech or expression
   to life, 39
   to one's bodily integrity, 15
   to privacy. *See* Privacy, right to
   to respect for private and family life, 43,
      44, 46–50

welfare, 98
Right to respect for one's private life, 54
   balancing against freedom of expression, 53–61
Ross, Alf, 82, 83

Saint, Emma, 127n20
Schiffren, Seana Valentine, 102n31
School desegregation, 145
Searcy, Dianne, 151n3
Secularism, 45, 149
Serious publication, 151–53
Simpson, A.W. Brian, 39n6, 40n8
Smith, Adam, 6, 85
Smith, Peter J., 86
Society
   basic structure of, 103
   democratic. *See* Democratic society
   social mores of, 125–26, 128
Souter, Justice David H., 60n2, 142n40
South Africa, constitution of, 19n12
Sovereignty, 20
Spatial isolation and privacy, 60, 61
Stanley, Paul, 65n45
Stare decisis, 132
State-action problem, 9
State responsibility, 51–52
   for actions of private persons, 52–53
   protection from "inhuman treatment or punishment," 52
Stevens, Justice John Paul, 7, 132n3, 137, 138–39n27
Stone, Julius, 121nn2 and 4
Strict liability
   for miscarriage of dangerous activities, 111–12
   for physical injuries, 92
Summers, Robert S., 83
Supreme Court of the United Kingdom. *See also* Court(s)
   decision of contentious questions, 7
Swiss Civil Code, 84n15

Thaman, Stephen C., 127n21

Thomas, Justice Clarence, 137
Tort law, 91, 147
Trespass, constructive, 156
Trial by a judge, 21–28
   criteria for review of trial court findings of fact, 22–23
   finding of specific facts, 23–24
Trial by jury, 22–23, 38
Trial courts, traditional deference to the decisions of, 22–23, 24
Truth, convergence theory of, 6
Tulkens, Judge Françoise, 44, 45n22

United States Supreme Court. *See also* Court(s)
   decision-making processes of, 7
Universal Declaration of Human Rights, 17
Universal discourse, 5
Universal human rights, 5, 17. *See also* Human rights; Rights
   structural impediments to consistent application of, 21–33
Universal values
   human characteristic of appealing to, 4–5, 86

Veil of ignorance, 98–99
Vidmar, Neil, 127n22
Violence
   immediate or imminent, 148, 149
   threat of social, 150
von Jhering, Rudolf, 107
von Savigny, Friedrich Carl, 106
von Puffendorf, Samuel, 6

Watkins, Floyd C., 163n34
Welfare rights, 98. *See also* Rights
Williams, Andrew, xivn3
Williams, Bernard, 85
Wolfe, Thomas, 163
Wood, Gordon S., 143n42

Zupančič, Judge Boštjan, 61